C

Harlem HEYDAY

A Pictorial History of Modern Black Show Business and the Apollo Theatre

By Jack Schiffman

Foreword by John Hammond

Prometheus Books

700 East Amherst St. Buffalo, New York 14215

Credits:

The quotations from *The Devil's Music: A History of the Blues,* by Giles Oakley (Taplinger Publishing Co., Inc., 1977), © 1976 by Giles Oakley, are reprinted by permission.

The quotations from *Jazz Dance: The Story of American Vernacular Dance,* by Marshall and Jean Stearns (New York: Schirmer Books, A Division of Macmillan Publishing Co., Inc., 1979), are reprinted by permission.

Library of Congress Card Catalog No. 83-63557
ISBN: 087975-247-5

Acknowledgments

Many friends, knowingly or unwittingly, have been responsible for much in this book. With great patience, they have responded to my proddings and have added anecdotes, comments, and observations. I am grateful to one and all, but to no one more than Francis "Doll" Thomas, who at ninety, still has his enthusiasm and love of the theater, as well as an incredible memory for events long past, which is evident throughout the text. There is no way I can ever thank Doll enough for his help.

Nor can I forget the contribution of my friend Henry Frankel. Scarcely a week passed while I was preparing this book without my soliciting from him an answer or a comment to some notion of mine.

I also feel infinite gratitude to my brother Bobby, who read the entire text and made many helpful comments and suggestions, including one that led to the writing of one last chapter when I thought the text had long been completed. He always supported my sometimes flagging spirits with his own enthusiasm.

More than casual thanks go to my friend Charles "Honi" Coles, who at long last has "made it." He was always willing to jog my memory or add wonderful little fillips. Nor can I omit a grateful bow to former Apollo manager, Leonard Reed.

Lastly, thanks are due to a full complement of musicians, performers, and theatrical personnel who shared experiences and memories and made useful comments. Harry "Sweets" Edison, Bunny Briggs, Sandman Sims, Buddy Tate, James Moody, Illinois Jacquet, Benny Carter, Ernestine Allen, Kenn Freeman, Flip Wilson, Nipsey Russell, Juanita Uggams, and Stephanie Mills are just a few of these.

Producer, manager, and friend Berle Adams was part of this group of friends who added grist to the mill. So, too, are songwriter Henry Nemo and stagehand Hans Nielson. To one and all, my grateful thanks.

To Charles

Contents

Foreword

This foreword is done out of love for the theater and out of penance, which I will explain later.

Going to the theaters in Harlem was my first real liberation from a very stuffy family upbringing. The first times I went to the various theaters owned by the Brechers and their associate, Frank Schiffman, was back in the early twenties, when I was barely a teen-ager and unable to get to nightclubs and speakeasies where I could find my favorite performers. It was the time of Prohibition, needless to say, and small boys were not exactly welcome either in Harlem or downtown New York.

My interest in Harlem theaters coincided with my first awareness of the Civil Rights Movement and the second-class status of black performers and musicians, and I had always assumed that Frank Schiffman was like all the other exploiters that managed theaters in those long-gone days.

It took me many years to realize that in this extraordinarily tough and competitive business, Schiffman and his sons were among the most honorable people in the history of show business, despite the fact that Frank could be fairly ruthless as competitor with other people trying to reach the same market. The result, of course, was that Frank and the Apollo survived as did nobody else in the theater business who catered to black audiences.

One of my closest friends, after I left Yale, was Vivian Brecher, the daughter of Leo Brecher, who owned every kind of theater in New York, from the Plaza, the Little Carnegie and the 68th Street Playhouse to at least six of the few prosperous theaters in the Harlem area: the Apollo, the Odeon, the Lafayette, the Harlem Opera House, and the Roosevelt. Excepting the Apollo, there is not one single existing motion-picture theater in Harlem today—not a single one. They were either torn down or converted to churches (all denominations) or are now stores.

It was so good to read that Doll Thomas, age ninety, who is the custodian of the Apollo, still goes to work every day. I got to know Doll back in 1932 when he was the electrician handling lights during my first venture in black show business. After the old Public Theatre was closed, Doll went back to the Lafayette Theatre, where he had had his first job in 1913. He was the very first black member of the Stage Hands Union (IATSE) back in the late thirties.

For nearly thirty years there was rarely a week that I didn't get to the Apollo either to check out an act or to "shoot the breeze" with Lena Horne's uncle, one of the managers of the theater, and Abraham Frankel, who actually was one of the greatest people I ever met in show business. Imagine my surprise when I found out that his son was the late Charles Frankel, one of the great

9

historians of our generation and a true intellectual.

The penance I referred to earlier is what I really owe to the memory of Frank Schiffman, who kept Harlem show business alive when it had been officially pronounced dead. As I grow older I'm beginning to realize what an extraordinary show business phenomenon Frank was. A true feisty independent who never gave up until Harlem disappeared around him. Frank was very lucky to have had two such honorable sons as Jack and his brother Bobby, and show business is much poorer without their continual influence and example.

Now that the Apollo is occasionally opened for special events, I can urge everybody to take a look at this fascinating edifice at 261 West 125th Street. No building in New York contains more extraordinary echoes of show business greats, even in the days before 1935, when it was a raunchy burlesque theater on the island of Manhattan. Frank Schiffman did clean up the shows—but not too much, thank goodness!

JOHN HAMMOND

Introduction

"I May Be Wrong"

When I was a very little boy, perhaps five years old, my father, Frank Schiffman, took me to a rehearsal. My recollection of it is still sharp and clear. It marked the beginning of a disease from which I have never recovered. I'm not sure I want to.

I can still see half a dozen muscular men, clad only in leotards, leaping and whirling and seeming to defy gravity itself. And the sinuous movements of a bevy of dark-skinned female dancers intruded in my dreams then and forever after.

Scenery simulated the deck of a ship: rigging, thole pins, and other paraphernalia of the sea reached all the way up to the "fly gallery" high above the stage. My imagination soared way past that narrow platform—and on into outer space, I believe.

It was my first association with that special place called the theater. In my family's lexicon there was only one theater in the entire world. Of course, the Roxy, Radio City Music Hall, the Paramount, Capitol, Palace, and Strand were all in New York, but *the theater* meant the Apollo—the Harlem Apollo—the 125th Street Apollo Theatre. It was the dominating force in our lives. Had my family been the only ones so affected, it would be of small moment; but the Apollo was, for more than forty years, the commanding force in black show business and a leading institution in Harlem.

As if my initial exposure weren't enough, there were periodic visits to the

---

"I May Be Wrong" was the Apollo's theme song. It was played before each and every show by whatever band was featured that week. To generations of Apollo theatergoers, it was the signal to blot out the unimportant, scrunch forward expectantly, psych oneself in preparation for the show. It was more than an overture; it was an electrical current discharged into an expectant crowd as musician after musician picked up a chorus and rode out the theme in his own manner. Often it was a moment of sheer joy.

theater. Dad would become engrossed in his tasks, and I was left to wander and wonder. I did a lot of both. I wondered, for instance, about a little bent man, all scrunched up among his drums and cymbals, making blood-rushing sounds roll forth from his flailing sticks and brushes. They called him Chick, and I was totally hypnotized by the rhythmic sounds he produced. I wondered too about the small dark man with the gravelly voice who was always mopping himself with a white handkerchief—one of dozens he kept piled on a corner of the piano. He played a horn and sang a song called "Ole Man Mose Is Dead." But if Mose were indeed dead, nobody seemed very sad about it. Indeed, everybody laughed and clapped their hands and yelled something to "Satch."

There were ladies, too—most especially two ladies who sang. One of them was very tall and very thin. They called her "Sweet Mama Stringbean," and she sang a song called "Stormy Weather," her head thrown back, her dark eyes looking sad, her head framed only by one spotlight, which cut a white cone-shape out of the darkness way up near the ceiling. Another lady was much heavier, with black hair pulled tight against her head. There were times when she sang that I felt like crying and I didn't really know why. Sometimes, though, she made people laugh. They said she sang the blues, but the blues weren't always sad, I discovered. Some of the people in the audience laughed and slapped their knees and said, "Bessie, yo' is a mess!"

A continuing kaleidoscope of memories tie me irrevocably to the theater. A phone call at home one night when I was in my teens, and my sad-faced father telling us that Chick Webb, the hunchbacked drummer of earlier recollection, had died. I felt as though a member of my family had gone. Then there was a drive into Harlem late at night, followed by a stop at the Lafayette Theater "for just a few minutes," Dad said. It lasted an hour! I didn't mind, though, for I could watch all those fancy-dressed men and women milling around, flashing smiles, moving gracefully, talking to a huge man with a gold tooth right in the middle of is mouth. He was called Jack Johnson.

All my life there were connections with artists—the great, the near-great, and the not-so-great. Some of them I treasure: backstage chats with Duke Ellington and Jimmie Lunceford, a lunch with Bill Robinson just two weeks before he died, a chance meeting with Lionel Hampton, a funny encounter with Joe Louis at Frank's Restaurant, a block from the Apollo. I may seem to be name-dropping, but that is not my intent. For a moment here and there, sometimes for an hour, frequently on and off for a week, these people were a part of my life and I was a part of theirs. The meetings and the events that surrounded them tell part of the why of my love affair with the theater. The how, and the particulars, are the rest of the story.

The Apollo Theatre was almost fifty years old when my father and his partner, Leo Brecher, took it over in 1935. It had previously been operated under the name "Hurtig and Seamon" as a burlesque theater and then a variety house.

The real Apollo Theatre story begins in the middle thirties. If you doubt that the Apollo is a unique institution in American history, ask any black performer, ask any jazz aficionado, ask any lover of entertainment—ask anybody! Says dancer Honi Coles, whose roots go deep into the theater: "As far as I'm concerned, the black show business that I know had its origins at the Apollo. All the great, great, great performers who really were the beginning even of the Apollo and the Lafayette are dead. Like the Bill Robinsons, the Bert Williamses, and other performers of the teens and twenties—they're all gone, and a whole new type of show business sprang up with the ascendancy of the Apollo."

Adds theatrical booker, former hoofer, and all-around show-business expert Henry Frankel: "The Apollo *is* black show business. Without it there is no black show business as we know it."

Ernestine Allen of the Negro Actors Guild, herself an ex-singer, said, "You could make it at the Howard [in Washington] or the Royal [in Baltimore], but you *never, never, never* really made it until you made it at the Apollo."

Another kudo comes from Peter Long, whose roots are also deep in the entertainment business: "I worked at the Apollo for seven years, and they were the most stimulating, the most challenging years of my life."

In the mainstream of the history of black show business were the Apollo, the Savoy Ballroom, Connie's Inn, the Cotton Club, and a few theaters outside Harlem: the Howard, the Royal, Chicago's Regal, and Philadelphia's Earle. All the rest were peripheral. The last of these titans to survive was the Apollo, and on its stage entertainment history was enacted. The Cotton Club, spawning ground for Duke Ellington, Cab Calloway, Ethel Waters, and a host of others, has a unique place in show-business history. It must be remembered, however, that it was always a for-whites-only showplace while it was in Harlem; only the performers were black. The Cotton Club didn't "integrate" until it moved to the Broadway area in the thirties. It was there for only a short time. At the Apollo, as my father was fond of saying, "We never draw the color line." The distinction is important.

Almost every black entertainer in modern history at one time or another strutted across the Apollo's stage, parading his or her talents before an audience so "hep" as to be legendary—as legendary perhaps as the artists themselves. Even so recent a star as Stephanie Mills, who made it big in Broadway's *The Wiz* in 1976 (and who was a graduate of the Apollo's Amateur Hour), put it simply enough: "I think that the Broadway audience is catching up with the Apollo's."

But if the Apollo was the mecca for black entertainers, it was also a lodestone for whites. The likes of Benny Goodman, Charlie Barnet, Buddy Rich, Chris Connors, Louis Prima, Keely Smith, Harry James, Artie Shaw, Maynard Ferguson, and Dave Brubeck were applauded and respected Apollo stars, and they were proud to be so regarded.

Time after time my path crosses with that of a famous white musician. A frequent response to my identification with the Apollo is "Oh yes, I played there years ago." Many a musician highly regarded in the jazz and entertainment fraternity did his bit "uptown" at one time or another. I'm referring to musicians like Gerry Mulligan, Doc Severinsen, and Eddie Safranski—the list is almost endless.

Judging from its physical appearance, the Apollo seemed an unlikely place to house a legend. It was shabby and dingy, and the lobby was sometimes heavy with the smell of urine rising from the men's room. Can there be charm in grime? If so, perhaps grime is one reason for the theater's allure; it was there in abundance. All that dirt wasn't there because we didn't try to remove it, but the stuff seemed ground in seventy-five-years deep. Somehow the dirt and dust that were only redistributed nightly by seven porters was eternal. I rather liked it that way; in fact I resented it when every few years a new coat of paint was slathered over the old. I needn't have resented it, though; it didn't change a thing!

The auditorium was probably as grime-laden as the lobby, but its true appearance was hidden by the dim lights. Just before entering the auditorium, one passed a huge montage, perhaps twenty feet long. It contained a graphic history of the Apollo; on it were pictures of every starring act to appear there for more than forty years. Only a real aficionado could recognize them all, but aficionados abounded in the Apollo's lobby.

The most fascinating part of the auditorium was the second of two balconies, affectionately called the "buzzard's roost." You had to be related to a mountain goat even to get to it; the stairway was sure death to those with emphysema, heart trouble, incipient catarrh, or hernia. The view down to the stage was shaded by the billows of smoke coming from dozens of cigarettes or reefers. Far below, the stage seemed like an oversized boxing ring.

Whenever the stage show started, the second balcony's denizens leaned forward expectantly, ready to pronounce sentence on the performers below. The artists knew it and played to them. As one superstar put it, "You either make it with that bunch in the second, or baby, you're dead." A shake of the head. "Without them, Jim, you kin go home."

Backstage at the Apollo was like backstage in most theaters, only more so. The switchboard on stage right was a bewildering panel of knobs, handles, buttons, and lights. The controls for the mikes were on the opposite side of the stage, and before another smaller panel, replete with its own switches and buttons sat its operator. Responsible for the volume of sound on half a dozen mikes, he was under the constant surveillance of the ghost of one Norman Miller, whose domain it was for many years. Mr. Miller was a short, pudgy, incredibly profane man who went under the name of "Porto Rico." Rico was a legend all by himself. The reader will meet him later, for he was the first and greatest of the executioners at the amateur-night program. Behind Porto Rico was a pedestal with a polished piece of wood on it—a log, to be accurate. But no, it was not really a log at all; rather it was the last remnant of the "tree of hope," another relic of Harlem history and a link to Bill "Bojangles" Robinson and an era long departed.

Above the sound system's switchboard and up a spiral iron staircase was the "fly gallery," that precarious perch from which the scenery was raised and lowered. From there one could see a bewildering array of curtains, drops, ropes, and sandbags, and you could see a performer only from his or her head straight down to the toes. They looked like gnomes from the flies.

On the street, the Apollo dominated the block of 125th Street between Seventh and Eighth Avenues, dominated it rather completely, although at one time there were three theater marquees on that one block. The Apollo's marquee wasn't the largest on the street (the Loew's Victoria's was), nor the brightest, for all three turned the juice to high as soon as the sun went down. It dominated the entire block because it was there—and everyone knew it was there. It *commanded* you to read the glitter of names by day or night. Flashing on and off, there was the marquee by night—and the marquee by day. And each tells its story.

For Nancy Wilson the Apollo audience was an inspiration and an emotional experience. Time after time she wept on stage and off, at the overwhelming outpouring of affection and respect accorded her. As for Aretha Franklin, her wet-eyed comment to my brother Bobby on seeing the caption on her marquee was, "You know, Bobby, it's true—I *am* home!" (See Illustrations 1a and 1b.)

If this faded old building on a dirty, noisy street seems an inappropriate subject for a legend, the dominating force behind the legend, my father Frank Schiffman, seems even less so. Shortish, pot-bellied, Dad looked a lot more like a high school principal than a showman. Until his forties, he wore pince-nez glasses, and when he switched to horn rims, he looked even sterner than before. He was the supreme anachronism for a show-biz type; he was educated, articulate, and straight-laced. He could ooze charm; but he could also cut you down with a glance or skewer you with a phrase.

To most performers he was a study in contradictions, and their attitudes toward him betrayed that fact. They loved, feared, and sometimes hated him simultaneously. As Ernestine Allen put it, "If he put his arm around you after the first show, you just *knew* you wouldn't be on stage for the second." And, said Pete Long, "I learned more about show business from those years with your father than in all the other years put together."

If lack of patience was his weak suit, keen observation and an analytical mind were his strengths. He may have looked like a pedant, but he was a showman to his fingertips, and a tough one at that. The slovenly, the careless, the unplanned, and poorly executed disturbed his sense of order. And in a world replete with crudities and vulgarities, he was a prude. Yet occasionally he would flash out with an impatient "that's a lot of bullshit!" Dad's using that phrase seemed somehow out of place, but there it was, hanging up like a slow curve just when you were expecting a blazer.

Sometimes he threw you off stride, Dad did. Impatient, short-tempered, he terrified the ushers, projectionists, and stagehands, who nonetheless often

1a. Marquee of the theater on West 125th Street in Harlem.

1b.

ambled into the office for a loan ("jist till payday, Mister Schiffman"); he rarely turned them down. When our chauffeur and general factotum George Moore looked ill, Dad sent him to his own doctor for an examination and then picked up the bill. He hovered over George so much that my brother Bobby and I sometimes wondered if he wasn't part of our family. We will never know the extent of the loans Dad made to musicians, singers, and other performers, including major headliners. Most of the loans were in his head when he passed away.

If show business and the Apollo are covered with legends, they were merely frosting on the cake. From the outside, it may have seemed all glamour, but for performers and operators alike it was a rough grind. Perhaps it is a little easier in theaters today—although I doubt it. But in my experience and my brother Bobby's and Dad's, it was a constant mishmash of problems, tensions, and fatigue all mixed and simmered together in a life-dominating brew. For every minute of "glamour" there was an hour of stress. We worked against the odds, not because it was so glamorous but because the theater was a kind of disease and we had it. Dad called it a "slavery business," but he wouldn't have had another. I left the theater for twenty years, but it never left me. Every trip to New York was "going home," and first stop was 125th Street—always!

I have tried to describe the theater, something of its appearance and its character, but perhaps the most compelling lure of all was the audience. As one of my writer friends expressed it, "The audience is almost as interesting as the show. In fact, the audience *is* a show in itself!" Little Stephanie Mills put it succinctly: "The Apollo audience *always* reacts to whatever is good, never to what is bad." To which I would add, "excepting during the amateur show, when it was permissible to ride the bad."

Performers have always spoken of the unusual rapport between Apollo audiences and them. Sometimes the reaction was highly emotional, as with Nancy Wilson, or when Bill Bailey (Pearl's dancing brother) made a triumphant comeback. In many an Apollo engagement, members of the audience would rise and seemingly float down to the edge of the stage, demonstrating by their eager presence the respect, delight, affection, and kinship they felt for the artist in the spotlight. At others, the audience reaction was so electric you fairly quivered from it. As a result, it was almost axiomatic that the artists responded in kind. One of them remarked to me in awe and wonderment, "You give out more than you even thought you could, at the Apollo. Sometimes I've sort of listened to myself and wondered if that was really me up there."

It's hard to say just what does happen, what magic current passes from artist to audience and back. Billie Holiday, in her autobiography *Lady Sings the Blues,* put it as well as it can be: "There's nothing like an audience at the Apollo. They were wide awake in the morning. They didn't ask me what my style was, who I was, how I evolved, where I'd come from, who influenced me or anything. They just broke the house up."

There's your intro—the stage is set—artists, personnel, owners, audience, theater, locale. Look then and behold my Harlem, my Apollo—all its jazz, song, dance, comedy, the whole wonderful potpourri. What follows are the sights, sound, highs and lows of a portion of show biz that was the Apollo's heyday.

The Heyday Years

2

"Ain't Misbehavin'"

From the depths of the Great Depression, on through the aftermath of World War II there occurred an entertainment explosion, which shook up jazz, rattled the dance, and rolled a galaxy of singers, comics, gospelers, and performers of every description to fame and fortune. Its epicenter was Harlem. Its ripples spread through New York City, then the country, and finally over much of the world, enduring from the mid-thirties to the mid-sixties and beyond. I call them the "Heyday Years."

There were, of course, artists of both races in this exciting mix, but it is hard to deny that the major thrust came from the fast-emerging blacks. There was a stunning development of talent among them, and a gradual but increasing white recognition and acceptance of their artistry.

Right in the center of the explosion stood our faded showplace, the Apollo, the spawning ground for an incredible array of talent. The Apollo survived not only an exciting group of Harlem nightclubs (The Cotton Club, Savoy Ballroom, Connie's Inn, Small's Paradise), but it was still going strong in the seventies when the Roxy, Paramount, Capitol, Palace, and Strand, Broadway's finest theaters, had either closed up shop or been converted to ordinary movie houses. Even the Radio City Music Hall was, by then, struggling along under varying and shifting policies, trying to stay alive.

The Heyday Years, a forty-odd-year span, witnessed the rise and fall of the big bands, followed by successive waves of singers, vocal groups, gospelers, and finally, comics. And throughout this entire period, a stream of jazz artists and dancers appeared, developed, and strutted across the entertainment horizon.

From the turn of the century on, Harlem presented a changing face. It

---

"Ain't Misbehavin'" is the theme song for this chapter. It is, of course, associated with Thomas "Fats" Waller, who, along with lyricist Andy Razaf, wrote it. Perhaps more than any other artist, the irrepressible Fats is connected with this early period in the history and evolution of jazz. Fats was a towering figure, all six foot two of him, and his spiritual stature still hovers over this early era.

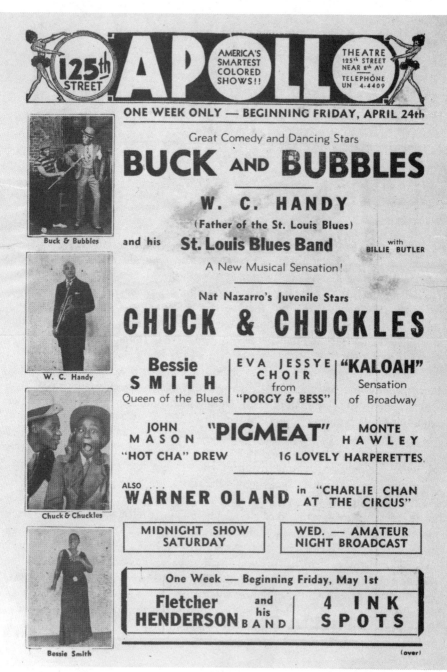

APOLLO
125th STREET

AMERICA'S SMARTEST COLORED SHOWS!!

THEATRE
125th STREET
NEAR 8th AV
TELEPHONE
UN 4-4409

ONE WEEK ONLY — BEGINNING FRIDAY, APRIL 24th

Great Comedy and Dancing Stars

BUCK AND BUBBLES

Buck & Bubbles

W. C. HANDY

(Father of the St. Louis Blues)

and his **St. Louis Blues Band** with BILLIE BUTLER

A New Musical Sensation!

W. C. Handy

Nat Nazarro's Juvenile Stars

CHUCK & CHUCKLES

| Bessie **SMITH** Queen of the Blues | EVA JESSYE CHOIR from "PORGY & BESS" | "KALOAH" Sensation of Broadway |

JOHN MASON   "PIGMEAT"   MONTE HAWLEY

"HOT CHA" DREW   16 LOVELY HARPERETTES.

Chuck & Chuckles

ALSO . . .
WARNER OLAND in "CHARLIE CHAN AT THE CIRCUS"

| MIDNIGHT SHOW SATURDAY | WED. — AMATEUR NIGHT BROADCAST |

One Week — Beginning Friday, May 1st

| Fletcher **HENDERSON** and his BAND | 4 INK SPOTS |

Bessie Smith

(over)

2.

began as all-white in the early days, turned to grey in the teens and twenties, and finally the "invasion" of blacks turned it into the world's most famous black ghetto. It took decades for deterioration to set in and show its grim face. In the thirties and early forties Harlem had many areas with a lot of "class." Our one-time manager and former dancer Honi Coles, speaking of the Harlem of that period, told me: "In those days, Harlem was clean and respectable. Nobody would even *think* of going out on the street without a shirt, tie and jacket. As for us dancers, we were the most particular of all, always up on the latest fashions."

Harlem began to rot and grow bitter when it became economically deprived as other areas were progressing. The disease started during the Depression, but Harlem's poor reputation was a long time in coming. During the fifties and sixties, we Schiffmans could walk its main streets without fear. On many a weary night in the fifties, I would leave the theater after a late rehearsal, walk to the subway nodding to the ever-present prostitutes on the street, and travel up past the George Washington Bridge with nothing more worrisome on my mind than the desire to get home to sleep. To be sure, mere prudence prevented us from going into the many side streets—especially after dark—but we wouldn't have gone onto similar streets in many other parts of Manhattan either. In those days, if Harlem was not the friendliest of locales, it certainly wasn't the most hostile either.

The Heyday Years saw the accelerated development of the black entertainment genius. It is true that in the late twenties black artistry was on the rise, but it seemed to gain a full head of steam as the thirties really got rolling. The more these artists rolled, the wider their acceptance; the wider their acceptance, the more exciting and innovative became their artistry.

Take, for example, an Apollo show that graced the stage in April 1936. It was a well-balanced, entertaining show at the time, but from a historical perspective, it is chiefly interesting because of the number of acts that became famous later on.

Buck & Bubbles, the headliners, was the greatest comedy-song-dance team of the decade—or several decades. The two strutted across the stages of niteries and theaters from Broadway to Radio City Music Hall, from Hollywood and the silver screen to Germany, Paris, and London. Audiences both black and white responded to John Bubbles' plaintive song, whose lyrics proclaimed: "Because my teeth are pearly, because my hair is curly, that's why they call me 'Shine'." They responded, too, to his fantastic dancing; some people believe he was the greatest dancer ever!

Equally noteworthy in this '36 show was the band headed by W. C. Handy. Trumpet-player William C. Handy is enshrined in history as the composer of "The St. Louis Blues" and scores more; he was the father of *all* the blues, those plaintive heart-songs that are the universal expression of the black man's misery and frustration, the black woman's grief. The blues became the most enduring of all modern musical offerings.

The last time I saw W. C. Handy was a short time before his death. He had come to visit my father at the Apollo about some matter. Honored in his time, recognized, celebrated, but almost totally blind, he heard someone talking about the then-current musical rage, bop. "Guess the scene has passed me by," he muttered. "I think I'm too old to understand it."

What could I say but "You're way ahead of them, Mr. Handy." We both knew it was a lie, or at least a half-lie—but was it? The blues that W. C. Handy had composed would live at least as long as bop; in all likelihood, singers will be wailing the blues when bop becomes a mere footnote to jazz history.

The peerless interpreter of those blues was another of the show's head-liners, Bessie Smith, the "Empress of the Blues." Bessie was as commanding a person on the stage as I have ever seen. From her voice to her manner, she was large. With head thrown back and eyes sometimes shut tight, she often projected an image of ineffable sadness. Indeed, jazz and record producer, John Hammond said of her: "There never was a singer like Bessie. She could make whole audiences weep."

Of the others in that show, Chuck & Chuckles was another of Nat Nazarro's acts (he managed Buck & Bubbles); the choir from *Porgy and Bess* was bringing George Gershwin to Harlem; and Dewey "Pigmeat" Markham, one of the most enduring black comics, almost deserves a chapter of his own. (The reader will meet him later.)

Over the years the face that show business presented to the public has changed often, but the Apollo always labored under a policy known in the trade as a "grind." The term is almost self-explanatory. It was, after all, a grind to do four, five, six, and occasionally even seven shows *per day!* It was a grind to present production numbers complete with a dancing chorus, with several costume changes, and often with the entire cast of singers, comics, and dancers working through the entire show. And if the grind format changed slightly from show to show or from year to year, the end product in terms of physical and emotional strain was the same. But then nobody who knew could ever claim that show business was easy.

In those early days when every show had production numbers the only time for rehearsals was between shows. That meant endless hours at the theater: early morning rehearsal calls, shows running from noon to midnight punctuated by dance rehearsals, musical rehearsals, costume fittings, and finally, a dress rehearsal before the new show began. It's no wonder that old-timers in the business look at the youngsters who complain about doing three shows a day, and shake their heads in wonderment. Three shows a day would have seemed like a vacation to them. The pressures to complete one and to open with a new show each week were enormous.

I recall a show, years ago, which Lew Leslie (who later produced such successful Broadway shows as *Blackbirds*) staged for Dad. All during the week, he and Dad did a little "Smith & Dale act," arguing, cajoling, disputing, until the final dress rehearsal on a Thursday night. Each thought himself a better showman than the other; each was determined to prove it! Dad later remarked to me, "It was just awful. Everything that could go wrong with a show went wrong. Comics forgot their lines, the music sounded as though each musician was playing a different tune in a different key, the costumes didn't fit properly, the lighting cues were all snarled up."

Finally, Lew turned around to Dad and the cast and announced: "It's no use. We're going to put the opening off for a night and open on Saturday instead!" It wasn't the first time Frank Schiffman bellowed, and it certainly wasn't the last.

"Mr. Leslie, sit down!" Dad shouted "This is *my* theater and this show will open tomorrow as scheduled." With that, he dismissed the cast, told them to get some rest, and stomped out of the theater followed by a fuming Lew Leslie.

On Broadway shows could be postponed and frequently were; but this was Harlem, and not only did the show always go on, it went on on time! And it did this time too. It was, according to Dad, a smash hit! Somehow the performers rose to the challenge and proved the boss right.

Nowhere was the grind more apparent than in the rehearsal hall itself. As a veteran of hour upon hour spent there, I qualify as an expert in that department. For some reason, rehearsal halls usually have low ceilings. (The Apollo's hall had been a nightclub at the turn of the century and afterwards—a club which, according to our projectionist Francis "Doll" Thomas, once sported a sign over the entrance reading bluntly "NO NIGGERS!" In the early days that club had a piano player and singer named Jimmy Durante.) The sound of the music bouncing off these low ceilings always seemed to whirl around the room a few times, gathering momentum I guess, and land—klunk!—right at the base of my skull. Rehearsal halls always have a lot of dust swirling around, and the stuff is agitated by the incessant shuffling of dozens of dancing feet. The halls are always smoke-filled, and the smoke mixed with the dust and stirred by the music makes an exotic, sound-filled mixture that is superb for h-e-a-d-a-c-h-e-s!

After a couple of hours, especially if they "just can't get the damned music right, Mr. Schiffman," or if your headliner has called to say he'll be an hour late and you know that meant he wouldn't make it until tomorrow morning at 10:30 and the first show is scheduled to go on at noon—well, after a few hours of *that,* you know what those sweat boxes they talked about in the chain gang were like. As I mentioned earlier, show business is a disease and if you've got it, you've got it! You can suffer from it exquisitely.

Sometimes we were privy to incidents that occured around rather than in the theater, incidents that tell a good deal about the character of the locale or the times. Leonard Reed, the Apollo's manager for a number of years, told me that there were always crap games going on up on 126th Street. You could hear the sound of dice being tossed up against the walls, coupled with the laughter, the curses, the entreaties of the players. The problem was that from time to time the police would take a run down that street, breaking up the games and arresting a

3a.

3b.

few of the participants.

The guy who was in charge of the game (he was "cutting the game," that is, he had a piece of the action) came to Leonard with a plan and a request. He would station someone at each end of the block to play "chickie" and let him know when a patrol car was seen. At that time, would Leonard permit the "players" to knock on the exit door, enter the theater, and stay just inside the door until it was safe, then leave? Leonard would. Leonard did.

For a number of years this was almost a nightly occurrence.

"Believe me," said Leonard, "these guys had no interest at all in the show. All they wanted to do was to get back outside and continue their game." Added Leonard with a laugh, "I could walk out on 126th Street at any time of the day or night, with my wife, and be perfectly, absolutely safe." (126th Street was known as one of the most dangerous streets in Manhattan.)

By the way—the guy who was "cutting" the game was Malcolm Little, known later as Malcolm X.

Over the years, the format of our shows varied. In the thirties and early forties, they almost always had a line of chorus girls; only the type of headliner changed. Sometimes the headliner was the show itself if we presented the Cotton Club Revue or the popular Ubangi Club Revue.

Willie Bryant was one of the most popular personalities ever to hit Harlem. He was tall, lean, hawk-nosed, and his skin was so light that he could easily have "passed." He was an orchestra leader—and a good one; he emceed our Amateur Show along with Ralph Cooper for years; and he was a smash on Broadway when he joined Ethel Waters and took the male lead in *Mamba's Daughters*. Gladys Bentley was as well known on Broadway as in Harlem. She was an early sporter of men's clothing, she knew how to belt a song, and she did it to what *Variety* would call "heavy mitting" (applause) by audiences, black and white. Gladys specialized in singing songs then known as risque. Today they would seem mild, or silly, depending on your tolerance.

Avon Long, whose name was on Broadway until he died early in 1984, was one of the peerless dancers of the American stage. He followed John Bubbles as Sportin' Life in the original Broadway production of *Porgy and Bess*. Later I will have comments about Leonard Harper, Andy Razaf, and Addison Carey, who were responsible for staging, writing, and presenting the show that opened April 17, 1936. Incidentally, the phrase "added comedy by Jackie Mabley" means that my beloved "Moms" was hard at work.

The announcement, casually scattered around the lobby in 1936, indicates one of the main reasons for the Apollo's enduring place in the history of show business. Six consecutive weeks of bookings that included Armstrong, Duke, Ethel Waters, Lunceford, Fats, and Bojangles—what can you add to such a list?

Nor were we necessarily tied to entertainers for our headliners. Over the years sports figures such as Sugar Ray Robinson, Kid Chocolate, Henry Armstrong, Kid Gavilan, Eddie Tolan, Jackie Robinson, and Joe Louis graced our stage. So too did some makers of history. No more sensational newsmakers

4a.

4b.

hit international headlines in 1937 than the Scottsboro Boys. Nine young men accused of raping a white woman on a train in Alabama were convicted and brought back on appeal. They saw their case dragged through the courts for years. Their attorney, Samuel Leibowitz, became an internationally known figure. In 1937 four of the Scottsboro Nine got out on bail and were brought to the Apollo stage, there to receive the emotional support of the black community, which fearfully followed the torturous ins and outs of their trial.

In the history of show business, there are few more illustrious names than the Mills Brothers. But, as a write-up in *Variety* in 1940 indicates, they had to share top billing with Claude Hopkins and his band at that time, since "Hopkins' 14-piece crew ranks among the top bands the Apollo has recently presented." The Mills Brothers were originally four brothers, or, as their billing put it, "Four Boys and a Guitar." Brother John Mills died in the midst of a European trip and his place was taken by Skipper, the boys' father.

In the early days John "made" the act with his rhythmic imitation of musical instruments. "No one had ever heard anything like that before," explained an excited Pigmeat Markham to me one day. "They were a new and unique act." But in the long run it was their distinctive harmony that became the trademark of the Mills Brothers. One musical bar and you *knew* it was them. No one else had that sound.

Illustration 5a is an old shot of the Apollo chorus line in action in 1940. The line always was made up in multiples of four so that every four weeks or so one group of girls had the week off. After all, even though young and beautiful, they could hardly have stood the grind without that kind of a break.

Illustration 5b is my all-time favorite show-business picture. It is, of course, the magnificent Ella Fitzgerald being greeted at a function by my father. Ella was always one of Dad's (and my) favorite people. Her personality and her voice are the same: smooth and mellow. Always inclined to be nervous before each performance, her nerves almost "got" her one night in Miami. She was playing an engagement at one of the hotels, where trumpet star Roy Eldridge and his band were in the show. Suddenly Roy saw Dad and Mother walk into the house, and he whispered to Ella that "Frank Schiffman just came in." Twisting her handkerchief and perspiring more than usual, Ella then confided to the crowd that "the man who gave me my start in show business just came in— and I'm so nervous I don't know what to do." She did what she always does better than almost anyone: she sang. But she confided to Dad backstage that "I didn't sing very well because I knew you were there listening." Even the mighty and famous have nerves!

When I speak of production, I mean p-r-o-d-u-c-t-i-o-n! "Production shows" were original, Broadway-type extravaganzas, complete with a theme (sometimes a story line) and special material written just for that show. They were also called "tab shows." Music for *Tan Manhattan* was written by Eubie Blake, who with Noble Sissle did the music for the mighty 1921 Broadway production *Shuffle Along*. (In 1983, Eubie died at the age of a hundred, an

5a. They did 31 shows a week and, in their spare time, rehearsed for the next week's show! The old chorus line.

5b. My favorite picture. My dad with his favorite singer, Ella Fitzgerald. Billy Taylor is behind her.

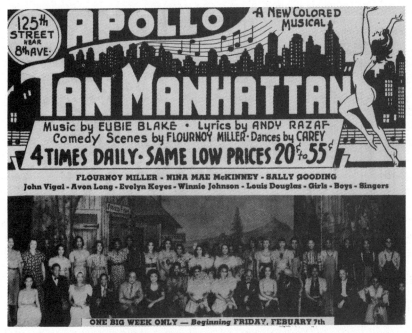

6a.

6b.

6c.

international celebrity of rare talent, who performed up into his nineties.) Lyrics were written by Andy Razaf, who was the lyricist with Fats Waller when they composed such gems as "Honeysuckle Rose," "S'posin'," "Ain't Misbehavin'" and dozens more. Flournoy Miller, who wrote the comedy scenes, was a partner with Aubrey Lyles, the two forming one of the greatest of all black comedy acts. Dances for this 1941 show were by Addison Carey, another of the black theater's creative geniuses. And you could dig the efforts of all these along with performances by such notables as dancer Avon Long, comic Johnny Vigal, and singer-actress Nina Mae McKinney for 20 cents—55 cents if you were a sport and could afford it.

Tan Town Topics, also presented in 1941, is notable on several counts. Years later, one of the stars, Juanita Hall, played Bloody Mary in the hit Broadway production *South Pacific.* She stood that street on its ear with her marvelous and amusing rendition of "Happy Talk." But the real star of *Topics* was the bandleader, James P. Johnson. Along with Willie "The Lion" Smith, dapper James P. Johnson was the prime exponent of what is known in jazz circles as "stride piano," in which the left hand and its chords is equal to the right and its melody. The left seems to "stride" along with the right. An exquisite artist, Johnson also befriended a young and eager musician, gave him piano lessons himself, and helped his burgeoning career. That pianist was Thomas "Fats" Waller.

But that wasn't the end of the Johnson story. He also wrote such songs as "Charleston" (thereby helping to popularize that dance), "I'd Like to Be with You One Hour Tonight," and, to cap it all, wrote the overture for Orson Welles' production of *Macbeth,* set in a Haitian setting and produced at the Lafayette Theatre a short time after Dad had moved from it to 125th Street. The story of the entertainment business, as is the story of science, music, or history, is of one creative soul feeding on another, transcending talent, building, expanding, creating ever widening horizons.

In 1941 we presented, at bargain prices, *Up Harlem Way,* which, in addition to its producers and writers, is interesting for the stars it presented. It was not Billie Holiday's first appearance at the Apollo, but it came in the midst of a stormy life. She was perhaps the greatest jazz singer of them all. If, as some lyricists and poets have suggested, the saddest sound of all is a freight train in the night, to me the saddest person I've ever known was this sensitive, talented, inspiring, and enslaved person. Just as Bessie Smith "could make whole audiences weep," Billie could make them sob.

Not so Slim and Slam—Slim Gaillard and Slam Stewart. Remember "The Flat Foot Floogie with the Floy Floy?" Remember "Cement Mixer, Puttee Puttee"? They were the work of this talented pair. Slim Gaillard possessed a rare combination of talents; he could sing, he could dance; he could play the guitar, the bongos. He could wiggle his muscles—he could break up the house! Slam Stewart wrote songs and played bass.

This won't be the last time you'll see the name of Lena Horne, but aside

7a.

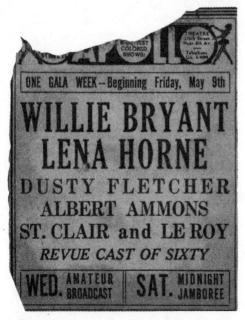

7b.

from a much earlier announcement, you'll never see her again as number two on a bill! She came out of the old Cotton Club, where she was a soubrette. Once a singer with Noble Sissle and Charlie Barnet, she became one of the stage and screen's most gorgeous women.

Note another member of this 1941 cast, Albert Ammons. Ammons was one more in a long list of talented pianists who added spice and inventiveness to the jazz scene. He was one of the originators of the style called boogie-woogie. He also had a son, Gene Ammons, who until his untimely death, was one of the best tenor saxmen in the world of music.

The 1942 show titled *Salute to Negro Troops* was almost the beginning of the end of the "production shows"; it was becoming increasingly difficult to put together chorus lines, and on a weekly basis, it was almost impossible.

Harlem Cavalcade was not the only show Broadway columnist and TV personality Ed Sullivan brought to the Apollo, but it was the one with the largest cast. Of particular note are Tim Moore, one of the greatest of the black comics, who, in his later years, played the role of "Kingfish" in the television show *Amos 'n Andy*; Avis Andrews, who for some years sang with the Cab Calloway Band; pianist Garland Wilson; and singer Jessie Cryor.

The year 1941 seems to have been an extraordinary one at the Apollo, perhaps a "last fling" before the war, which everyone knew was coming, and everyone dreaded. Witness, for example, the announcement for *Hot Mikado*. It was a show capable of setting the town on fire—a swinging, singing version of Gilbert and Sullivan's *Mikado,* which featured the world's number-one black entertainer at the time, Bill "Bojangles" Robinson.

Entertainment at the Apollo was not always singers, dancers, musicians, or comics. Sometimes, as with the Scottsboro Boys, it was the presentation of people in the news; sometimes it was a popular black personality. When the final history of Harlem and black America is written, no one will deny that the great Joe Louis surpassed most others in popularity and human appeal. On the nights when Joe was fighting, the streets of Harlem were deserted, and in his prime gawking, worshiping hordes followed him wherever he went. Nor is anyone more deserving of the adulation Joe received; he was always a source of pride to Americans of any background. In 1953, as detailed in *Variety,* we presented a couple of shows starring Joe. He was assisted by Leonard Reed, one of the cleverest performers I've known and a walking encyclopedia of show business.

No one should have expected Joe Louis to be a great public speaker, and yet some people concluded that his lack of speaking ability indicated a lack of intelligence. I recall, however, that at the time we were negotiating our contract for Joe's appearance we explained the "deal," which consisted of a guaranteed salary plus a percentage of the gross over a stipulated amount. The first one at that meeting who said "In other words, if we take in———[and he named a figure] then we can make———" was Joe. He had picked up the essence of the deal before anyone else in the room had.

By the fifties the chorus line was gone, and the format of the Apollo

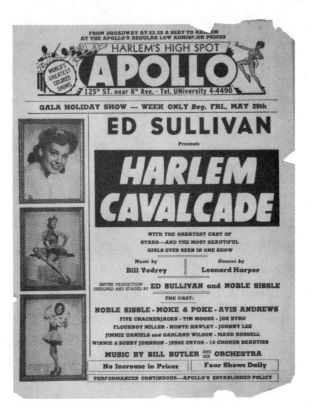

8a.

8b.

9a. Charles Parker ("The Bird")

9b. Nat "King" Cole.

shows had shifted from production number to headliners as the box-office lure. They were a varied bunch, including such great personalities as Nat "King" Cole, a swinging singer whose popularity among Apollo patrons never faltered, and Charlie "Bird" Parker, one of the greatest alto saxophonists in jazz. Charlie played the Apollo with a number of bands, including Earl "Fatha" Hines' and Billy Eckstine's, as well as with several of his own. The history of the saxophone in modern jazz virtually starts with "Bird" and ends with John Coltrane, with Coleman Hawkins, Chu Berry, and Lester Young thrown in for good measure.

But genius will always out; and if John Coltrane had genius, so too had Stevie Wonder. He started out as "Little" Stevie Wonder, but the *little* was dropped when physical maturity and artistic growth made Stevie one of the most respected and sought-after personalities in modern show business. Musician, composer, personality—Stevie Wonder has it all.

The Apollo wasn't all music and song. Long before Sidney Poitier had become a household name the world over, he headed an all-black dramatic production of *Detective Story* in August 1950. Nine years later, he was on Broadway starring in *Raisin in the Sun,* well launched into one of the most successful careers in show business. Nor was this the only departure from our usual format into the realm of the legitimate theater. *Tobacco Road, Anna Lucasta,* Canada Lee, Ossie Davis—these are but a few of the names that were written into the Apollo Theatre's book of legitimate shows. Harlem had seen "legit" at the Lafayette back in Depression days, but that was a long while back.

In 1960 we were still presenting the major headliners of the day, such as that delightful pixie and blues queen, Dinah Washington. A veteran of the stage, alumna of such bands as Lionel Hampton's, Dinah remained until her tragic death one of the most consistently popular stars to appear at the Apollo. Every time her career reached a lull, she would cut another disc and see it soar to the top of Harlem's hit parade. From the early "It's Too Soon to Know" to the later "This Bitter Earth," Dinah's hit recordings rolled out like clockwork.

But if the show that opened June 24, 1960, with Tommy Smalls, Jimmy Jones, Mary Johnson, and the rest didn't *start* a revolution, it certainly illustrates one. In the early sixties, the Apollo's format once again changed. This time the change was radical, and in the history of the business, it was probably unfortunate. In place of *variety,* which in the presence or the absence of "production" had remained a staple part of each show, we presented a procession of vocal groups. The idea was not entirely ours; it was spawned by Tommy Smalls, a disc jockey, whose stock in trade was the vocal group and who suddenly had become a personality on his own. Working on the assumption that a disc jockey could serve a dual role, as publicizer of the show and as master of ceremonies, we brought in a succession of deejays who each headed his own hand-picked show.

As my brother Bobby put it, "You could have brought on the same act over and over again, after a costume change, and hardly anyone would have known the difference." It may have been lousy showmanship, it may have bored me, but to our audiences the new format was dynamite. We may not have liked

10a. John Coltrane ("Trane")

10b. Miles Davis

10c. Stevie Wonder

For One Week Only
OPENING TODAY
(Fri. Sept. 9th)

The Apollo Theatre Proudly Presents

The "QUEEN"
MISS DINAH
WASHINGTON

11a.

11b.

11c.

it, but I must confess we liked the long lines of hep cats into who flocked into the theater, shrieking and bouncing as their favorite group sang, shouted, and gyrated before them. It was an orgy of noise that left me gasping. "Turn down the mikes," I hollered at Bobby during one show. "I can't understand a single word."

"You're not supposed to hear them, you're supposed to know them," he shouted back.

He was right. At that moment in show-biz history, I *was* supposed to know the words, or I wasn't supposed to care. I didn't. And if the new format started a revolution in popular music, it also made another one possible. I will talk about the gospel show in a later chapter, but it would never have happened in the form it took, unless preceded by the rock vocal group of the sixties. *They* brought the curtain down on the Heyday Years.

History 1 A

"Ole Man Mose Is Dead"

At the turn of the century and into the early teens, Harlem was exclusively white. It was not only white but elegantly so. Shortly before World War I a few black families (known then of course as Negro and later as colored) moved into the vicinity of 135th Street and Lenox Avenue from the area called San Juan Hill. Though not especially hilly and bearing no special resemblance to the real San Juan, San Juan Hill was roughly an area in the Fifties between Sixth and Tenth Avenues. (Incidentally, the area around Pennsylvania Station, not too far south, was then the red-light district.)

Shortly after this initial invasion, some landlords around 142nd Street in Harlem, struggling against hard times (which were partially caused by the greed that sent real-estate values skyrocketing to absurd heights) rented to an increasing number of black families. There was no shortage of those, especially since a substantial number of blacks from the South, like foreign-born immigrants, were moving to New York looking for "streets paved with gold." Of course, they were also looking for a freer atmosphere for themselves. In the short space of ten or twelve years, the area between 130th and 145th Streets, from Eighth Avenue to Fifth became almost solidly black.

There was an astonishing number of theaters in Harlem in those days. At one time, for instance, four theaters stood on the single block of 125th Street between Seventh and Eighth Avenues. The Harlem Opera House building housed two of them; the Victoria and Hurtig and Seamon's (later to become the Apollo) were the others. And if one added the nearby Orient Theatre, the Alhambra (around the corner on Seventh Avenue), and the West End, just two blocks west, there was a total of seven theaters all within a three-block area! Then there was the Douglas on 142nd Street (the Cotton Club was upstairs over

---

Towering above all but a select few in the list of jazzdom's greats, was Louis "Satchmo" Armstrong. His recording of "Ole Man Mose Is Dead" sets the theme for this chapter. This comical recording exhibits the showman side of Louis' genius, but soaring over the fun is the Armstrong trumpet.

its lobby) and the Odeon on 145th Street and Lenox Avenue. The Lafayette (with Connie's Inn in its basement), the Roosevelt, the Lincoln, and the Renaissance were all part of the scene, and of these only the little Orient Theatre didn't have live stage shows at one time or another.

Francis "Doll" Thomas, a former roustabout with carnivals and minstrels, then a stage hand, and finally a motion-picture projectionist had worked for Dad since the early twenties. Laughed Doll, "In 1931, your dad put some shows on at the Douglas Theatre and with its 3500 seats [all on one floor] was able to make money with a mere ten-cent admission charge."

In May of 1925, Dad put on the first black vaudeville-type stage show at the Lafayette Theatre. Its cast included a small orchestra, a line of chorus girls, and several acts. The show included an organist who had worked at the Lincoln Theatre, who went by the name of "Fats." It was some time before he agreed to permit use of his last name, Waller. There had been live shows at the Lafayette before Dad and Leo Brecher took it over, but for the most part they had been more serious productions. There was, for instance, a production of *Faust* (with an all-black cast), which was produced back in the teens and which then went on tour. The modern equipment we take for granted now wasn't yet in use. There were no microphones, for instance, and singing acts used megaphones to project their voices outward. "Still," said Dewey "Pigmeat" Markham, veteran comedian, "it was often hard to hear their voices beyond the second or third row!" He continued, "The first act to use a mike at the Lafayette was the Mills Brothers. They started their act by jumping through a huge replica of a [Decca] record, then started singing. It broke the audiences up!" That was back in 1931.

Pigmeat adds a graphic description of the Harlem of the day:

I've been here since 1927. At that time everything was nice here. There was the Cotton Club, Connie's Inn, Small's Paradise—all the nightclub life was up here. At twelve o'clock, after the Broadway shows closed, Broadway went completely dark. People would come up here with their chauffeurs and limousines and everything, and they'd come to the Cotton Club, Connie's Inn, and the [Lafayette] Midnight Show. There was no stealin', no dope, no breaking into cars. And if you wuz sittin' in at one of the shows and you saw a gal you liked, you'd call the headwaiter and he'd make the arrangements, and when the show was over he'd get whoever was in charge, in order for the chorus girl not to show up for the next show. She'd turn a trick and go back for the show after that. Yes, everything was fine then!

A more idyllic but still poignant description of the Harlem of those days is added by Doll Thomas' description of a Sunday outing in Harlem in the twenties:

We'd get up about three o'clock in the morning and w'd have all kinds of fried chicken and other food and we'd put them in shoe boxes to take along. We'd get a big bottle of beer for ten cents and then we'd hire a carriage for the day for about two and a half bucks. We'd start from the Fifties and drive up to what is now the speedway [what is now the East River Drive] and we'd have a picnic. We'd play ball and dance and just have a good time of it. The only thing was, though, that we had to be outta that neighborhood by dark!

In the "free" atmosphere of New York, some "freedom" still had its limits.

The great Bert Williams, star of the *Ziegfield Follies,* was a frequent visitor to Harlem and the Lafayette, coming uptown after his stint at the Follies was done. Bert was a close friend of J. Lubrie Hul, whose *Darktown Follies* was one of the early masterpieces of the black theater, and Bert would go out of his way to see Hul's shows, trying to pick up ideas for himself. Doll Thomas relates that Williams frequently brought his boss, Florence Ziegfield himself, uptown and that Ziegfield was so impressed with one of Hul's productions that he bought a finale and put it into his own Follies. In 1930, when the original cast for the Broadway production *Green Pastures* was being hired, a good deal of the casting was done on the island in front of the old Lafayette Theatre and in front of the "tree of hope."

After Dad moved his operations from the Lafayette to the Harlem Opera House, the Lafayette continued to be operated under the aegis of Hallie Flannagan and the WPA Theater. It all happened during the depths of the Depression. Productions of various plays with black casts were staged, the idea being to offer work to black actors and inexpensive shows to a demanding but impoverished public. One of the problems was that, as Doll Thomas put it, "there were no qualified blacks to serve as directors and producers." Whites were brought in to do the job. Their names? Orson Welles and John Housman. In fact, Orson Welles presented a production of *Macbeth* in 1936 with an all-black cast.

Jackie "Moms" Mabley was a comedienne whose career transcended time, generations, and race. She appeared at the Apollo and its predecessors during the thirties, wrote comedy material for many of the original shows that appeared there, and was already well launched into a career that eventually became legendary. Moms, like many black performers, was brought up on a theatrical circuit, of which there were several. The most prominent of them was called the Theatrical Owners Booking Association, the TOBA, the TOBY, or "Tough on Black Actors." Sometimes it was bitterly called "Tough on Black Asses." The TOBA (and the CVBA, another circuit) was an extension of the old minstrel tradition, which had its roots back in pre-Civil War days.

Travel has always been an integral part of the performer's life; it is regarded as curse and lure simultaneously. Talk to any of the old-timers, and they will eventually reminisce about the days of the carnivals and minstrels. Said one old-timer, "On the TOBY, you learned. You had at least a month's work, maybe several, and you developed your poise, your stature on the stage." Tours run by the TOBA and the CVBA swung through the major cities like Richmond, Washington, Baltimore, New York, Pittsburgh, and then through the rural South. "We played as many as ninety one-night stands in a row, and you learned to be a performer," says Doll Thomas. "Music, dancing, and comedy were developed, sometimes out of the daily situations you faced on the tour." Jingles like this came out of the experiences:

> The longest train I ever saw
> came down the Georgia Line.
> The engine came 'round five in the mornin',
> the Caboose didn't get there 'til nine!

Or perhaps:

> There's the love of a mother,
> and the love of a brother.
> But there's no love like
> the love of two drunks,
> for one another!

Traveling anywhere in the country was no bed of roses for a black performer in those days, but traveling through the South was a particular hell. Doll Thomas tells a graphic story of the trials and tribulations that were then the black performer's lot:

I was stranded in a "turkey" in Atlanta while on the TOBA. The drummer in the band and I made the mistake of coming around and trying to enter the theater through the front door one night before the show started or the public was even entering. The man at the door couldn't stand that and he started hollering, "You niggers ain't allowed through the front door" and he was carrying on something awful. When the drummer started bowing and scraping and saying "yassuh" I figured that was no place for me. So I wrote a friend in Newark and arranged for a job.

A week later, I went to the railroad station, put my money down and said, "Give me a ticket to New York." That red-faced cracker looked at me and said, "Ain't no niggers leavin' here. We don't allow them out." That man refused, absolutely refused, to sell me a ticket.

Man! I walked forty miles to the next depot, but before I went in I decided to use some of my show-business training. I got out my banjo, put on some false whiskers, walked into the station, and said to the man there, "You know Aunt Lucy, don't you?"

"You must be one of them red niggers of Lucy's, huh?"

I said, "Yessir, and I'll tell you what happened. One of Lucy's boys went to New York and he got sick and I wanna go and git him."

He said, "Man, you go on up there and bring that nigger back here where he belongs." Then he walked out to the platform and waited for the train, flagged it down and put me on board. It was the first time that train had stopped at that particular station in forty years!

Such southern travel was a nightmare for the black performers. Hops of five hundred miles or more between engagements were not uncommon; they were made on buses that left late at night (or early in the morning) from a dance hall or theater, ran throughout the next day, and arrived in time for the next night's performance. Most of the sleeping was done on the bus, and rest stops were frequently met with "No Niggers Allowed" signs at the men's and ladies' rooms and cafes.

"It got so that I didn't drink coffee very much, although I needed it to stay awake, because drinking coffee meant having to use the men's room and having to use the men's room meant an argument or being threatened at the next filling station," said one musician.

A famous singer related this tale:

I remember traveling with my Momma when I was a little child. We were tired and hungry, so we walked into the restaurant at the bus station and stood waiting while the white man waited on the whites who came in, some of them after we did. Finally, after they had all been served, he turned to us, looked Momma square in the eye and said, "All right, what do you niggers want?"

Momma looked at him, turned on her heel and said "Nothing," dragging me out of the room.

"But Momma, I'm hungry," I said.

"Then you'll jest have to stay hongry," she said. "Ain't nobody gonna talk to us like that and get our money too."

I remember visiting with Billy Eckstine while he was on tour in the South. It was before he was to appear at a dance. His dressing room was the bus! There he was, earning more money than the president of the United States, and he was changing his clothes on a bus. He wasn't the first or the last black entertainer to note the irony.

But Doll Thomas pointed out a supreme irony:

And if you think prejudice was confined to the South, forget it. Back in the twenties you couldn't buy anything to eat right here on 125th Street, and if you walked into a store and touched something, you'd bought it. A dress, shoes, fit you or not, if you touched it, it was yours! Traveling with Bessie Smith was a pleasure in those days, because she had three Pullman cars—two sleeping cars and a diner. You didn't have to go to the local restaurants and run into *that* prejudice. You know, you ran into it from the local black people too, because in the years I traveled around, it was only recently that show-business people were accepted as more or less normal. I mean, people would invite you into their homes and they were very hospitable. They'd feed you and then they'd ask you what you did, and when you told them you were connected with entertainers, they'd exclaim, "O Lord, Child, you can't stay here in my house. You're bringing the devil in here with you." I worked with a lot of white performers too in my time, and the same prejudice against performers existed among white folks as among black.

Kenn Freeman was the historian of the Negro Actors Guild and a descendant of a distinguished theatrical family. I talked to Kenn and to the NAG's secretary, Ernestine Allen. Formerly a vocalist with Lucky Millinder's band, which had traveled extensively through the South, Ernestine is a thoughtful and articulate lady.

"Why did you put up with it?" I asked. "Didn't it make you mad enough to tear them limb from limb?"

Replied Kenn, "There are all kinds of hates today, but we just didn't have them when I was growing up. Everybody loved everybody else."

Ernestine responded differently to my questioning glance.

You don't accept it. You're angry at that particular moment because you think, "Why do I have to suffer?" And you cuss like a sailor. And then you get on the bus and you see other white folks and you don't carry it with you, because you weren't taught to hate—and you don't—you can't. You really don't know how. Listen, when I was growing up, Broadway was called the "Great White Way" and Brother, that's exactly what it was—white. And there was a million dollars worth of black talent running around. A black couldn't get a job because that's exactly what it was—the Great White Way! I had the experience many times of talking over the phone, thinking I got the job and when I showed up, they took one look at my face and boom! there goes the job!

I kept thinking about Ernestine's remarks about not having learned how to hate, and somehow I thought that said it all. Somehow I came away from that meeting feeling an infinite compassion and love for the lady who could have said it, could have thought it. Her humanity transcended mine, and I was ashamed and glad all at once. I couldn't help thinking that if I were black and had to put up with that crap I'd be ready to commit mayhem. I recalled an incident from my own past.

It was Christmas time and I was home from college and had stopped by the theater to ride home with Dad. On the way out he introduced me to Dan Burley, a writer who was then working for one of the local Harlem papers. We shook hands and exchanged pleasantries and Dad and I got in the car. As we pulled away, Dad remonstrated with me over a transgression that would never have occurred to me. I had, he said, forgotten to take my gloves off while shaking hands with Dan Burley. Dan might think I was unwilling to have my skin touch his! In my imagination I have told Dan Burley a hundred times that I intended no slight, but I have never been able to expunge that moment from my recollection.

Many people are unaware of the fact that one of the great levelers and integrators (of blacks and whites) are show-business people themselves. They were sometimes in a position to *demand* better treatment for themselves and open a few doors while so doing. Ex-trouper, ex-comedian, master of ceremonies, producer, and Apollo manager Leonard Reed tells the following story.

After World War II, Josephine Baker was playing her first engagement at a Miami Beach hotel. Standing in the wings just before her very first show, she peered out front as performers are wont to do, then called the assistant manager over and said, "Isn't it odd? This is my first appearance here and I don't see a single black person in the audience."

"Oh, that's not odd," he replied. "You're not likely to see any during your entire engagement."

"Why not?"

"Because we don't *allow* Negroes in here."

Josephine looked at him, turned and walked back toward her dressing room, tossing over her svelte shoulder, "You can tell the manager I'll be in my dressing room."

When the frantic manager rushed up, Josephine said to him, "I understand you don't allow any colored people in here."

"That's right."

"Then I don't go on." Silence.

There were hundreds of people in the dining room waiting to hear Miss Josephine Baker, one of the greatest artists on the stage that first night. They came back to see her the next night and the next and the next, along with dozens of black couples who were literally bused from the black sections of Miami and environs to see the great Josephine. They never were denied entrance again.

The same type of situation existed in Las Vegas, which was long known among black performers as a "Jim Crow town." That is, it was so known until one Louis Jordan headlined there in 1952. Overnight the doors came tumbling down. Louis played before integrated audiences—he was the hottest thing in show business at the time—followed by the Mills Brothers, Nat "King" Cole, Lena Horne, and others. It seemed that the bosses at Vegas would do *anything* to appease the demands of some of the most powerful citizens of these United States—our performers. They are, after all, America's royalty.

The move in 1934 from the Lafayette at 132nd Street to the Harlem Opera House on 125th Street was not made lightly. Moving a theater's activities is not done with the ease that one changes a shirt. Sheer necessity demanded it. The commercial center of Harlem had shifted and though a mere seven or eight blocks comprised the shift, those blocks represented a whole new world. Business at the Lafayette had fallen off badly and the lure of "downtown," although only eight blocks away, was strong. Furthermore, the Harlem Opera House, though built in 1889, was a larger and better equipped theater.

My father's tenure there was fairly short-lived, for up the street in what had been Hurtig and Seamon's Burlesque, the Apollo was now actively competing by presenting black shows too. In those Depression days, two competing theaters on the same block was an invitation to mutual suicide. After a run at the Harlem, a "pooling of interests" was arranged, and Dad's activities shifted to the Apollo, the larger and better theater, while the Harlem wound down, eventually becoming a movie house, then a bowling alley and, about twenty years

12a.

12b.

12c. Believe it or not, this is the much-loved
Jackie "Moms" Mabley, before she lost her teeth.

ago, being sold and razed to make a small office building. So ended the Harlem Opera House, whose long history went back to the days when it was part of a "wheel" of Broadway shows put on by the Shuberts; it later saw the arrival of one of jazzdom's superstars via its amateur hour.

The Apollo already had a long history and its own traditions. There was, for instance, a nightclub in its basement in the old days. It was called Joe Ward's Swannee Club. Around the corner at the Alhambra Theatre site was once a club called the Spider Web, which was reputed to be the headquarters for the New York mob. But if the Apollo had a history and a set of traditions, they were dwarfed by the events that followed Dad's arrival in 1935. Looking back at the first years of his tenure at the Apollo, one realizes that almost every major black headliner and a number of white ones graced the Apollo's stage. It was the start of the Heyday Years.

Sometimes you meet a person who has the sweet innocence of a child and wonder how he was able to keep it. And when you consider his history, you can't believe it. "Pops" Armstrong was raised in poverty, exposed to gangsters, played his horn in whore houses ("sportin' houses" as Louis laughingly called them), and was privy to every seamy act in the book. It never rubbed off! Lionel Hampton used to read the Bible before every show; Louis Armstrong always acted as though he had written it. Said his manager, the late Joe Glaser, "I've known Louis for years and years, and I've never seen him mad!"

Illustration 12b advertises a show presented back in 1935 at a time when Louis' voice lacked the harshness that characterized it in later years, when his horn was sweet and pure and agile as a dancer. His friend Dizzy Gillespie once said, "If it weren't for him, none of us would be here." In the early days, Louis was a superstar to black audiences, but as often happened, his box-office appeal faded with Harlemites as it zoomed with whites.

There was no more glamorous name in show-biz history than the Cotton Club. It started in the teens as the brainchild of Jack Johnson, the heavyweight boxing champ; but it was taken over later by Owney Madden, George "Big Frenchy" DeMauge, Sam Sellis, and their ilk for the mob. Its shows were produced by a variety of talented men like Lew Leslie, Herman Stark, Leonard Reed, and many others. Until it moved downtown to Broadway in 1936 it was a club for white patrons by black entertainers.

The revues featured such stars as Duke Ellington, Cab Calloway, Ethel Waters, Bill Robinson, Louis Armstrong, Buck and Bubbles, Jimmie Lunceford, the Nicholas Kids, and many others, either starting or headlining there. Lena Horne was a soubrette in the chorus line; she did an act later with dancer Avon Long. Also in the line was Bessie Buchanan, whose husband, Charlie, ran the Savoy Ballroom. Bessie became the first black assemblywoman in the New York State Legislature. With her was Lucille Watson, who later became Mrs. Louis Armstrong. Lucille, a particularly beautiful woman, had a rare distinction at the Cotton Club: she was probably the first dark-skinned woman to join the mostly light-complexioned chorus line at the Club.

Each year, the Apollo, as had the Lafayette before it, presented *The Cotton Club Show,* the one on August 9, 1936, headlining Claude Hopkins and his band. In the supporting cast were dancer Babe Mathews, singer Jessie Cryor, Lena Horne, and a dancer named Cora LaRedd who pioneered a dance called "Truckin'," which during the thirties and early forties was a craze that swept not only Harlem but the entire country. The 1936 show also headlined one of the most beloved comedy acts ever to appear on the black stage, Butterbeans and Susie. (Their names will appear throughout this book for I, like all aficionados of black talent, grew to love them as people and as an act.) Nor can I let this show go by without mentioning Flournoy Miller (of the comedy team Miller and Lyles) and Mantan Moreland, a veteran comic who played in many of the Charlie Chan movies.

I have already mentioned the influence of the mob in some portions of show business. It ran and controlled the Cotton Club, which was known for its racially restrictive policy. Doll Thomas tells a story to illustrate:

> I had a contract on the Blackwood Lewis Band from Missouri; I was supposed to be their agent. We auditioned them for the Cotton Club and the audition was successful, so I went there to see what was doin' and to get some money. I showed my management contract to Jack "Legs" Diamond. He looked at it a minute, then tore it up. Then he pulled out a pistol, stuck it in my ribs and said, "You black motherfucker; you ain't got no band. This is gonna be our band." End of matter.

It's hard to argue with a .38, and Doll's presence today is mute testimony to the fact that he didn't.

Songwriter Henry Nemo, who speaks the original "jive" and is the prototype of Mr. Five by Five, offers this recollection of the world of Tin Pan Alley:

> I was just a dumb kid back in the twenties and I was writing lyrics for some songs that Duke [Ellington] wrote. I was raised in New York, but I really didn't know anything about show business, the mob, and like that. Dukey was working under Irving Mills, the music publisher and so was I. Mills was payin' me off in the dark but I didn't know the difference. I did know that winter was coming; it was gettin' colder every day and I was shiverin' because I didn't own an overcoat and didn't have enough dough-re-me to buy one. Well, Dukey is in there talkin' to Mills one day and I'm cooling my heels out in the lobby when this man walks in. He's well-dressed but I didn't know who he was.
>
> He starts talkin' to me. You know, like "What's your name, kid? Whatcha doin' here?" That kind of stuff. Well, he was friendly enough, so I keep talkin' to him.
>
> Then he asks me, "Where's your coat, kid?" Guess he must have noticed I was shiverin' or something. Well, when he finds out I haven't got one he sez, "How much money they payin' you anyway?"
>
> I laughed. I guess they were payin' me about fifteen bucks a week and that's what I told him. He just stares at me; then he grabs me by the arm and marches me right into Irving Mills' office. He starts roaring at Mills and I'm scared.

13a.

At The **125th** STREET **APOLLO**

AMERICA'S SMARTEST COLORED SHOWS!

THEATRE 125th Street Near 8th Av. — Telephone Un. 4-689

WEEK ONLY — BEG. FRI. MAY 9th

CHARLIE DAVIS PROUDLY PRESENTS

Willie Bryant

MEADE LUX LEWIS--JOE TURNER

IN A NEW MUSICAL COMEDY HIT

Swinging in Society

WITH THE GREATEST CAST YET

EARL BOSTIC AND HIS BAND

TIP, TAP and TOE SENSATIONAL DANCERS

BILLY DANIELS SWEET SINGER

Dusty Fletcher - Jimmie Baskette

Sinclair & LeRoy -- Edna Harris

NEW BROWNSKIN CHORUS

in **CHARLIE CHAN** in "DEAD MEN TELL"

Wed. Nite: Amateurs | Sat. Midnight Show

13a.

13b.

1935

125th STREET **APOLLO**

AMERICA'S SMARTEST COLORED SHOWS!!

THEATRE 125th STREET NEAR 8th AV. TELEPHONE UN. 4-4409

ONE WEEK ONLY — BEGINNING FRIDAY, MAY 29th

Today's Outstanding Star of Stage, Screen and Radio

"FATS" WALLER

APPEARING WITH

Turner's Arcadians

with

Emmett Mathews

And Another Unbeatable Revue

PIGMEAT JOHN MASON JIMMIE BASKETTE

Three Kanes ACROBATIC MARVELS

DINK, BLINK & DINK · PEARL BAINES · BOBBIE EVANS and CLARENCE ROBINSON'S BEAUTIFUL DANCING GIRLS

Also the Gripping Drama of Reckless Adventure

"The House of a Thousand Candles"

MIDNITE SHOW SATURDAY | WED. AMATEUR NIGHT

ONE WEEK BEGINNING FRIDAY JUNE 9th **Earl Hines** AND HIS BAND | ERNEST WHITMAN

13b.

"Whatya mean, paying this kid like that?" he sez. "Nobody can live on that."

"All right, all right, I'll tell Arthur [his brother, who was the bookkeeper] to give him a raise."

But that didn't satisfy this character. He makes Mills himself take me out right then and there an' buy me an overcoat. And it was a cashmere no less! Jeez, I never saw a cashmere coat in my life. [Nemo doubles up with laughter.] And then he makes him give me a raise. To two hundred bucks a week! I didn't think there was that much money in the whole world. And when I got home my mother thought I was stealing the money. She wouldn't believe me when I told her I was makin' it honestly.

When the Neme finished, I asked, "Who was the guy? The one who befriended you?"

"Oh, that was Dutch Schultz," he shot back.

There is no more important genius among Apollo Theatre headliners than Fats Waller. Fats started by playing the organ at the Lincoln Theatre; his accomplishments are so numerous that not one but at least half a dozen books have been written about him. There are many notes to be made about his accomplishments, which are especially impressive when you realize that he was only thirty-nine when he died. With lyricist Andy Razaf he wrote a song that to my mind is one of the greatest compositions to come out of this period of American musical history. Its title and principal lyric asks, "What Did I Do, To Be So Black and Blue?"

It was probably back in the twenties that an amusing incident involving Fats took place. At that time Dad was running a movie theater in the Yorkville section of Manhattan called the Verona. The area was populated by many members of the mob. It was in the silent-movie days when an organist played along with the picture, blending his music in with the picture's theme to add another dimension to it. Suddenly the organists began quitting, one after another. In desperation, Dad sent up to the Lincoln Theatre and hired Fats to do the job for a while. After a single show, Fats appeared in the office and announced, "I'm quittin'."

"The hell your are," said Dad, "at least not until you tell me why."

Fats refused; Dad refused to permit him to leave. Finally, Fats said, "Mr. Schiffman, you've always been good to me. I can't tell you why I'm quittin', but if you'll come down to the pit during the next performance, maybe you can figure it out."

Dad went down and discovered guns, dozens of them, all resting neatly between the foot pedals. It was a scary scene and it had an obvious explanation: the mob. None of the gangsters who frequented the theater wanted to be caught with guns on them. They were using the organist as a "gun checker," who was understandably terrified. I don't know how it was done, but the practice was stopped.

On October 11, 1936, a show opened with more than one performer of note. Willie Bryant was "Harlem's Favorite." The young Nicholas Brothers,

14a.

14b.

Harold and Fayard, already had a fairly long history. Known earlier as the Nicholas Kids, when they broke into show business, they were the most sensational dancing act the stage had ever seen. They starred at the Cotton Club, but when still youngsters they had become internationally known movie stars. As they grew into manhood, the quality of their act grew.

One star of that show, Muriel Rahn, had to wait until 1943 to achieve due recognition. This lovely and talented singer starred as one of the alternating Carmens in the Broadway production *Carmen Jones,* a modern version of the Bizet opera. Muriel, who died tragically young, played at the Apollo on and off for many years. Both as an artist and as a person, she brought that rare and elusive thing called class to whatever she appeared in. (I will talk about other stars of this show later.)

Another original production show, the *League of Rhythm Revue,* was produced in December 1936. None of the stars of this show were thought at the time to be famous enough to dominate the marquee. This is ironic in terms of subsequent musical history. The mere mention of the name "Bessie Smith," for instance, is enough to make any jazz aficionado jump for joy, and the history of the bands could hardly be written without a bow in the direction of Erskine Hawkins, one of the best trumpeters ever to come along in America. The appearance of Hawkins, Bessie, Pigmeat Markham, and the other acts were worth the price of admission many times over.

In 1936, one Huddie Ledbetter, better known to the public as Leadbelly, was languishing in a Texas jail, having been tried and convicted of murder. Leadbelly played the twelve-string guitar and he wrote songs, lots of them, some of them pretty good. One was titled "I'm Coming Home, Mary." It was brought to the attention of Governor Neff who, the story goes, was so impressed that he pardoned Leadbelly. The Apollo booked him while he was on a nationwide tour. But don't let the blurb on the ad fool you; Dad thought he was awful.

"The first time I heard him sing was on stage at the Apollo," he related. "We had constructed a prison scene in which Monty Hawley played the part of the Governor and Leadbelly sang before him. When he started to sing, I thought I'd die. I never heard such awful wailing. But even though I didn't like him, the audience did." He shook his head. "Maybe they were right." He added, "This man was the only man I ever met who physically scared me; there was something sinister about him."

Sinister or not, Leadbelly had a successful tour; he also had a successful career as a songwriter. You may not know "I'm Coming Home, Mary" but the world knows "Goodnight, Irene," Leadbelly's most successful creative effort.

Out of the Cotton Club another band leader emerged to become one of the nation's most popular and famous personalities. He was the "King of Hi De Ho," Cab Calloway. Although he was known principally as a singer and entertainer, Cab was also a fine musician and, at various times, he hired some of the greatest musical figures of their day. Tenor saxman Chu Berry, for instance, has become legendary, but he was not the only outstanding star in the Calloway

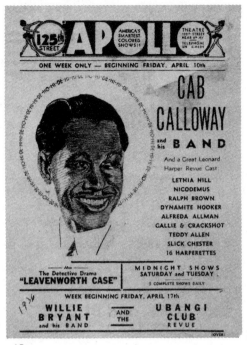

15a.

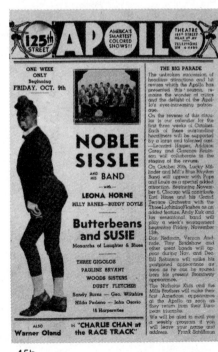

15b.

organization. For starters, how about trumpeters Dizzy Gillespie and Jonah Jones? Jazz buffs will recognize the names of pianist-arranger Buster Harding, saxophonists Ben Webster (for years, one of Duke's stalwarts) and Hilton Jefferson, bassist Milt Hinton, and the great drummer Cozy Cole. There is hardly a show-business personality who characterizes the jazz age better than Calloway. The lexicon of jive talk, precursor of terms like *cool*, and *right on* was fathered by him. He even wrote a dictionary listing all the slang, and every school kid in Harlem probably knew the words by heart. In the ad for the April 10, 1936, show notable names are his vocalist, Lethia Hill; a stalwart of Cab's organization for years, Nicodemus; and the dancer Ralph Brown.

Noble Sissle became a Broadway figure as part of the composing team of Sissle and Blake, who wrote the music for *Shuffle Along*, produced in 1921, and who wrote "I'm Just Wild About Harry." But for years before and after his association with Eubie Blake, he was known as an orchestra leader. In his October 1936 revue at the Apollo his vocalist was Lena Horne, then known as Leona. (Said Lena, in a conversation with me, "Noble never liked the name Lena, so he changed it to Leona.") For her talents, Lena received the Depression sum of $35—for the week, but in cash!

Lena later left Noble's band to do vocals with Charlie Barnet. When she left Charlie it was to become the spectacularly successful singer who endeared herself to audiences all over the world through films and stage appearances.

The man in Illustration 15b is Butterbeans. "Butter" as he was known on stage and off, worked in blackface in the thirties, as did most black comedians. He later abandoned the cork.

If you examine "The Big Parade," Dad's blurb for coming attractions at the Apollo, you can see why *Apollo* and *black show business* became synonymous terms.

With but one exception, none of the cast of the *Hot Chocolates of 1936* were to become superstars. The original Hot Chocolates appeared on Broadway in 1929 (the first trumpeter in the orchestra was Louis Armstrong), and this version was an Apollo standout in 1936. It was written by Fats Waller and Andy Razaf. Louis Jordan was in the cast; for years he was the Apollo's number-one headliner. Louis recorded "Is You Is or Is You Ain't My Baby," and later recorded other smash hits such as "Run Joe" and, with Ella Fitzgerald, "Cold Stone Dead in the Market."

In October 1936, the Sunset Royal Band and its revue was a standout show. The band was fronted by Doc Wheeler, who later became one of the best-known gospel disc jockeys and a creative force in the gospel movement. The band itself used a skillful blend of jazz and show biz savvy to achieve its effectiveness. They worked out an arrangement of "Marie," which was used later by the Tommy Dorsey Band that became a national hit. This is merely one more in the long list of cases in which a creative effort by a black organization was picked up and capitalized upon by a white band. That practice was long a source of frustration and bitterness among black artists, justifiably so. It was

16a.

16b.

tough for blacks to stand by and see white artists make millions and achieve enormous popularity for doing what they'd been doing for years, for a lot less than millions.

Rex Ingram, featured in the same show, had a long and distinguished acting career prior to his appearing as "De Lawd" in the movie *The Green Pastures.* He appeared a few years later, in the Broadway production of *Cabin in the Sky* with Ethel Waters. No stranger to Dad, Ingram had appeared in many earlier dramatic productions as part of the Lafayette Players.

One of the most colorful (and controversial) figures to come along in the thirties was Stepin Fetchit, whose real name was Lincoln Perry. The sad-eyed Stepin Fetchit was the headliner in a December 1936 show, and it was no exaggeration to bill him as "America's Greatest Colored Screen and Stage Star." Stepin Fetchit appeared in dozens of Hollywood films, in which he always played the part of a lazy, slothful black, whose decision on whether to go from "here" to "there" was made on the basis of how much effort was required to do so. Many people have claimed that Fetchit did a grave disservice to black Americans by appearing in such demeaning roles. I cannot quarrel with that opinion. There are, on the other hand, those who claimed that he made a contribution by becoming a black star and personality, and thus was a pioneer. It should also be noted that if he appeared lazy in his roles, at least he always "won" in the situation he found himself in.

Notable in the same show were Bardou Ali, a veteran dancer who also fronted the Chick Webb Band at the Savoy Ballroom, and Sandy Burns, one of the Apollo's most stalwart comedians for many years.

On February 12, 1937, Louise Beavers opened at the Apollo in *Brownskin Models of 1937,* one of a series bearing that name. Its producer, Irvin C. Miller, was as distinguished a producer as there was in the black theater. Miss Beavers, a truly talented actress, became a notable Hollywood star, but the condition of the times dictated that she play her roles dressed as a maid. There is, of course, nothing wrong with maids; they are—or were—a part of the scene. But there was something wrong when a talented woman was restricted to maid and colored Mammy roles. Louise did star in some independently made pictures but in "major" Hollywood productions, she remained a part of the servant class.

In the thirties there was no more famous radio program than that of Major Bowes. For years millions of Americans listened faithfully to his "Amateur Hour." Bowes organized some road shows and sent them touring. On July 23, 1937, he brought one of them to the Apollo. I do not know of a major black star who came from this show, but it is possible there was one.

Teddy Wilson's appearance in March 1937 caused excitement at the Apollo; it headlined one of jazzdom's great pianists. Teddy was the first black artist to hit "downtown," playing with the Benny Goodman quartet and sextet, making records with Goodman and on his own, and backing Billie Holiday in many of the classic sides she cut during her career. In the history of jazz, Teddy Wilson must be ranked alongside such great pianists as Art Tatum, Fats Waller,

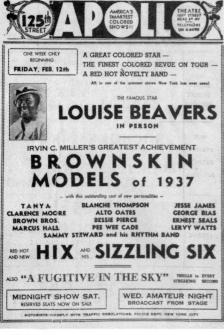

17a.

17b.

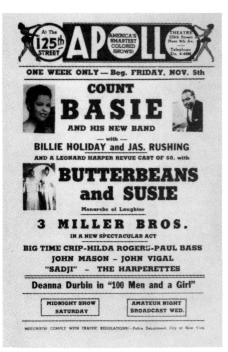

17c.

17d.

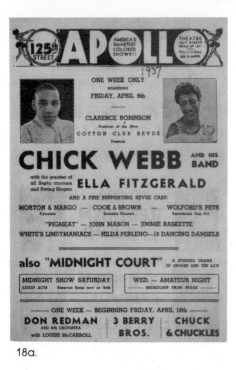

18a.

18b.

18c.

James P. Johnson, Willie "The Lion" Smith, and Earl "Fatha" Hines.

Billie Holiday starred in a November 1937 show along with Bill "Count" Basie, one of the most innovative and popular jazzmen of them all. Among his many interests, Basie researched and pioneered in the presentation of the blues, for which Jimmie Rushing was for years Basie's prime vocal exponent. The Miller Brothers formed one of the thirties great dancing acts. They were always known in the trade as a "class act." One of its members was one of the Apollo's greatest friends, Honi Coles, who danced at the Lafayette, the Harlem Opera House, and the Apollo, and who worked for a number of years as the Apollo's manager. Fitting recognition of his talents came in 1983, when he won a Tony Award for his past in *My One and Only.*

In 1934, a scared, skinny, young girl won the amateur contest at the Harlem Opera House. She started out dancing, but then switched to singing. In 1937 that young performer, Ella Fitzgerald, on her way up, was a regular member of the Chick Webb Band. Chick, probably one of the greatest drummers of all time, had a fabulous group that featured an entertaining alto saxophonist named Louis Jordan. Thus from the Chick Webb organization, two of the most famous stars in the Apollo's history emerged.

The war clouds were gathering when "News and Notes," part of an Apollo handbill, was written. In August 1941 *Variety* reviewed a show starring the Four Ink Spots. Adelaide Hall, mentioned in "News and Notes" was a product of the Cotton Club and Lew Leslie's famed *Blackbirds.* Old-timers may recall her rendition of "Dig-a-Dig-a-Doo." As for the Ink Spots, in their prime Bill Kenny, the tenor, and Deek Watson led them as they became a legend at the Apollo as well as in general.

Not one, but *two* white headliners led a 1942 show into the record books. They were the "Old Rockin' Chair" gal, Mildred Bailey and her husband, the vibraphonist Red Norvo, and his band. Red once told me that John Hammond used to bring him and Mildred to see the Apollo's shows frequently, especially when Charlie Barnet was there, but it wasn't until some years after his first visits there that he became an Apollo headliner himself.

But if Red Norvo and Mildred Bailey were early on the list of white entertainers to become Apollo favorites, they weren't the first. Charlie Barnet was! The great Charlie Barnet also brought in the first mixed band. Typical of the Barnet touch was the inclusion of Edith Wilson as a featured singer with his show. A veteran of the twenties, she only missed being a superstar because there were so many top-notch singers at that time. At various times Charlie's vocalists included two other thrushes to thrill Apollo audiences: Lena Horne and Kay Starr.

Charlie's first appearance, in 1940, at the Apollo is a story in itself, not without its touch of irony. Charlie had wanted to play the theater but Dad was somewhat dubious—not because he doubted Charlie's ability but because he was white. Although we had played white acts before, we had never played a white headliner. Charlie finally won however. He offered himself and his band

19a.

19b. Ethel Waters appearing as the star of
"Cabin in the Sky" in 1940.

during the pre-Christmas week (normally, a bad week for stage shows since people were spending their money on gifts). He also accepted a percentage, with no guarantee. It was an offer too good to refuse, since all of the gamble was on Charlie's side. Much to Dad's surprise, Charlie and his racially mixed band was a smash hit. The irony of the story is that not only did Charlie at once establish himself as a major Apollo headliner but also he had won the right to play always on a percentage, a deal which we used only in connection with Hampton, Ellington, Basie and Calloway at that time.

A star-filled show played the Apollo on April 3, 1941. It included John Kirby, a bassist, one of jazzdom's greats, whose band was among the more popular black bands of the early forties; "Peg" Bates, who fell just short of being a headliner himself; the Delta Rhythm Boys, a popular gospel-oriented vocal group, one of the early precursors of the groups who made history in the sixties. But perhaps the most interesting name that week was that of Shelton Brooks! Brooks wrote a song called "Some of These Days," which was immortalized by Sophie Tucker! In his later years Shelton fell on bad times but was finally found by Miss Tucker, who searched for him for years. She saw to it that he lacked for nothing from that point on. It was a generous acknowledgment, too rare in our business, of the gratitude and loyalty one performer owes another.

One of the superstars of the thirties, one of the greatest all-around performers ever to appear at the Apollo was Ethel Waters. Ethel, who died in 1977, will be remembered by many as a very large woman who sang with the Billy Graham Troupe and who was once an actress. Such a recollection would do an injustice to this lady. In her early days Ethel was known as "Sweet Mama Stringbeam," for she was a tall, skinny woman. But could she sing! If you want to get a feel for the history of jazz singing, go back to the early Ethel Waters recordings and you will hear traces of artists who came along later to build upon her artistry. If you have time for only one song, listen to her "Stormy Weather," the song that rocked the Cotton Club, Broadway, and the entire country.

Ethel was a many-faceted woman. She was dynamic, forceful and, at times, bitter. In her autobiography, *His Eye Is on the Sparrow,* she reveals a complex personality fitting somewhere between the bedrock of her deeply held Christian faith and the bitter legacies inherited from experiences suffered in the seamiest of America's black ghettos. Once, in the forties, she was rehearsing to open in a Cotton Club Revue downtown, with her boyfriend, Eddie Mallory, and his entire band standing in the wings. The trouble was that Eddie's was not the featured band, a fact which caused Ethel more than a little pain. Now Ethel could spew forth language that would make a marine sergeant blush, and on this occasion she did, referring to the antecedents and the abilities of the band that was playing her music. Her ploy must have worked, because the management discharged the band and on opening night Eddie Mallory and his crew were playing. The original band? Oh, just a fellow named Duke Ellington!

Nor can we forget her career as an actress. *Mamba's Daughters, As*

Thousands Cheer, Cabin in the Sky—they all shook Broadway. But in the last analysis, it was Ethel Waters—the person and the artist—who triumphed the most. An event at which I was a witness typifies, to me, the glory of Ethel. It was in the early fifties that a testimonial dinner was given for her and Ralph Bunche, at that time our ambassador to the United Nations. Our whole family went to it.

The first award was presented to Dr. Bunche, and during his acceptance speech my heart sank. I knew Ethel Waters, although not nearly as well as my father did. With all due respect to her, she was an artist, a singer, an actress, but not a public speaker. I thought, here was Dr. Bunche, a highly educated, articulate gentleman, used to making speeches—he's simply going to "upstage" Ethel, without intending to.

Then it was Ethel's turn to speak, and she taught me a lesson that night. Not four minutes had passed when Miss Waters had us mesmerized. She spoke of her childhood and its hardships. She spoke of her career and its obstacles. She spoke of her triumphs, her defeats, her profits, and her losses. And then she spoke of her faith, of her God. She toyed with us, bounced us around like so many rubber balls, manipulated all of us like a bunch of marionettes, and then gave us the *coup de grâce*. When she sang "His Eye Is on the Sparrow," there was no way anyone in that hall could have seen an eagle, let alone a sparrow. It's hard to see anything if your eyes are filled with tears, and that night Ethel Waters sang to the wettest-eyed audience in New York City! On the way out, it occurred to me that perhaps I should have felt sorry for Dr. Bunche.

CODA

It is easy to look back at the Harlem of the Heyday Years and glamorize it in your imagination. There were the speakeasies of the early days, the black-chauffeured limousines with their "slumming" white passengers. There were those dances that swept its streets: the Black Bottom, the Charleston, the Shim Sham Shimmy, and the Suzie Q. There were the Cotton Club, Connie's Inn, Small's Paradise, and Dickie Wells'.

Harlem was glamorous for only one brief period of its chaotic history and that was at the turn of the century when it was rich, white, and law-abiding. Actually, it was only glamorous then if seen through the myopic eyes of history and nostalgia. It was probably quite dull! From the late twenties on, Harlem was on a roller-coaster ride and the tracks were mostly pointed downhill. Its streets were better and safer during its heyday than they are today, but they were better still during the teens and early twenties. If the Harlem of today is riddled with crime, cursed by dope, and characterized by fear, it has seen poverty, struggle, bitterness, and frustration throughout most of its history. It has long been one of our country's most tragic and blighted areas. Some of its citizens speak of it in impassioned terms.

Bobby Robinson is a short and slight brown-skinned man with a slightly oriental look. He owns a record shop (which was once combined with a shoe-shine parlor) on 125th Street, and he has managed such acts as Gladys Knight and the Pips and others of lesser stature. He is a pleasant, articulate man with the sensitive outlook of the writer, which he has also been for many years. Like others, Bobby has been shocked, hunt, and bewildered by the disintegration of Harlem. Sometime about 1980 he said to me:

> From five o'clock in the evening until midnight, we always used to do a tre-mendous business at the store, especially when the Apollo had a big show. Today, at seven o'clock in the evening—earlier during the winter when it gets dark at five-thirty, it's like a desert out there. It's not so much that people are afraid; they've got nothing to come out for.

I argued about the last statement, but Bobby continued thoughtfully:

> I try to suppress the thought that Harlem is a frightening place now. But I used to walk the streets to get ideas; I used to make it a point to walk the streets around four-thirty or five in the morning—often. I loved to watch the people sitting on their stoops, talking; I'd listen to the winos and their conversation, catch the whores on the street, listen to them talking to their pimps. I'd walk under the El when it was dark. I wouldn't dare now! It's a goddam shame!

Dewey "Pigmeat" Markham, one of the greatest of the black comics, came to Harlem in 1927; he stayed a Harlem fixture, until he died in 1981. Said Pigmeat, "I never dreamed that I would ever be scared to come to Harlem, but I'm scared now and everybody knows me."

"And you're the right color," I added.

"That's right. I'm the right color, and I'm still scared."

To understand the how and the why of Harlem's descent into the mael-strom, you have to search back, far back. You can start off with the Depression. The Depression was a horror for most people in our society, but for black men and women it was indescribably worse. The notion that "blacks are the first to be fired and the last to be hired" is tragically still true; when its truth hit Harlem in the twenties it was devastating. Perhaps it is easier to endure your own misery if you can look down on someone else, so instead of whites and blacks finding a kinship in their mutual misery, the lower position of blacks in the economic spectrum served to bolster white egos at the expense of blacks'. The better-off whites who traveled to Harlem for a glimpse of the nightlife at the various Harlem clubs did so not to mingle with blacks but to view them. The owners and managers of the Cotton Club were well aware of this desire and with rare exceptions, blacks were excluded—except for those on stage or carrying trays. The irony is that while the whites were "slumming," they were actually paving the way for future integration. They liked the entertainment and that made its later move downtown possible.

But, basically, two events paved the way for black artists' move from the ghetto of Harlem and into the consciousness of white America. These were the Harlem Riot of 1943 and World War II.

No more graphic description of the riot exists than is found in *The Autobiography of Malcolm X,* which was ghostwritten by Alex Haley, author of *Roots.* It is not my intention to try to describe that event, which has already been described far more graphically than I could. (I must add that during the riot I was at the Naval Training Center located at Columbia University, which is on the very edge of Harlem. The officials at the school were so frightened of the riot that they went so far as to put live bullets in the .45s the midshipmen on watch carried. The only casualty was sustained by a midshipman who managed to shoot himself in the foot; his curiosity about the suddenly lethal weapon was a bit too much for him to handle.)

The riot was a natural and perhaps inevitable outcome of the years of frustration built up in Harlem. One of its major results was that the many whites who had been traveling uptown to see the shows at the Apollo and the various nightclubs no longer went. The riot of 1943 engendered fear that has remained unshakable. The increase in crime, the lurid tales of the drug trade, the economic stagnation of the area, and the latent prejudices of many New Yorkers made further integration impossible. The worst tragedy of all is that the victims of crime in Harlem are usually black. With the downtown movement of black artists well under way, the riot succeeded in making ghetto Harlem more isolated than ever. Indeed, as economic integration picked up pace, the more prosperous people living in Harlem moved out in increasing numbers, moved to St. Albans in Long Island, to nearby Connecticut, New Jersey, and into Westchester County.

History sometimes works in devious and ironic ways. Take for instance the impact of World War II. It was a great leveler. Suddenly, whites who were either prejudiced against blacks to start with or who had never given them much thought because they'd never met any were thrown into contact with blacks. Both had an opportunity to observe each other. "The skin might be black, but the color of the blood is the same," marveled a Virginian with whom I came in contact while overseas. With knitted brow and troubled face he added, "Look, I've thought about it and I've listened to what you've said and I think you're right. But you gotta realize, I never had contact with blacks before and—well, it takes time to get used to the idea." Time there was aplenty for him and also for the many blacks who had never come in contact with whites before.

It's a simple equation with complex answers: take growing acceptance of black artistry, mix it with the sudden postwar awareness of downtown merchants that both black and white money is green, and you have the movement of black artists and patrons out of Harlem. Take growing postwar prosperity and, as just mentioned, you find people moving out of Harlem. Ironically, the integration taking place downtown meant increased ghettoization of Harlem itself.

But history, like Mother Nature is rarely in a hurry, and the movements I have described in sketchy detail took years and years to achieve their maximum thrust. In the meantime, post-World War II saw the country return to normal and to relative prosperity, and even Harlem was to share in this bounty for a while. Not that Harlem was prosperous, but relative to its former and later poverty, it was briefly less poor. The winds of change were already blowing up their little eddies, but the potential for the gross changes that later affected Harlem took some time to effectuate.

In the meanwhile, the Heyday was rolling along! Harlem, New York, the entire country was moving to a beat—the beat of swing. Just prior to World War II was the heyday of the big bands and for every Benny Goodman and Harry James, there were dozens of less well-known (but nonetheless highly talented) black groups in addition to Fletcher Henderson, Louis Armstrong, Duke Ellington, and Cab Calloway. Let's swing along and take a look at those bands.

The Bands
and All
That Jazz

4

"Mood Indigo"

You don't have to look hard to find an important facet of American life that has been dominated by blacks. That is jazz. In jazz the black man stands supreme; the products of his creative energies are sought after by musicians and listeners of every hue. Of course, jazz didn't start at the Apollo or even in Harlem. Its origins lie deep in the history of New Orleans, Kansas City, Chicago, and New York; its ancestral roots are buried even deeper in the musical traditions of West Africa and the Latin countries. But the Apollo was one place that provided a home and an especially receptive atmosphere in which its practitioners felt at ease, where their art could better thrive and flourish. They could try out their musical wares knowing that nothing was arbitrarily rejected, everything would be heard out. In today's parlance, "the vibes were right."

And that was vital to its growth, for although jazz is a uniquely American phenomenon, it was formerly held in relatively low esteen by a certain intellectual elite who found it both "exciting" and "primitive." I cannot escape the conclusion that this relatively low appraisal of jazz' value was made because most of its practitioners were black and its critics white. It was one more of the "put-downs" heaped on the head of Black America. The status of jazz among so-called "serious" critics and listeners has improved, as modern composers began to take an interest in it. They have recognized that its spontaneous, creative, and inventive values exist in no other musical form. Composer, arranger, and pianist Billy Taylor has quite accurately called it "American classical music."

Although the Apollo was essentially a black theater (audience and performers), our interest was always in quality rather than color. Many white musicians were accepted with respect and affection by Apollo audiences. The

---

Of the large (14 pieces or more) black bands, only those of Duke Ellington, Count Basie and Lionel Hampton were able to continue without being whittled down to combo size. And if the immortal "A Train" became a kind of theme song for the Duke, "Mood Indigo" was among his most recognizable works. With its slow blending of harmonies, it was Ellington at his suave best.

Benny Goodman Band never played the Apollo, but Benny himself did. His brother-in-law, John Hammond, told me that Benny once played an engagement as one of Count Basie's musicians, just to "have the pleasure of jamming with Lester Young, Buck Clayton, and others." The number of other white musicians and singers who played the Apollo is impressive; a partial list would include Harry James, Artie Shaw, Gene Krupa, Maynard Ferguson, Stan Getz, Buddy Rich, Woody Herman, Dave Brubeck, Doc Severinsen, Louis Prima, Boyd Rayburn, Charlie Ventura, Terry Gibbs, Gerry Mulligan, and the all-time favorite Charlie Barnet. The late Bunny Berigan was another white musician who played "way back yonder." His "I Can't Get Started with You" is one of the great jazz classics.

Our stage manager, Hans Nielsen, told me of a midnight show benefit in which Tony Bennett walked out and sang a song. "The audience reaction was so terrific," said Hans, "that a pleased Tony turned around and asked, 'Would you like some more?' To the accompanying roar, Tony took off his jacket and tie and sang for one solid hour to an audience which simply wouldn't let him go." As more than one artist has remarked, "there's no audience like an Apollo audience." Stephanie Mills, star of Broadway's *The Wiz,* said, "Apollo audiences always react to what is good."

Despite the fact that jazz was predominantly the creation of black musicians, the amount of interracial jazz was relatively small throughout early jazz history. Teddy Wilson, that great pianist, was one of the first blacks to play with a white band (Benny Goodman's), and John Hammond has pointed out that he almost had to trick his brother-in-law into using one of the early, guitar-playing geniuses, Charlie Christian, with his group. Certainly this was not because Benny Goodman was prejudiced; rather it had to do with the prevailing climate of the times. Nevertheless, every one of the four members of the Goodman quartet (Teddy Wilson, Lionel Hampton, Gene Krupa, and Benny himself) played at the Apollo. Lionel, the peerless vibraphonist, held the all-time attendance record for a week's engagement at the Apollo for many years.

If there is an artistic, a creative thread running through the history of jazz, it has to do with the interdependence of jazz men on each other. They shifted, they moved, they played with one band, than another, and with each move, the seeds of creative genius were dropped on fertile soil. It is not my intention to write a treatise on jazz; many writers, most more qualified than I, have written on that subject. But there are musical "parlays" (my term), which deserve to be pointed out anew. They have to do with the creative interdependence of artists, one on another. They would include such a one as this: Louis Armstrong to Roy Eldridge to Dizzy Gillespie to Miles Davis, a quartet of trumpeting geniuses who each built on the work of his predecessor; sometimes they added, embellished, developed certain musical ideas. (Louis himself leaned heavily on King Oliver and Buddy Bolden for *his* creative spark.)

Or, consider the singer who, in my book, was the jazz singer beyond compare—Billie Holiday. Hers is an interesting parlay too. It reads: Ma Rainey to Louis Armstrong to Bessie Smith to Billie. Ma Rainey, blues-singing queen of the "Rabbit Foot Minstrels" (a legendary group of a bygone era), passed her torch to Louis Armstrong. Billie always said that she wanted to sing exactly as Louis played his horn. And she did! The "Empress of the Blues," Bessie Smith, was another musical voice out of her childhood, whose star "Lady Day" followed. Indeed, Billie talks of Bessie in her autobiography *Lady Sings the Blues,* and Bessie's early mentor and teacher was Ma Rainey.

To follow another thread even further back into history, there is a fascinating parlay among the pianists. It is a long one, but historically authenticated. James P. Johnson and Willie "The Lion" Smith were strong influences on the mighty keyboard and composing genius Fats Waller. They were once "cut" by perhaps the greatest of them all, Art Tatum, the one whom Duke Ellington called "Boss." The skein continues with Earl "Fatha" Hines, a major innovative wizard, and it moves along with the addition of Duke Ellington, Count Basie (who learned to play the organ by watching Fats' feet at the Lincoln Theatre), and Thelonius Monk. Today's wizards, such as Oscar Peterson, Bud Powell, Cecil Taylor, Keith Jarrett and Billy Taylor, would be quick to acknowledge their debts back down the musical line. So, too, the early ones would glance back toward Jelly Roll Morton and Lucky Roberts. There are more, for there is nothing static about the history of jazz. You can't leave out Eddie Heywood, Mary Lou Williams, or Hazel Scott.

It might come as a shock for the reader to learn that, although Louis Armstrong is regarded by many as perhaps the greatest figure in the history of jazz, he saw his popularity slide down the drain in Harlem long before his death. We could play Louis (and did) in his later years and, as one of our ushers remarked, we "could have thrown basketballs around the place without hitting a soul—'cept maybe, one of us." My father always felt—and I agreed with him— that since Louis' music was basically Dixieland and since Dixieland went back to a period long gone, a period when the black man's situation was even worse than it became later, the audiences didn't want to be reminded of the past, when misery was mated with hopelessness! In any event, by the fifties, the modern musical styles, built on the early "Satchmo," had branched off into a dozen new directions.

Other jazz greats managed to hold their popularity much longer than did Armstrong. Duke Ellington, for example, was never a gate-buster, but he always attracted an interesting crowd to the Apollo during his engagements. You could look at the patrons—a little more conservatively dressed, a little more sophisticated, a bigger sprinkling of whites—and know that Duke was headlining.

Non-aficionados may be surprised to learn that the Apollo, in times past, had a large white following. Indeed, there were times, such as the Wednesday Night Amateur Show and in particular, the Saturday Midnight Show, when whites equaled or even exceeded the black patrons. But that, I hasten to add, was during the thirties and the very early forties, prior to World War II.

William "Count" Basie was another perennial favorite, who held onto his popularity when some of the others had faded a bit. On the other hand, we played Cab Calloway and Ethel Waters in the fifties to less than smashing box-office results.

By the mid-thirties, the era of the big bands was in full swing. Of all the personalities we ever played at the Apollo, none was more colorful, more personable, or more talented than Fats Waller. Fats' history with Dad goes back to the Lincoln, the Douglas, the Lafayette, and the Harlem Opera House, those show places before the Apollo. Fats got his nickname because he was a huge man, weighing about three hundred pounds. His musical compositions ran into the hundreds and include "Ain't Misbehavin'," "Honeysuckle Rose," "S'Posin'," "Black and Blue," "I've Got a Feelin' I'm Fallin'," "Keepin' out of Mischief Now," "All That Meat and No Potatoes," some written with Andy Razaf, some with Clarence Williams, some with Ed Kirkeby, and others. He was a movie personality, an entertainer par excellence, an undisputed genius who died tragically young, at thirty-nine.

There was never any question about Fats playing the Apollo; it was a semi-annual engagement, which he never missed. Sometimes, to be sure, his engagements were interrupted in midstream, but Fats always "made them" at the Apollo. There was a time, however, when he left in the middle of a show. That was when his former wife started down the aisle brandishing a pistol. When he saw her coming, Fats took off at a speed seemingly impossible for a three-hundred-pounder. Why such an uproar? Well, once again he had forgotten a small item, one he forgot month after month—alimony. Fats, it must be admitted, was not always the most responsible of performers, but his loyalty to Dad and the Apollo was eternal. This can be illustrated by telling a little story about him.

Fats didn't reach three hundred pounds by abstaining. His appetite for food and booze was prodigious; not only did he need the stimulation of liquor, he brought it on stage with him. His valet was stationed in the wings with a tray, a bottle, and a glass, so that a bow could also include a swig. My father was a bit straight-laced about such things (almost a teetotaler himself), and he once remonstrated was Fats about having liquor on the stage. Fats' answer was typical, final, and what's more, it made its point. "Mr. Schiffman," he said, "if the booze is out, then I'm out. And if I'm out then you're out. But if the booze is in, then I'm in and if—" Dad held up his hand, shrugged his shoulders, and left. The matter, was of course, dropped.

It's an amusing story but if amusement were all there was to Fats, he would have been forgotten long before now. He wasn't forgotten because he was a musical genius. Without Fats, there would have been less of Duke Ellington, less of Count Basie, less of a lot of great musicians who followed him, added to his contributions, broadened the musical base of jazz. Just listen to his records: a lilting and tinkling series of cascading arpeggios with a right hand as light and airy as he was big and ponderous; a left hand that rolled with power, that was capable at any moment of taking the play away from the right hand. Fats

20a.

20b.

despised a "one-handed pianist," as he called anything less than a "stride pianist."

In the history of jazz, "cutting" became an important incentive in fostering the experimentation and change that made jazz a live and vital force. "Cutting" was the name given to contests, in which musicians or even whole bands were pitted against each other in an attempt to see whose inventiveness would give out first. The cutting contests probably came out of the early "rent parties," in which musicians showed up at someone's apartment where, for a fee, people came to hear them, thus helping pay the rent of the tenants. In the early days, Fats Waller, Willie "The Lion" Smith, James P. Johnson, and others probably made their livings playing at rent parties. They also vied with each, stimulated each other, tried to "cut" each other to prove they were the best. "Move over and I'll show you how to play that" was the Lion's favorite phrase.

But one night Waller, Smith, and Johnson invited a young pianist to join them—a guy they'd heard was "pretty good." He was. Complacently, the three listened to the cat, thinking he "wasn't bad," but not *that* good, when suddenly this dude cut loose. In one fell swoop, the three greatest jazz pianists of the day were "cut" by the greatest of them all—Art Tatum! It was a moment Fats, in particular, never forgot. Of later vintage was the legendary battle between two great tenor saxmen, Coleman Hawkins and Lester "Prez" Young. It lasted all night and when it was over, the new generation in the form of Prez had won. That contest is still spoken of in awe by those privileged to have been there.

Without the great Fletcher "Smack" Henderson, the whole history of jazz and the thirties might have been different, for his band was the spawning ground for talents so prodigious, so varied, so influential in jazz history as to be little short of astonishing. Just to list the people who played with Fletcher at one time is to name a Who's Who of the middle period of jazz: Louis Armstrong; saxophonists Coleman Hawkins, Bennie Carter, Buster Bailey, Lester "Prez" Young (very briefly, however); trombonists Benny Morton and J. C. Higginbotham; arranger Don Redman; and trumpeter Cootie Williams. Fletcher even had Clarence Holiday, a banjo player and the father of Billie Holiday.

That's not all of Fletcher Henderson's gifts to jazz. He made some early recordings with Fats Waller and employed such musical greats as tenorman Ben Webster, bassist John Kirby, drummer Big Sid Catlett, and his brother, pianist Horace Henderson. Fletcher was probably more responsible for the "sound" of the Benny Goodman Band than perhaps Benny himself, for he was the peerless arranger of many of the Goodman classics. Jazz aficionados will recognize that such musicians as Ben Webster and Cootie Williams were long-time members of the Duke Ellington Band, while such a genius as Lester "Prez" Young must be numbered among the all-time greats of jazzdom's long history.

People are always being snubbed or misplaced by history, and although Earl "Fatha" Hines has been recognized as a great pianist—one of the greatest—he must also be acknowledged as an early pioneer of the music that later became known as bop and still later as progressive jazz. Indeed, if you listen to Earl's recordings of as late as 1980, you will be struck by the modernity of the man.

21a.

21b.

Earl died in 1983, but his musical perception and his modern conceptions were as vital to the end as they were forty years ago. And when one further considers the quality of the people in his organization, it is hard to come away with anything but profound admiration for the musical gifts of Hines.

Years ago he hired an alto saxophonist whose position is secure among a small handful of the most influential jazzmen of all time, Charlie "Bird" Parker. He also had the foresight to hire, groom, and present two highly inventive singers, Billy Eckstine and Sarah Vaughan. Budd Johnson, his tenor saxophonist and arranger, also worked for Basie, for Dizzy Gillespie, and many others. At one time Earl hired Gillespie himself, plus trombonist Trummy Young and the late arranger Jimmy Mundy, who also arranged for Goodman, Harry James, Doc Severinson, Count Basie, and Lionel Hampton. In more than one conversation, Nat "King" Cole acknowledged Earl Hines as "my idol."

Students of jazz and old-timers will recognize two bands that played the Apollo in 1937. Teddy Hill, like many a less well-known bandleader, was more important for the musicians he employed and encouraged than for his personal musical talents (which were good enough). Teddy, in fact, once played tenor sax with the Luis Russell Band. More to the point, however, is that he hired "Little Jazz," the great trumpeter Roy Eldridge, as well as tenor-sax legend Chu Berry, who later became the backbone of the Cab Calloway Band. In 1937, the man whose name keeps cropping up in band after band, Dizzy Gillespie, was a member of Teddy Hill's Orchestra.

In 1940 Teddy retired as a bandleader and ran a nightclub called Minton's. In the history of jazz, Minton's must rank at least on a level with the Savoy Ballroom, for week after week, night after night (morning after morning would be more accurate), it was the scene of jam sessions and "cutting" contests, which drew the great, the near-great and the also-rans of jazzdom. It is no exaggeration to say that modern jazz was born during the jam sessions at Minton's.

The Luis Russell Band was one that had been put together to star Louis Armstrong. It played a 1937 engagement at the Apollo without Louis, who had left it by then. It did, however, include clarinetist Barney Bigard, who later starred with Ellington; Big Sid Catlett, who also played with Hines, on drums; and the talented trumpeter Henry "Red" Allen.

Illustration 21b is the ad for another of the many shows (1942) we played featuring Louis Armstrong. (Note the appearance of Louise Beavers, who, despite the limited roles she obtained in Hollywood, was the most famous black actress in America at that time.)

Along with Duke Ellington, Armstrong is probably one of the two most influential men in the long history of jazz. Louis played with them all because they all wanted to play with the master. In 1949, for example, Louis' band in an Apollo show included such legendary figures as trombonist Jack Teagarden, the only white artist whose blues singing was acceptable to blacks; Cozy Cole, who came to Louis after the untimely death of drummer Big Sid Catlett; Barney Bigard on clarinet; Earl Hines on piano; and Arvel Shaw on bass. A jazz lover

22a.

22b.

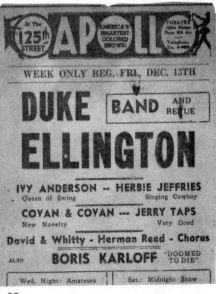

22c.

can only marvel at such a lineup. Louis influenced everyone, even the singers. This jovial genius had a vocal trick of finishing his songs with "Oh yeah!" It was a little like the end of a hymn, a musical blessing, an "Amen." He was one of the most lovable characters I ever met, a man filled with human kindness and always in a good humor.

He played a concert once in Orlando, Florida, where I then lived. Afterwards, at my home, he regaled me and my friends with hours of jokes and music. Many times he was asked which was his favorite band. The reader will never guess his answer—but Satchmo was serious. It was Guy Lombardo—who, incidentally, according to long-time Apollo emcee Leonard Reed, once played an engagement at the Apollo.

An Apollo favorite was Louis Prima, who was a real clown. He did songs in an Italian dialect, and had more fun on the bandstand than almost anyone I can think of. He was a fine trumpeter, a good all-around musician, and he had an ear for talent. His vocalist (and wife) for a time was Keely Smith, an ultratalented offbeat thrush, who was equally at home with a torrid ballad or as a straight-faced foil for Louis' clowning. His vocalist in a 1940s Apollo show was Herb Jeffries, who later starred with Earl Hines and then Duke Ellington. A supporting act on the bill was the Will Mastin Trio, which starred a little known youngster named Sammy Davis, Jr.

Andy Kirk's choice of "Clouds of Joy" for his band was an apt title; Kirk was a talented and popular bandleader. He featured one of the greatest of all jazz pianists, Mary Lou Williams, who must be ranked along with Earl Hines in musical inventiveness. When she was a kid, hanging around the band, Andy had called her "the pest." Andy also hired rotund singer June Richmond, who enlivened every show she was in. In the forties, his band had such brassmen as Shorty Baker, who married Mary Lou Williams, Howard McGhee, and Fats Navarro. For a while, after Andy left the musical world, he managed the famed Hotel Theresa, scene of Fidel Castro's one-time visit to the United States; then he was an official with the American Federation of Musicians; he ended up as a church leader.

In 1936 Duke Ellington played the Apollo. He had played there and at the Harlem Opera House and the Lafayette and, of course, was a legendary figure at the old Cotton Club. He was to play the Apollo again and again and again, almost until his untimely death. One of the giants, one of the transcending figures in jazz history, he is one of the people I genuinely miss.

In about 1962 Duke played a concert with the local symphony orchestra in Orlando, Florida. I spent the afternoon with him while the orchestra rehearsed and arranged to pick him up the next morning and drive him to the airport. He was slightly late when I arrived and was embarrassed because he had female company in the room with him. As we departed he said, "Please don't tell your father about this, he'll think I'm an old reprobate."

"Don't be silly," I said. "He *knows* you're an old reprobate."

"How is your dad?"

23a. Louis Armstrong

23b. Duke Ellington

23c. Count Basie

"Getting older. We're trying to get him to write his memoirs. Bought him a tape recorder and———"

Duke exploded. "Memoirs, hell! Listen, I've been writing my memoirs for years, and I hope to hell I never get them finished. Memoirs are for looking backwards and I'm too busy planning what I'm going to do tomorrow!" (He did, of course, write them. Appropriately, they were titled *Music Is My Mistress.*)

We drove to the airport and sat quietly talking while waiting for his plane to be called. People kept coming up, asking for an autograph, congratulating him on his performance of the night before. When he finally walked to the plane, after giving me a double embrazzo, it was with the springy step of a young man. Duke was in his seventies, I knew he had had only three hours of sleep the night before, he was carrying a briefcase full of blank music pages, which I guessed he would fill up before reaching Washington—oh, he was the youngest man I ever met!

One cannot talk about Duke's musical genius without a glance at the incredible number of musical compositions he penned. In the entire history of music, perhaps no one has composed more songs than Ellington. There are over two thousand of them. Some people have belittled his contributions; some have claimed that most of his compositions were written by Billy "Sweepea" Strayhorn. Rubbish! Without diminishing the memory of that talented, delightful man, I must point out that Duke had written hundreds of tunes before he ever met Billy and that many of his major musical works were written long after Billy died.

Illustrations 23a, b, and c are a trio of the mightiest jazzman in the history of that art: Edward "Duke" Ellington, William "Count" Basie, and Louis "Satchmo" Armstrong. If you took all three of them out of jazz history, there would scarcely be any history left.

After being the featured vocalist with drummer Chick Webb and following Chick's death in 1939, Ella Fitzgerald took over the band and toured as its leader for almost a year before giving it up and launching her career as a "single." She led the band at a show at the Apollo that opened September 12, 1940.

There are, of course, many women jazz artists. Most of them are singers, the major exceptions being pianists Mary Lou Williams and Hazel Scott. The International Sweethearts of Rhythm, who opened the week before Ella, were more a novelty, but unfortunately they didn't go very far. Their featured star was a tenor saxophonist named Vi Burnside, who could blow a torrid horn. Only the prevailing prejudices prevented the Sweethearts from becoming a major attraction. (Phil Spitalny and his white all-girl orchestra attained box-office success, but they were not a true jazz orchestra.)

Another talented jazzwoman was the late Blanche Calloway, Cab's sister. Although Blanche frequently copied Cab's style as a leader, she was a serious musician, and at times had a band as good or even better than Cab's. Later, Blanche ran a club in Washington and brought us Ruth Brown, who became a major Apollo attraction.

In the age of the big bands, there were many of good quality who never became major names in the business; at least they didn't achieve fame outside Harlem and other black communities. One such was Lucius "Lucky" Millinder, who was about as fine a showman as I ever saw. Lucky had the charm of a snake-oil salesman and, in fact, he could sell just about anything, ending his career selling the Gospel. Lucky was an athlete on the stage, rushing back and forth at a pace rapid enough to make Cab Calloway appear to be standing still. He waved his arms, called out cues and encouragement to his musicians. He couldn't read a note of music; but in rehearsal, he'd hold up the score and instruct his men to "take it from B," just as though he could read all the notes. It didn't matter to his musicians for, as one of them remarked, "Lucky reads music by ear."

The Negro Actor's Guild's Ernestine Allen was a one-time Millinder vocalist who worked under the name Annisteen Allen. She recalled touring the South with Lucky. "I'd be sitting next to him on the bus and Lucky'd be sound asleep. Suddenly, he'd open one eye, poke me on the arm, and hum six bars of a tune. 'Remember that, Ernestine,' he'd say. And pop right back to sleep! Lucky might have seemed asleep, but he didn't ever forget those six bars!"

Back in the fifties, a memorable Millinder show featured Sidney Bechet, one of the truly legendary jazzmen (a New Orleans product). He returned to the Apollo from France playing his torrid soprano saxophone. It is an interesting side note that Lucky Millinder joined talents with Sidney, who also couldn't read a single note himself.

No recitation of the legend of Lucius Millinder would be complete without recounting the tale of how he temporarily vanquished segregation while Harlem laughed. Lucky was playing a concert in Atlanta, Georgia, back in the forties, and he was sick of the accommodations—or lack thereof—accorded black artists. He sent his road manager, Irv Siders, into the best hotel, to inform them that his boss, an Indian Maharajah, wanted to stay there. Before an awestruck room clerk strode Lucky, replete in his best suit, his head wrapped turban-style in a towel. It worked! When Harlem learned of the trick a few days later, it would have elected him mayor, governor, or president without hestitation.

Another great showman was Tiny Bradshaw, who could have sold suntan lotion to the Eskimos and who, according to popular legend, also couldn't read music.

Charlie Barnet was a serious musician, who was the most popular white bandleader in Apollo history—and deservedly so. For Charlie, as more than one jazzman pointed out, lead "the blackest white band of all." Possessor of a keen ear for musical talent, Charlie presented at the Apollo such musicians as trumpeter Maynard Ferguson, who also played with Boyd Rayburn and later headlined himself; Doc Severinson, later television star with Johnny Carson; clarinetist Buddy de Franco; bassist Oscar Pettiford; saxophonist Peanuts Holland; and the singers Kay Starr and Lena Horne. Charlie was the most

24a.

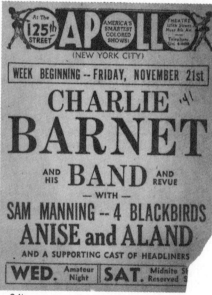

24b.

24c.

unlikely tenor saxman you might ever meet. Scion of a wealthy family, he loved music too much to be chained to a desk. He had the advantage of being colorblind where musical talent was concerned. Many an engagement was turned down because the promotors didn't want a racially mixed band. Charlie's response, so I'm told, was unprintable!

Of all the shows in Apollo history, the one that opened November 28, 1941, the week before we plunged into World War II, is probably the one I would most like to see replayed. Headlining it were the Apollo's box-office champ (at least until years later) and the greatest jazzsinger of all time. The champ was Lionel Hampton; the singer, Billie Holiday. In the normal course of an Apollo week, thirty-one shows were presented, but for this one sensational engagement, the Lionel Hampton crew put on forty-five. In every theater, the "half-hour," that is, the time one-half hour before the next show is to begin, is posted on a bulletin board. During that week, the half-hour was already "in" as the show was just ending! Lionel fairly chortled with glee at the prospect of doing another show. Before the first show was even on, he'd come out front and egg everyone on: "Let's do six shows today. How about seven?" The lines were so long and so constant that some merchants up the street complained that they couldn't get into their own stores, but the complaints were never in earnest. 125th Street had never seen such a week.

At various times, Lionel had some of the best jazzmen in the music business. Bass player Charlie Mingus, for example, was featured with Lionel long before he rose to stardom in progressive jazz. Quincy Jones is today among the most highly regarded of musical arrangers, but he was then a sideman with Hamp. Illinois Jacquet's tenor sax solos on such numbers as "Flyin' Home" almost started a riot each time he stepped from the band car to stage center. "Cat" Anderson played with Lionel and was long one of the stalwarts of the Duke Ellington Band. And Lionel also had several fine singers, like O. C. Smith, Joe Williams, considered by some to be the finest male jazz singer in the business, and the beloved Dinah Washington, who rose to individual stardom after being featured with the Hampton band. Riding herd over all of them was Lionel himself, one of the most inventive and exciting musicians of the day.

When Lionel, toward the end of each show, wheeled out his vibes, a long expectant sigh invariably arose from the audience. Fans knew that what was coming was a musical treat punctuated by Lionel's unmusical grunts. An opening series of riffs, with Lionel's face bent low over his instrument, seemed to blend with the flashes of light thrown upward as the spotlights hit the metal strips, caught those little whirlers as they twirled inside the tubes. The riffs seguayed into a rhythm tune ("How High the Moon" perhaps), then into a slow ballad like "My Funny Valentine," and finally into the rocking, swinging "Flyin' Home," the frantic finale of every Lionel Hampton show. It always left everyone limp—except Lionel, of course.

William "Count" Basie remains one of the living legends both in Apollo history and in the history of jazz. It is safe to say that when John Hammond (who heard him on a car-radio broadcast from Kansas City and immediately changed course and went driving in that direction) and Willard Alexander brought Basie to New York, they were presenting one of the revolutionary figures in jazzdom. Basie's free-rolling swing was jazz at its most exuberant best. He pioneered in the playing of "head" arrangements, those spontaneous, unwritten arrangements that were made up as he went along. His interest in the blues and his presentation of them through Joe Williams, Jimmie Rushing, and Helen Humes brought a marvelous dimension to jazz fans. An Apollo show, presented April 25, 1941, was typical of the rocking Basie style, puncutated by the suave, understated Basie piano. Even today Basie records are guaranteed to increase your pulse rate and make your feet want to get up and go. The Basie Band was the forerunner of the swing music of the thirties that rocketed Benny Goodman and others to stardom. At one time or another, with the Count were drummer Joe Jones, trumpeters Harry "Sweets" Edison and Buck Clayton, tenor saxophonist Illinois Jacquet, and Billie Holiday.

Before his first Apollo appearance in the thirties the name of Basie was already on every Harlemite's lips. The first ten rows were filled with screaming, jumping "hepcats," who were in danger of wrecking the seats with their movements even before the show began. In those days, Apollo shows followed a rough formula. An opening number (sometimes called the "opening shout"), a dance act of some sort, followed by a vocalist, a novelty act, a comedy scene, and then the star's appearance. But when that first Basie show began, the hepcats gave verbal notice that they weren't about to permit the "usual" format to be followed. At a sprinter's pace, Dad, potbelly and all, raced backstage, beckoned Basie to the wings, and said to him, "Bill, forget the rundown; go ahead and do your band specialty now. These kids will never sit through the rest of the show waiting for it."

Poor Basie! He sat at his organ and listened to all that racket; he looked down at those bobbing heads and smiling faces and was almost overcome. In his very first Apollo appearance, Basie learned that an Apollo audience would have its way—and its way was to pay homage by demanding that its newest hero, William "Count" Basie, do his thing—and now!

When Dad went backstage after Basie had finished to congratulate him and to rearrange the rest of the show, he had to wait in the hallway while the star composed himself a bit. The shock of the Apollo audience was still with him.

Sometimes Apollo shows were panned; sometimes the reviewers cheered. Even its most partisan supporter (namely this writer) wouldn't claim that all Apollo shows were equally great. *Variety* reviews sometimes reminded me of a theater marquee I heard about in a small midwestern town during World War II; about a double-feature program, it proclaimed, "Same old story: one piperoo, one stinkeroo." In 1940, *Variety* roasted Teddy Hill and gave Cab Calloway a rave.

Calloway was always known as a great showman; what some people do not recognize is that he also had a superb band. It featured such musicians as

25a. Johnny Hodges

25b. Don Redman

Chu Berry, the tenor saxophonist regarded by almost all jazzmen as among the greatest; a young trumpeter named Dizzy Gillespie, whose music Cab didn't quite dig (he called it "Chinese" music); the drumming of one of the best, Cozy Cole; and still another trumpeter who rose to stardom later on, Jonah Jones.

Out of the Chick Webb Band of the thirties came an alto saxophonist who became the Apollo's number-one star during the fifties. He was Louis Jordan, whose group included such fine musicians as drummer Chris Columbus and tenorman Paul Quinchette. Managed by one of the canniest personal managers I've known, Berle Adams, Louis Jordan's name on the Apollo marquee was the guarantee of a box-office smash. When performing Louis would stare down at the audience with eyes popping; he would feign anger, terror—any emotion—and make you believe it. He sang and composed calypso songs, novelty songs—almost anything rolled off his pen with ease. They rolled from his throat with a humor and spirit no one could match. His sense of timing was superb; once the musical momentum started, he never let it fade.

His recording career started with "Knock Me a Kiss" and "I'm Gonna Move to the Outskirts of Town." These ballads began a run of smash hits that went on without interruption for more than a decade. The biggest of them was a calypso number called "Run Joe." With the aid of Berle Adams, Louis parlayed his hits into a headline position at Broadway's Paramount Theatre and top billing in Las Vegas, one of the first black stars to be so featured. But the greatest compliment to Louis Jordan is to note that almost every week, even the week just after he had played, calls would come into the Apollo switchboard asking, "When ya' gonna play Louis Jordan?" When the curtain went up and Louis was standing in front of the mike, eyes popping, horn at the ready, his right foot already pounding out the beat for his men, the sound from the audience was always the same—a delighted roar—Louis Jordan was back!

Don Redman was known as the "Little Giant of Rhythm." It was an apt title, because Don was tiny in stature but a giant in the music world. His band was moderately popular, but it was as an arranger that Don made his biggest mark. He arranged for Harry James, Fletcher Henderson, Jimmy Dorsey, Charlie Barnet, and Jimmie Lunceford, as well as many special arrangements for his friend Pearl Bailey.

Perhaps the most interesting of his musical experiences came when he made some arrangements for Paul Whiteman. Whiteman thought the arrangements were great; there was only one trouble. His musicians could play all the notes, but they couldn't play the music! A Redman arrangement that would have lifted you out of your seat if played by Benny Goodman or Harry James or Jimmie Lunceford sounded like musical mud when played by the urbane gentlemen of the Paul Whiteman Band. It is no exaggeration to say that Don's arrangements for Fletcher Henderson set the pattern for the movement known as swing, which was picked up by Basie and then Goodman. Once again, however, the big financial rewards went to the white bands that had merely picked up on the idea.

26. The tall man is the great Jimmie Lunceford. The bald one is my father.

Johnny Hodges was known as "the rabbit." I guess he looked a little like one. As for his music, it is safe to say that no one could coax the tone out of a saxophone that Johnny Hodges did, save for Sidney Bechet, and Bechet (soprano sax) was Johnny's mentor. Johnny played the alto sax. He made a few recordings with Woody Herman; he had his own band for a short while; but the Rabbit was known primarily as Duke Ellington's man. It was with Duke that he shone; it was with Duke that his musical expertise achieved its greatest development, adding a dimension to the Ellington Band that was distinctive and important.

One of the most enduring alto saxophonists was Bennie Carter. A prodigious musician who also played a sizzling trumpet when the mood and occasion suggested it, Bennie's musical roots are as durable as those of Johnny Hodges. He had not one, but a number of bands. Bennie told me that it was his band which was featured in the very first Apollo show my father presented. His stars included Teddy Wilson, Cozy Cole, and Chu Berry.

Bennie also hired pianist Eddie Heywood, who, if he had contributed nothing else but his superb arrangement of "Begin the Beguine," would have contributed enough. Eddie must be included on anyone's list of great jazzmen. And then there was Dickie Wells, known to jazz aficionados for a dozen reasons, the best of which was his handling of the slide trombone. In addition to his instrumental talents, Bennie Carter also made arrangements for drummer Chick Webb and Fletcher Henderson.

When I was a kid, my sister and I had a couple of favorite records we played until we almost wore out the grooves. One of them was "For Dancers Only" and the other was "By the River St. Marie." They were both part of a long-lost collection of recordings made by the great swinging band of Jimmie Lunceford. It was, visually and musically, the swingingest band of its day. You not only heard Lunceford, you watched him. The reeds would stand up and move their horns in one direction as they blew, while the brass stood up and swayed theirs in an opposite direction. And all the while that swinging, rocking sound! I can hear it still.

Lunceford, pictured in Illustration 26 presenting a plaque to Dad at the Apollo, was a retired athletic director who found his niche as a conductor. He was one of the few bandleaders who used a baton, one of which lay on my sister's night table for years, a souvenir of our first evening's outing to hear the great Lunceford! Jimmy, a large, quiet man, had the good sense and musical judgment to hire one of the great jazz arrangers, Sy Oliver, who played trumpet and arranged such jazz classics for Lunceford as "Marie" and the two numbers my sister and I were so fond of. Sy, by the way, made some fine arrangements for Tommy Dorsey and later for Harry James, Charlie Barnet, Ella Fitzgerald, and the Four Ink Spots.

Lunceford also had the good musical sense to hire, at various times, Willie Smith (sax), Trummy Young (trombone and vocals), Jimmy Crawford (drummer), Eddie Wilcox (piano), and Joe Thomas (tenor). The last two tried to keep the band going when, in 1947, Jimmie Lunceford died of a sudden heart attack, leaving the musical world in the lurch. In its heyday, Lunceford's band had the greatest spirit of any band in jazzdom and it was *made* for dancing! Perhaps the band's spirit is best explained by the title of one of its biggest hit records, "It Aint Watcha Do, It's the Way Howcha Do It."

When I think of the peerless arrangements by Sy Oliver, it brings to mind a sore point among black musicians: the number of arrangements and compositions that were played unacknowledged to the public. I have already mentioned a few of them: the ones Fletcher Henderson made for Goodman and others; those made by Mary Lou Williams for Goodman, the Dorseys, and Glen Gray, as well as Calloway, Gillespie, and Lunceford; and those of Redman and Carter. I would feel neglectful of his memory if I failed to mention the late Jimmy Mundy, who arranged and composed for Harry James and Doc Severinsen, then for Basie and Lionel Hampton. I would be neglecting musical history itself if I failed to mention that hundreds of black musicians have made thousands of arrangements for the big white (and black) bands of America with barely a mention in the press.

Not all the bands of the thirties and forties achieved the eminence, of course, of the Lunceford, Basie, Hines, or Ellington bands. One of the better ones was led by Willie Bryant, who became one of the most popular figures in Harlem. Willie even succeeded Bojangles Robinson as the unelected "mayor" of Harlem. He was also a popular disc jockey as well as a bandleader. Among Willie's early musicians was pianist Teddy Wilson and drummer Cozy Cole.

In the early forties, Billy Eckstine was singing with Earl Hines, but in 1944 Billy decided to strike out on his own. He formed a band, which became one of the most important, most interesting, and most highly praised bands in the history of the big bands. Mr. B. picked up on the "bopish" strains of the Hines group and extended them into as yet unexplored realms. Although Billy became a highly successful and popular singer, one who profoundly influenced the course of popular singing, in some respects it is a shame that he didn't stay in the band business. The list of young musicians Billy had in his crew was impressive: Dizzy Gillespie (isn't it amazing how often his name keeps cropping up as he moved from band to band dropping his musical pearls on the way?), Charlie "Bird" Parker, trumpeter Miles Davis, drummer Art Blakey, and a whole coterie of super jazzmen like Budd Johnson, Howard McGhee, Fats Navarro, Gene Ammons, and Dexter Gordon—not to speak of Sarah Vaughan, who has said that her experience with Billy Eckstine was among the most important, musically, in her entire career.

Sarah later spent some time singing with another unsung hero, bass player John Kirby, who had a successful band, a mildly, rather than wildly, swinging band. It also featured Kirby's wife, Maxine Sullivan, who in the early forties became a nationwide star when she gently swung "Loch Lomond."

By the end of World War II, the revolution that had already been started with the bands of Billy Eckstine and Earl Hines became a full-fledged move-

27a. Dizzy Gillespie

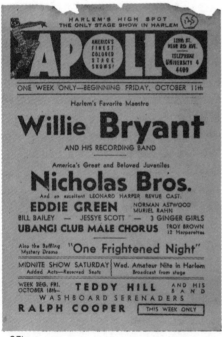

27b.

27c.

ment, aided and abetted by such innovators as Dizzy Gillespie and Thelonius Monk. As with all radically new movements, it shook the musical world to its roots. Although some detractors claim that bop was an antisocial movement, no truly revolutionary movement like it could have stayed alive a week if it had not had ardent admirers and superbly talented musicians to play it. One should simply realize that the big bands were designed first of all for dancing; the new bop bands and combos were designed for listening. The uniqueness of the new sounds, plus the economics of the business, dictated smaller bands.

Almost anyone who is "into jazz" would claim that Lester "Prez" Young was one of the most influential men in the history of jazz. Lester had a way of holding his head and horn off at about a 40 ° angle, staring off into space, but eliciting from his horn a cacaphony of thin sounds of such startlingly different musical quality that you either sat up and took notice or you were tone deaf. His "duel" with Coleman Hawkins is one of great historic "cutting" sessions of all time. His nickname, Prez, was reputedly given to him by his musical "sister," Billie Holiday. When he opened at the Apollo on June 25, 1948, there were no long lines straining eastward toward seventh Avenue; however, he did bring in a keen-eared crowd of jazz buffs, who were convinced that their hero was a genius. They were right, for Young was the musical bridge between the two saxophone giants, Coleman Hawkins and John Coltrane. It is our loss that all three are gone.

Another musician with a tilted horn played a trumpet and the tilt was manmade. He was also a major, transcending figure in jazz—the droll, sometimes humorous, and always dedicated guy whose goatee and uptilted trumpet have become symbols of bop, Dizzy Gillespie. Dizzy slid from band to band, from Teddy Hill to Cab Calloway, from Earl Hines to Billy Eckstine and Boyd Rayburn. He leaned on Louis Armstrong, loaned to Miles Davis. Out of his own band arose the Modern Jazz Quartet (Percy Heath, John Lewis, Kenny "Klook" Clark, Milt Jackson), all products of the Dizzy Gillespie approach to music.

Not all of the jazz giants were bandleaders. We have already spoken of Ella, of Billie Holiday, of Sarah Vaughan. In 1949 at an Apollo show that opened September 30 a new name appeared to challenge the greats among jazzmen: Errol Garner. This remarkable guy was a jazz phenomenon, a delightful personality, a musical treat. He hummed outrageously while he played, and his humming was not a thing of beauty. We had an awful time trying to place the mike where it would pick up the piano but not his humming, but we never succeeded. He never was able to read music, and never wanted to learn. To a musician's inquiry at rehearsal, "What key is that in, Errol?" he merely grinned, walked to the piano and struck a chord. "That one," he said.

But what transpired at the keyboard between his left hand and his right would have thrown Mohammed Ali into utter confusion had Errol been a fighter instead of a musician. Errol not only took up the stride pianists' cry about the left hand being as important as the right but he also blended the two,

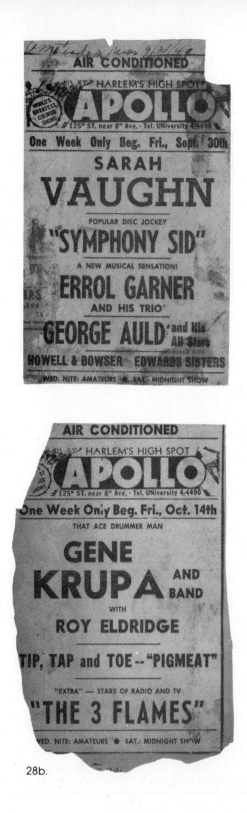

28b.

then rode them in seemingly independent directions, kept two rhythms going simultaneously, and created a unified whole out of the separate worlds of the right hand and the left. He was capable of mystifying a traditional-minded music lover. I once listened to two members of a symphony orchestra talking about Errol's music, and it was immediately apparent that their musical comprehension was never able to transcend the rigidities of their classical training. But to those able to open their minds and ears wide enough to his offerings, he had new and delightful dimensions to offer.

Symphony Sid, the nickname of deejay Sid Torin, enthusiastically backed Gillespie and Parker, George Shearing and Errol, thereby aiding their careers considerably. His nightly musical forays on radio, his broadcasts from Birdland and Bop City helped to popularize these new sounds that mystified some, thrilled others.

Nineteen forty-nine, a year of excitement and innovation for us, marked the first Apollo appearance for Gene Krupa, a man regarded as one of America's most dynamic drummers. Years earlier, a younger Krupa had said of Chick Webb, "He cut me to ribbons." Gene wasn't the only one so cut, for Chick was a past master of the art! Roy "Little Jazz" Eldridge was playing with Gene in 1949. Later, after a nationwide tour with Gene, he bitterly announced that he would never again play with a white band. The jibe was not directed at Gene, who was always a gentleman, but to the cruel people who had subjected a talented and sensitive man to indignities. (Roy's bitterness reminded me of that of Billie Holiday, who, in 1938, had toured with Artie Shaw with equally unhappy results.)

The art of drumming was always popular at the Apollo. From the early days of Chick Webb to the later times of people like Art Blakey and Philly Joe Jones to the exciting rhythms of the Nigerian, Olatunji, drumming throbbed on our stage. Of the fine drummers who made it big at the Apollo, none was more popular than Buddy Rich, who once startled our audiences for a whole week by doing his drum specialty with one hand, his other arm having been broken just before the engagement started. Buddy ingratiated himself by being more than a drummer. He danced, he clowned with each act, he even sang! His singing wasn't bad, but it convinced the audience that he was, after all, a drummer.

Nothing demonstrated better than the 1949 show "Jazz at the Philharmonic" that white and black musicians belonged together. This production was the brainchild of Norman Granz, one of the brightest and ablest men in the music business. (In handling the fabulous career of Ella Fitzgerald, no manager has done better by his client than Norman has done for Ella.) "Jazz at the Philharmonic" was a musician's and a showman's delight with Coleman Hawkins and Joe "Flip" Phillips competing with each other on their tenor saxophones in front of a wild Apollo audience.

In case the reader got the idea that all Apollo shows were great, let me set the record straight. Some of them bombed; some were dogs. When you book as many as forty-five shows a year, which we did in the Apollo's heyday, duds turn

Carmen McRae And Al Hibbler Sing Out At Apollo Nov. 27

Not one, but two great headliners of the music world, Carmen McRae and Al Hibbler, will be the featured fare on stage of the Apollo Theatre beginning on Friday, Nov. 27th. Also in the cast will be Pigmeat Markham and his comedy Co., Reuben Phillips and his Band and the Flying Nesbits.

Just two months before cutting her first record, Carmen McRae had decided to leave show business behind her. She was visiting relatives in Jamaica, British West Indies when the phone call came that changed her life. One night Duke Ellington heard her and gave her just the encouragement she needed to keep on singing to confirm her own belief that she had something to offer beside ambition.

It was just a coincidence that when some years later, she was singing at the Club Harlem in Atlantic City, the Duke's son, Mercer Ellington heard her and invited her to join his newly formed band. Carmen toured with the band as featured vocalist for more than a year in theatres and night clubs all over the country. When the band broke up in Chicago, Carmen was booked as a single in a club known as the Airliner.

But this was closing night and a discouraged Carmen had her piane ticket to Jamaica, little dreaming what plans were made for her.

CARMEN McRAE   AL HIBBLER

... recording contract in his pocket, he tried desperately to locate a girl with "the haunting voice." He called every Melba in Jamaica, Long Island and then learned tha this future star had headed for the West Indian Jamaica. It took one last phone call — fifteen minutes at three dollars a minute — to convince Carmen to return to New York.

Carmen has been the recipient of laurel after laurel. She has been voted "Singer of the Year," Place All Star Annual Poll, and other such glowing honors. She is a Jazz singer who has never lost sight of the essentials of her art, whether she is heard on recordings or in a life performance.

Al Hibbler has been a great favorite at the Apollo for many years going back to the days with the Duke Ellington orchestra. When he went on his own, Al became one of the country's outstanding song stylists and his great recordings has solidified his position as one of today's great vocal stars.

The Clovers are currently riding high as their recording, toward the top of every popularity "Love Potion," has skyrocketed poll. This group is regarded as one of the best singing groups in the country and has been for several years. Now with the added impetus of this smash recording they are sure to gain the national reputation they have so long deserved for they are indeed a talented and entertaining group.

The balance of the cast will include Pigmeat Markham and his comedy situations, the amazing acrobatic antics of the nation's top family troupe, the Flying Nesbits and last but not least our own musical director, Reuben Phillips and his wonderful orchestra.

29a.

29b.

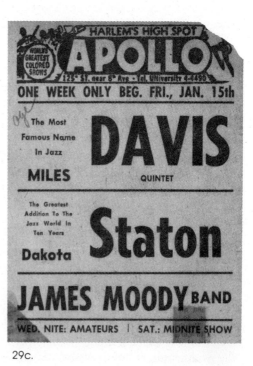

29c.

up. Early in 1950, we opened a pretty good show. It didn't bomb but it did flop. It flopped despite the fact that Sidney Bechet and Red Allen were two legendary figures in jazz. It flopped despite the fact that in Lucky Millinder it had a great showman and in Butterbeans and Susie it had one of the most enduring and best-loved acts on the black stage. And it flopped despite the fact that in Slim Gaillard (with his former partner Slam Stewart, author of many zany tunes) it had one of the kookiest, most talented, and irrepressible performers in show business.

By 1959, the Apollo shows contained many newer names, but some of the older ones were more popular than ever. A case in point was a show that opened November 27, starring Carmen McRae and Al Hibbler. Carmen was not new to the Apollo; she had played there in the early fifties, but her career never quite got off the ground then, despite the fact that she has always been one of the best and most courageous (musically) jazz singers around. Suddenly, lightning in a bottle, and Carmen was off and running, a star at last! As for Al Hibbler, he had been an important figure with Duke Ellington since 1943, and was regarded as a musician's musician, a singer's singer. Al had been publicly admired by Frank Sinatra, but what was more important was how he was regarded by audiences. When Hibbler was guided gently to stage center by Duke and started singing "Trees," there was one highly predictable response—bedlam!

By the sixties a whole generation of new names was gracing the Apollo marquee in twenty-four-inch letters. The "cool sound" of Miles Davis was an exciting and logical aftermath of the Dizzy Gillespie/Roy Eldridge/Louis Armstrong parlay. The late Cannonball Adderley's remark that "nothing happened in jazz between Bird and John Coltrane" was a historical postscript to the fantastic sounds emanating from Trane's tenor saxophone. The influences on his music came from way back, from Dizzy and Johnny Hodges, from Eddie "Cleanhead" Vinson and Earl Bostic, from Miles Davis, the "Bird," Bechet, and Hawkins. But John Coltrane's music developed chiefly from the prodigious gifts buried deep inside a talented soul!

Accompanying John on a September 1961 bill was a delightful newcomer, Miriam Makeba, who, with the clicks and melodic sounds of Africa emerging from a warm and vibrant throat, added new dimensions. The other stars in the January 1960 Davis show were Dakota Staton, a dark thrush with an exciting style, and a tenor saxman named James Moody, a slightly zany, albeit talented cat. I once asked James, "What've you been eating to get so fat?" He looked at me deadpan and responded, "Ain't been eatin'—been drinkin'."

As we left the forties and entered the fifties and sixties, the sounds of jazz were changing. The big bands and dance-music jazz were gone, a victim of economics and the lack of interest in dancing. They were gone in favor of a more personalized jazz with its accent on pure listening. Miguelito Valdes was never a big musical favorite at the Apollo, but he was one of a whole group of Afro-Cuban bands which were. They started with Machito and ran the gamut from Tito Puente to Noro Morales, Perez Prado, and others. (I will say more

30a.

30b. Oscar Peterson

about them later.)

One of the more interesting musical favorites at the time was Julian "Cannonball" Adderley, a saxophoning musical intellectual of power, force, and ideas. Cannonball and his brother, Nat, took their band on tour to many college campuses right up until Cannonball's unfortunate and shocking death. They explained the whole history of jazz to enthusiastic groups of young students. The Adderley show in May 1962, also starred Nancy Wilson, who became a superstar and an Apollo favorite, and the Ramsey Lewis Trio, one of the more delightful and exciting new groups.

Canadian-born Oscar Peterson (Illustration 30b) the living end of the piano-playing jazz tradition that spans the years from Fats Waller to Earl Hines, through Errol Garner, George Shearing, Eddie Heywood, Thelonius Monk, and countless others.

When I started this chapter, I indicated that this was not going to be a comprehensive history of jazz. I planned to present *some* of the people who graced the Apollo's stage, to indicate the breadth and scope of the talent we presented to a sophisticated and knowledgeable audience. Any jazz aficionado will notice that I have left many people out. They are missing not because they weren't important but because of the limitations of space. Some of them deserve a brief mention at the very least. Can I write about jazz without citing talented singer Nina Simone, trumpeters Cootie Williams or my good friend Harry "Sweets" Edison, tenorman Sonny Stitt, or another great jazz pianist, Hazel Scott? Two vocalists who sang with Dizzy Gillespie and then went out on their own, Joe Carroll and Eddie Jefferson, took musical ideas spawned in the early days of bop by Dizzy and Ella Fitzgerald (the only vocalist who knew immediately what to do with this strange new medium) and enlarged on them with a discursive, humorous, and highly inventive style. One couldn't listen to either without chuckling or laughing out loud.

Betty Carter was first introduced to Apollo audiences by Lionel Hampton as "Betty BeBop," and her name would endure in the history of jazz if her "scat" singing was all she added to its liturgy. But it wasn't all. Although Betty's style is sometimes hard to fathom, it is worth the concentration. She leaps, she soars, she dips and wavers. My candidate for the most overlooked jazz artist of the day, Betty has been an interesting, entertaining, and inventive vocalist.

It's hard to leave the subject of black artists used by white musicians alone because I became aware of so much of that during my father's tenure at the Apollo. For example, Doc Wheeler and his Sunset Royal Band recorded their version of "Marie" first, but it was Tommy Dorsey who won the prize with the same arrangement.

The hit record "Caledonia" was the product of Louis Jordan, but the record company refused to release the tune until it had been recorded by Woody Herman. Woody's recording was "engineered" by Berle Adams, Jordan's brilliant manager. (The irony was that a third recording, one by Erskine Hawkins, was the best seller of the three.)

An item called swing was the product mainly of Fletcher Henderson and Don Redman; it was developed into a fine art by Count Basie; but the biggest plum in that musical genre went to Benny Goodman.

Elvis Presley died a millionaire, having exploited musical ideas that were stock-in-trade for dozens of black musicians before him. Presley did openly acknowledge his debt to Bo Diddley and other black artists, but the public and press conveniently forgot that acknowledgement. The fault for these and scores of similar events lies, I hasten to add, not with the white musicians and band-leaders but with the public and the exploiters of talent. What the black musicians needed, I guess, were musical Jack Johnsons, to bludgeon their way into white consciousness.

A fascinating phenomena in jazz history is "pairings," those musical combinations in which creative energies from two people jelled into something extraordinary. In the scores and tunes of Duke Ellington and Billy Strayhorn, his remarkable composer, arranger, and alter ego sometimes the distinction became so blurred that one couldn't tell where Duke started and Strays stopped, although as I indicated earlier Duke was also a solo composer in his own right.

And there was the magic conjured up by Billie Holiday and Lester "Prez" Young. You can hear it in some of their recordings such as "He's Funny That Way," a musical coalescence that generated loving sparks between a pair of musical geniuses. There was the almost electric connection between Louis Armstrong and Earl "Fatha" Hines. Or, on a not-so-jazzy scale, between Louis and singer Velma Middleton, and in the earlier vocals done by two youngsters then with the Chick Webb Band, Louis Jordan and Ella Fitzgerald.

In earlier books on jazz, such serious authors as Marshall W. Stearns (*The Story of Jazz*) and Ralph J. Gleason (*Celebrating The Duke & Louis, Bessie, Billie, Bird, Carmen, Miles, Dizzy and Other Heroes*) have suggested that black musicians in both periods—the early thirties and forties and then the later era of bop—were primarily motivated by their desire to achieve acceptance in a white world. It is possible—considering the difficulties involved in making a living as a black musician—that this was so in the thirties, but to stretch that assertion into the period in which bop and progressive jazz developed is, it seems to me, to misread the thrust of black artistry. Indeed, I can hardly understand Gillespie, Monk, Parker, and Davis in these terms at all.

Some critics of bop have gone so far as to accuse its practitioners of being antisocial, so disdainful of the audience did some of them appear. If this is unfair (which it is), one can only make sense of their musical rebellions by viewing them as the acts of individualists intent on developing their musical ideas *in spite of the sometimes negative reactions of their audiences*. In short, they were completely engrossed in their creative labors—as musicians in the classical field have always been.

One cannot read Stearns or Gleason without sensing their passionate indignation at the unfair treatment accorded black musicians by white society. Yet their insistence that black musicians were eternally striving for integration, musically speaking, is typical of the preconceived notions of most whites—even the most sympathetic of them.

Like most other creative movements, jazz can be a lonely art. In the solitude of a room, or even the solitude of a crowded bandstand, the artist is usually creating alone. There are times, of course, when he is creating in conjunction with his fellow musicians, but the initial thrust of his art must spring from his own solitary wellspring. The progressive jazzman or bop musician was trying neither to please nor to displease his audience. He was trying to develop his own musical expression to the utmost; he was calling on all his creative reserves to bring forth the musical expressions latent in his soul, bred into his background, striving to be born into the world. We, most of us, approach the creative character in our midst with mixed emotions. He scares us with his new departures; he challenges us to hear, listen, and to give up the familiar. He makes us feel small and futile and inspires us with awe and frustration. We turn on him; we mock him; we put him down, but somewhere we are ashamed of the derision rising in our throats.

Dizzy Gillespie, for example, did more than become one of the founding fathers of the musical form known as bop. He did more than to inspire Miles Davis. He was bold enough to break with musical traditions, searching his own musical soul for new harmonies, new structures, new forms. And when that wasn't enough, he reached into the world of Latin music and bled its beat into jazz, thereby adding an exciting new dimension to the jazz scene. *That* action simultaneously released Latin music from its own fetters and allowed it to integrate into the exciting and facile world of jazz. No doubt Dizzy's introduction of the Latin element stemmed from the years he worked in the Cab Calloway Band with trumpeter Mario Bauza, the guiding spirit of the Machito Band of later vintage.

Finally, I would like to make a few comments on today's scene in the world of music. They are unhappy ones, and followers of some of the newer trends in today's music will, no doubt, put my comments down as "sour grapes." Worse, they may put me in the "old fogie" category, although I do not think I belong there.

What I hear in much of today's scene doesn't cut it in my book; and what I see is even worse! A knowledgeable friend of mine put it succinctly: "It's not really music; it's just plain noise." We are both referring to the use of electronic gadgets, speakers, and amplifiers piled so high that the stage is reduced to postage-stamp size. We are also referring to the bizarre costumes and styles that make a circus of some concerts, detract from the music and appear to be calculated for their shock value alone. Indeed, comments made by some of the managers and agents of the rock scene bear out that notion. "All those electronic gadgets are used to cover up the dearth of really creative musical ability," Henry Frankel said to me one day. Sometimes the pile of equipment becomes absurd, as when a stage-wait of a solid hour is needed merely to set it up. Before the amplifiers are turned on, the instruments tuned up, the switchboards collated, and the musicians adjust everything from their pics to their underwear, the audience has forgotten why they came there in the first place.

There is, it seems to me, a substitution at work that does a disservice to the true expression of jazz. In the recording studios of today, the blending and shading of sound is done not by musicians, but by technicians. A kind of mechanical dexterity takes place so that sound is not produced, it is manipulated. The object of it all is not musicianship; it is money.

Pianist, arranger, composer Billy Taylor—my candidate for one of the most exciting and creative musicians on today's scene—tells the story of a happening at the Newport Jazz Festival several years ago. After an hour's wait while great quantities of electronic equipment was stacked on the stage, plugged in, tested, and connected, finally the group preparing to perform asked the great blues singer-guitarist B. B. King to join them. B. B. did, carrying in one hand his sole electronic support, a three-foot-high amplifier. "When all was ready," said Billy, "B. B. King calmly stepped up and with his guitar and the little amplifier, just blew that group right off the stage!"

At the Apollo I remonstrated with my brother Bobby because there had been an interminable wait for the equipment to be plugged in and readied for not one, but successively, four rock groups. "Why can't you use one set of amps, one synthesizer, one organ, or whatever you have for *all* the groups and avoid all those set-ups?" I asked.

"Because the musicians won't put up with it. They want their own." He laughed. "You know, one guy says, 'But if I use his moog, I'll miss mine. It has a little nick on the left hand side of the C above middle C and without that nick, I'm lost.'" So was I. So was Bobby. So are all of us.

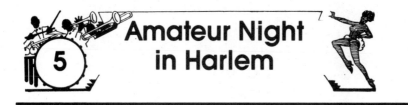

Amateur Night in Harlem

5

"Christopher Columbus"

The theater could have been empty all week. The show could have been a "dog," but almost without exception they were standing in the aisles when the show started on Wednesday night. For Wednesday night was Amateur Night in Harlem and that was always an event.

A character named Sandman was settled in Box C high above the stage, glancing around imperiously from under a huge, garish hat, as though daring the oncoming kids to be star stuff. A person called "Geech," dressed in bizarre and dowdy female finery lurched through the audience inquiring "RICH—ARD?" And an eternal presence known affectionately as Porto Rico was below stage dressing himself in one of the costumes he had concocted for that particular show (now a hula skirt plus a gigantic overstuffed bra, now a homemade costume consisting mostly of pots and pans). By showtime, 125th Street was invariably deserted, for as stage manager Hans Nielson put it, "You'd hear people talking on the street and one would suddenly say, "Listen, man! I gotta go home. It's almost time for the amateur broadcast!" That had been going on since 1936.

Amateur Night in Harlem was more than a mere contest, more than a mere show. It was virtually a way of life. You had a chance to be a judge, you could watch your imaginary stand-in trying out his wares before a live audience, or best of all, you could be on hand for the launching of a new star. So many had started there! Ella, Sarah Vaughan, Jackie Wilson, James Brown, Gladys Knight, Leslie Uggams, Dionne Warwick, for example. Maybe tonight? My brother Bobby says that Dinah Washington told him she had been on Amateur Night, and hardly a week went by when some performer backstage didn't claim

---

The Apollo's Amateur Night in Harlem show evolved into a melange of the carefully planned and the spontaneous. In the latter category belong the audience and its reactions; in the former, the amateurs, trucking off the stage when their number was completed. The trucking sequence was performed to the strains of a popular record of the forties titled "Christopher Columbus."

31a. Ella Fitzgerald

31b. Jackie Wilson

it as *his or her* point of origin. Like everything else about the Apollo, the Amateur Show has a history that is etched deeply into the stories of show business and of Harlem. Such latter-day programs as "The Gong Show" are, at best, feeble and humiliating imitations of the real thing.

The appeals of the show were many and varied; they were directed at audiences and artists alike, encompassing losers and anyone with a sense of history or the dramatic. (In some respects the show was dedicated to the losers, but more of that later on.) Still, the primary thrust was always upward, toward the stars. The following description of the first appearance of Ella Fitzgerald at the Harlem Opera House just before our move to the Apollo is supplied by one of the most colorful characters I have ever met, my friend Henry Nemo, known to the cognoscenti as the "Neme" and to the entire world as the lyric writer of the songs " 'Tis Autumn," "I Let a Song Go out of My Heart," "Blame It on My Youth," "Goin' out of my Head," and others.

I had gone down to the rehearsal hall before the Amateur Show began that night, to watch what was going on. They were rehearsing their music with Frances Welch, the gal who played piano for the show. This kid Ella was so frightened (it was during the time she was living at the orphanage), she didn't have any sheet music with her, and this Welch gal didn't like that. She asked Ella what key her song was in, and in response Ella hit a note—"hmmmmmm." By God, I swear to you I can hear that note yet—"hmmmmmm"—it went through me like an electric shock! I just had to be there for this chick's first appearance so I went upstairs and arranged for some seats in the orchestra pit, right in front of the stage. Then I went backstage and got hold of Chick [Webb] who was headlining that week. He was just getting ready to leave. I grabbed him. "Chickie," I said, "you'd better stay for the amateurs 'cause there's a gal who's gonna blow your mind!" Chickie wanted to leave, but I made him stay. Man! That theater was loaded—packed!

When they finally announced Ella she absolutely froze in the wings, she was so scared. She started out onto the stage, then she started to cry. And then she turned around to leave. She finally got out to the center of the stage, Frances Welch hit a chord, and Ella sang one note. Just one note and people jumped up and started screaming! She laid it right in there and she couldn't get past the fourth bar, the audience was hollering so loud. She sang "Believe It, Beloved"—no, she sang "Judy" and the audience made her sing it over and over again. They just wouldn't let her off the stage. I tell you, it was history!

Henry's story makes good reading, but he was undoubtedly talking about a subsequent appearance Ella made at the Amateur Show. For Leonard Reed and "Doll" Thomas both insist she first announced that she wanted to dance, only switching to a vocal when her legs refused to do her bidding. Undoubtedly on her first, fourth, or tenth appearance, the audience at the Apollo was electrified by a sound they had never heard before. As for the rest of the story, no less an authority than my father indicated that Chick Webb heard her and came running to him suggesting that he "sign her up—right away." To which suggestion he received Dad's standard answer: "I'm not in the management business.

32a.

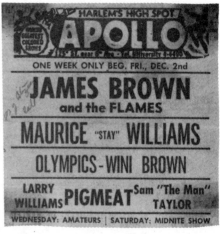

32b.

I run a theater. You sign her up." Chick did.

If Amateur Night in Harlem had only been the birthplace of dozens of stars, it would have been enough to enshrine the show in history. But there is a lot more to it than that. To begin with, it was a complete show by itself, a show packed with drama, humor, and the unexpected. It catered to show biz needs that transcended even our own need for new talent. As an example, consider Jackie Wilson. He won the contest hands down, won it for five consecutive weeks before being approached by another winner named Billy Ward. The result was that Jackie joined an early group called The Dominoes, which became one of the Apollo's strongest attractions during the fifties.

"One night," said comic Dewey 'Pigmeat' Markham, "I was havin' a drink at the Braddock Bar [around the corner from the Apollo's stage door] when Jackie Wilson came in, sat down alongside me, and ordered a drink. 'Pigmeat,' he says, 'I just quit the Dominoes and I'm goin' out on my own. Do you think I can make it?' I'm sure you can, I said."

It was the understatement of the decade, for Jackie Wilson in his short career did it all. He headlined at the Apollo, at New York's Copacabana, at the top spots in Vegas. He headlined wherever he wanted to because he was among the great performers of his era. His billing read "Mr. Excitement," and he lived up to every syllable of it. Entertainment was never quite the same after Jackie Wilson did his thing; only an act of God in the form of a stroke cut short one of the great show-business careers.

That story illustrates another aspect of the Amateur Program. It was a constant source of new talent for agents, managers, and others who were not always looking for potential stars but for supporting artists of various kinds. In the heyday of the vocal groups someone was always looking for a bass singer, a tenor, perhaps a baritone, and Amateur Night in Harlem was the place to find one. Said Bobby Robinson, "At one time I had thirteen acts under management and a majority of them I found on the Amateur Program. It was a weekly *must*." My brother Bobby added, "In the heyday of the rock groups, I'd guess that in the East, seventy percent of them had at least one singer who came off the Amateur Program."

Nor were agents the only ones to use the new talent that was always springing up on the program. Leonard Reed describes an incident (and its results) from some years ago.

> Roy Hamilton had been on the Amateur Show and had won a rather weak third place. But we had a show coming in with Ruth Brown, and we were looking for a supporting act, a "filler." Roy had a record out called "You'll Never Walk Alone," which seemed to be gaining momentum. I suggested to your dad that we use Roy who, after all, was a product of our own Amateur Program. When we put him in the show, his manager got the owner of the record shop across the street to play that record from morning 'till night. I mean, they played it from the time the store opened until they closed it at midnight, and by the time the show was ready to open it had taken off. In fact, Ruth Brown's manager came to me and offered me

fifty dollars to take Roy *off* the bill! He was frightened of what Roy would do to his star—and he was right. We were paying Ruth big money that week and Roy was getting a mere 250 dollars, but the audience just screamed and hollered for him and you just couldn't get him off the stage. Ruth, who was a full-fledged star and a great singer, didn't have a chance. We brought Roy Hamilton back three weeks later for 1500 dollars and that was just the beginning of his career.

The amazing part of the story is that Roy, a tall, handsome, and pleasant young man, had a fatal flaw as a singer: he went flat at the end of every song. I mean, there was no way in which Roy could keep his voice from tailing off. The result was not that he lost in popularity, but he started a fad. There was a whole generation of singers who intentionally sang flat because one Roy Hamilton became a first-magnitude star unintentionally doing so.

The final irony is that Ruth Brown was also one of our own Amateur winners of an earlier era. Like the aging champion who is knocked out of his title by a newcomer, Ruth was displaced by another Amateur winner, at least for that one show.

In the middle and late fifties there was no stronger Apollo headliner than Little Willie John. With an infectious style, Willie sang and danced. He was a fun-loving, talent-loaded young man. Leonard Reed has described an event that took place in the rehearsal hall, prior to a Willie John show.

A young fellow came in who had won the Amateur Show. He had a straw suitcase, a brash manner, a load of talent, and he insisted on our putting him in the show. You remember that part of the prize for a winner was to be given "a week." Well, I guess this was this guy's week. We put him in the show with Little Willie John. Put him in the last moment, unbilled and unadvertised. But then, what was there to advertise? He was an unknown. For the Apollo, it was a bonanza; for Willie it was something less. For the artist was a kid named James Brown, and he was so sensational that, like what Roy Hamilton did to Ruth Brown, he tied the show up in knots and poor Willie couldn't get on stage. James was so strong that we kept moving him around from one spot to another trying to help Willie. It was useless. That show simply belonged to the kid who insisted on his "Week," took it, and parlayed into one of the greatest careers in modern-day show business."

There was an interesting corollary to the story. Several years later, Willie John was arrested and accused of committing a capital offense. His biggest benefactor and a man who spent thousands of his own dollars to try and help him was James Brown. Unfortunately, it didn't help and Little Willie John, one of the cleverest and most infectious youngsters I ever met died in prison. No jail built could have contained that free spirit!

We are so used to thinking of show business in terms of stars that we sometimes forget the legions of talented people in other phases of the business who help make it all possible. Occasionally, in addition to being supertalented, you meet one who is a person extraordinaire. In my book such a one is Frankie

Owens. Because it is unlikely that many readers would know that name, let me explain that Frankie, an ex-Amateur of ours, is an arranger and a conductor. He was accompanist for lovely Barbara McNair (also an ex-Amateur), for Johnny Mathis in 1957, and for ten years beginning in 1965, he did all of the conducting and arranging for Petula Clark.

Frankie was number one on two consecutive "Amateur Night in Harlem" broadcasts in 1953. With his talent, he might have continued winning the contest for a month or so, but he forgot one thing. Frankie has laughingly recalled:

> I forgot that most audiences go for what is familiar to them and, wanting to vary my offering each week, I played something I loved and the audience didn't know it from a hole in the wall. At that time, I was studying with a man who was a member of the First Piano Quartet. I fell in love with the music from *Showboat* and for the third week I chose to play "Why Do I Love You?" Even though I played it in the style of Errol Garner, my idol at the time, the audience was totally unfamiliar with the tune. I don't recall who won the contest or what tune they were playing, but the winner wasn't Frankie Owens.
>
> But I had fallen in love with the Amateur Show and so I used to go to the rehearsal hall every Wednesday night while they were going over the music for that night's show. Now most musicians are decent fellows, but sometimes they get rushed or maybe they're a little short-tempered. I didn't think they were always doing justice to the kids' music. So I'd sit there and make myself obnoxious. You know, I'd holler out, "No! no! That's an A-natural chord!" Or I'd whisper in a stage voice you could hear to Grand Central Station, "That's B-flat, dummy— B-FLAT!" I don't know exactly why, but the guy who was running the show, Frank Parrish, finally came up to me and offered me the job of playing for the amateurs. Man! That was a thrill. In the first place, the job paid fifteen dollars and that was a lot of money to me, but more important, I felt that playing for the Apollo Amateur Show was a real honor. I still feel that way about it.

My brother Bobby later said, "Frankie was good. He was damn good. And after awhile he became too good! What I mean is that he made even the lousy amateurs sound good, and we were having trouble getting losers and losers are part of the show. We didn't put losers in on purpose, but on an average there would be at least a couple in each show—until Frankie came along." Laughed Bobby, "To tell you the truth, I didn't want to fire Frankie, but when he got the job with Johnny Mathis I was glad to see him go. He was too good for our show."

Frankie's attitude is really an admirable one. "I knew from watching them how much this show meant to these kids. Why some of them went over their song for weeks and weeks. I even recall some of them getting special costumes together and rehearse and choreograph dance steps, so that they would appear professional when their big chance came. All I wanted to do was to give them the best possible break, musically."

So Frankie Owens would rehearse those kids between rehearsal time and show time. He would make outside appointments with them, go over their

33a. Leslie Uggams

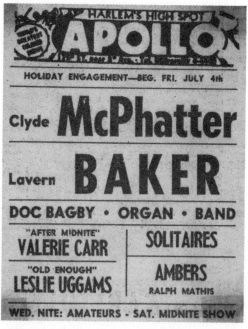

33b.

music, add embellishments of his own, and if he made things tougher for the program in the sense Bobby speaks of, he exhibited a human concern that is rare. It is the reason I love him.

If Frankie Owens presented minor problems for us, the little doll in Illustration 33a presented slightly larger ones. It is a childhood picture of Leslie Uggams. Leslie was good, very good, from age eight on. She was so cute that Ella Fitzgerald, Sarah Vaughan, and Dionne Warwick *combined* couldn't have beaten her in a contest. You can beat talent with more talent, but you can't beat a child in an amateur contest. And so, with reluctance, we laid down a rule: No child contestants. It simply wasn't fair to the other people on the show. The last child we had on the program was Leslie.

No less than four of the artists on the 1958 show (Illustration 33b) were Amateur Hour graduates: Clyde McPhatter started out singing with a popular group of the fifties called The Drifters; Lavern Baker once performed under the name of "Little Miss Cornshucks"; little Valerie Carr was a hit of the period, with the biggest voice for a skinny kid I ever heard; and Leslie's career is one of our pride and joys.

The Apollo's Amateur Night in Harlem was something special in the world of entertainment, evolving with a unique formula. Amateur contests, as such, were nothing especially new, because agents and artists were always looking for places to "try out" their acts, and showmen regard new talent as the lifeblood of their business. There is nothing quite as exciting, quite as luring at the box office as a newcomer moving up the ranks, attracting followers as he or she goes. Many a theater manager has solved the problem by occasionally "spotting" a new and promising act (which he had already auditioned) into a show for a performance or two, to see how it fared before an audience and how the audience might react.

In the twenties, for instance, the Fox Theatre at 105th Street and Fifth Avenue had a weekly amateur contest. And one week each month, it was open for colored performers.

An act called "The Three Dixie Songbirds" once won their contest. The act was made up of three singing sisters named Mills. The first name of one of them was Florence. That lovely bundle of talent tore up Broadway in the musical *Shuffle Along* in 1921 and again in 1926, when she plaintively sang "I'm a Little Blackbird Lookin' for a Bluebird Too" in Lew Leslie's production of *Blackbirds.*

As one old-timer once remarked to me, "They gotta start somewhere, an' if you wanna see the kids who'll make the big time, jest see a good amateur show. They're there."

On an island in the middle of Harlem—at Seventh Avenue just south of 132nd Street, to be exact—a plaque has been placed in the ground. Its legend tells the reader that the "Tree of Hope" once stood in that location. In terms of show business and Harlem, the plaque is a marker in history. For the "Tree of Hope" harkens back to the days of Bill "Bojangles" Robinson, who gave it its name, and to the casting of *Green Pastures*. Hundreds of performers stood under its shade in the heat of summer and touched it "just for luck" at any time of the year over a number of decades. Jack Johnson leaned against it; it was a witness to a real-life comic duel between Bill Robinson and Irvin C. Miller, producer of *Brownskin Models* (in which Bill's pistol was fired harmlessly in the air "at" Miller); and the Lord only knows how many scripts were born, deals were made, and hopes were kindled under its sheltering branches.

As far as I know, the only extant remnant of the tree is backstage at the Apollo Theatre. In the form of a small log mounted on a pedestal, it was one of the elements always present at the Amateur Program, for each and every contestant is required to "touch the tree, touch it for luck" as he walks or skips out to center stage to face the kindest, wildest, most critical, most sophisticated, most demonstrative audience in the world.

On the way off the stage, after his number has been performed, the amateur is required to perform one last rite. He doesn't walk off, run off, or crawl off. He "trucks" off to the tune of "Christopher Columbus." In case there is a soul in the audience who is unfamiliar with "truckin," I can only inform him that it is a dance, a dance done at an oblique angle, a dance done with both feet doing a kind of shuffle, a dance which *must* be performed with one finger—the index—of the left hand pointed skyward. As for "Christopher Columbus," it is a tune with a special rhythm all its own, which will go down in musical history as the theme song for Amateur Night in Harlem. Since that program went on roughly forty-five weeks per year from 1934 until about 1974, I leave to the mathematicians the calculation of how many times it was played and how many fingers pointed or dropped to its bounce.

Most readers have never heard of Norman Miller, though his place in history is as secure as anyone's in the theater. But, if I discarded his real name and inserted his stage name, bells would start ringing among Harlem theater aficionados. For Norman Miller is the true name of one Porto Rico. Now Porto Rico (known merely as Rico to his friends and even casual acquaintances) was what is known the world over as "a character." Short, brown, and a bit potbellied, usually chomping on a dead stogie, Rico's appearance was routinely nondescript. Not so his vocabulary. Although limited, it was triumphant. It consisted basically of two words, the first of which was *mother*; I will leave the second for your imagination to supply. Rico's intonation of the words, like the lilt of a voice, the inflection, the stress—all told the real meaning in a particular context. Sometimes *mother*——— could be like a mother's caress; sometimes it could be a blood-curdling curse. In Rico's lexicon, the two words were an infinite series of ideographs encompassing all the considerable nuances of his vocabulary.

Rico started working at the Lafayette Theater in 1913, in the first black show there. Show business flowed through his veins; it was all he know and that was enough. He started as a dancer, but in those days, black male dancers had a name that later took on other meanings. They were first called, for reasons which escape me, *pickaninnies*. Later, the term was shortened to *pics*. Rico was a dancer and, from conversations with Doll Thomas, I gather that he was a very good one. Truthfully, I don't need Doll's confirmation of that fact. Several generations of Apollo Theatre patrons can testify to the fact that Norman Miller could dance. Brother, could he dance! Porto Rico was the first, the most glorious, the most talented "executioner" in the history of the Apollo's Amateur Program. Like a Manolete Rico executed with style. His was the master's touch.

It all started one night when an especially poor amateur was on stage, in full sight of Rico, who worked the microphones on stage left. Some evil spirit began working on his innards and suddenly he could stand it no longer. With black eyes blazing, he ran out on stage brandishing a starter's pistol in his raised hand. He stopped, turned, and went into a grotesque dance. Round and round his transfixed victim he spun, weaving a tight magic spell. It is even likely that some incantations escaped from between his curled lips. It is certain that he fired off his weapon. There can be no question that the magic had worked. The amateur was dispatched before an audience that was convulsed with laughter yet fully aware that a device had been hatched, a myth born.

The first execution had occurred without a single drop of blood being spilled. On future programs, Rico's approach was signalled by a siren and sometimes bells, gongs, and other such riot equipment. Rico did more than shoo off a talentless amateur; he lionized both himself and his victims. If laughter followed on the heels of catcalls, the signals for his appearance and the amateur's "execution," the onus for the latter was now on Rico and off the amateur. It was no disgrace to be executed. It might be a disappointment, but at least one was skewered with artistry and style. An executionee could scarcely ask for more than that, could he?

If aging Porto Rico could have chosen his successor when he was required by infirmity to retire, he would have chosen Adam. I cannot imagine him choosing anyone *but* Adam had he been able to audition his successor. Now Adam was no carbon copy of Rico; he was his own man. With long and curved finger Adam would point at his intended victim, crooking it at him like a modern-day Monsieur DeFarge. Taller and thinner than Rico, his grotesque dance was sinewy, insinuating with all the generosity of a boa constrictor. Once, however, while wearing a Batman costume, his black tights split in the middle of his dance; they split, also in the middle of the tights themselves. It revealed— well, it revealed about everything including Adam's lack of dignity plus a few clues as to how much laughter an audience could sustain without destroying itself in the process. But a worse episode occurred on another night. That was when an intended victim refused to be executed. He continued his act as Adam approached him with increasing boldness, finally even plucking at his clothing. With unrestrained fury, the executionee turned on poor unsuspecting Adam and decked him with one solid blow. It required the efforts of several burly stage-hands to remove him from the stage. It was the first and last time a contestant failed to truck off to the lilting strains of "Christopher Columbus."

There was a long line of masters of ceremonies on Amateur Night in Harlem. Perhaps the favorite was Willie Bryant, who was one of Harlem's most beloved citizens anyway. Willie had a charm which, without being cloying, fairly oozed from his smiling visage. Not too far behind him in popularity were Leonard Reed and Ralph Cooper. Coop was another perennial Harlem favorite, whose varied offerings included acting in some of the early black motion pictures, fronting a band, playing straight man with various acts, and working as one of the more popular disc jockeys in town.

You could take the Willie Bryants, the Porto Ricos, and the amateurs themselves, put them all together, and they still wouldn't have made a show without the audience itself. It was the critical added ingredient that made the show the unique institution it became. Quick to react to the good *and* the bad, they would jump on a contestant who didn't measure up as often as they would explode joyously to one who rang the right bell. They were lukewarm to the relatively few white contestants who appeared, but when they were good, the audience rewarded them with the same enthusiastic responses they accorded the black ones.

Writer and gadfly George Plimpton once appeared as a contestant on Amateur Night in Harlem. He did so, George declared, because he wanted to know how it felt to experience defeat. He elected to play, of all things, "Clair de Lune" on the piano, thinking that an Apollo Theatre audience would never tolerate such "corn." How wrong he was! Much to his astonishment, the audience was not only listened, they applauded and capped it off by awarding him third prize!

But stagehand Hans Nielson tells of another white contestant with a different reception. "When she walked out," Hans relates, "the audience was pretty cool toward her, someone even started booing even though it was immediately apparent that she was blind. But when she started to sing, that changed it all. You could have heard a pin drop. I mean this chick could *sing!* As they usually did on hearing something extra-good, the audience broke into applause right in the middle of her song. It was like an explosion. Someone ran upstairs backstage and summoned our headliner, Nancy Wilson, who ran down, stood in the wings, and listened to the rest of her number." Continued Hans, "When she walked offstage, the audience really broke it up. Nancy Wilson talked to her for some time, encouraging her to continue her career, telling her how much she liked her voice and style. She never came back again; I guess someone heard her and put her to work, but I'll never forget that night when a blind white girl won it all."

"Do you think the audience gave her first prize because she was blind or because she was so good," I asked? "Because she was so good. No doubt about it," Hans replied.

When they were good, when they were very good, the audience would set up the cry, "Give them a week," because a week's engagement at the Apollo was frequently an added prize. When Stephanie Mills won the contest four weeks in

34a. Vivian Reed

34b. Sonny Til

35a. Gloria Lynne

35b. Isley Brothers

a row, her prize was a week with the Isley Brothers (also from the ranks of our ex-amateurs). The "week" was often but not uniformly offered to successful contestants. For with the best of intentions on our part, the deeper we got into rock-style shows with a dozen or so vocal groups on each show, the more difficult it became to place an amateur in a show. In the earlier days it wasn't so hard.

In 1940 the Apollo presented Lucky Millinder and his band with a whole group of contest winners and another, in 1947, featured Dizzy Gillespie's Band. That same year the "Divine Sarah," Sarah Vaughan, was a contest winner. It is hard for me to write about Sarah without reaching for superlatives, for few singers have grown to her stature over the years. At this writing, it seems to me that she hasn't come close to reaching the full scope of her artistry. Indeed, recent recordings make me feel that Sarah Vaughan's talent is close to being inexhaustible. There isn't an artist I know who inspires more genuine pride than this lady. She has always been known as a musician's musician; she is also an audience's *and* a management's musician.

And now I would like to present a roster of Amateur Hour winners. Lovely Vivian Reed has it all—talent, beauty, and ambition. In 1977, she set Broadway afire as the star of *Bubbling Brown Sugar*. Sonny Til, in the fifties, was the lead tenor with a group called The Orioles. In modern show-biz history, that group, their name now virtually lost, is of transcending importance. Without them, there would be no Beatles, Rolling Stones, or BeeGees, at least not in the terms we know them today. They set the vocal and choreographic style for hundreds of vocal groups that followed in their wake.

In the late thirties and early forties, Bill Kenny reared back and sang "If I Didn't Care" to international acclaim. He was lead singer of the Four Ink Spots. The Isley Brothers had enough energy and talent for six. My brother Bobby says that ultratalented Gladys Knight told him she had been an Apollo amateur winner. Her statement is typical of the many performers who point to their appearance on the show with pride.

From unknown to stardom and back to obscurity—that has been the story of Gloria Lynne. She started as one of the (four) Dorsey Sisters and became a major attraction at the Apollo and elsewhere during the sixties. She should be a superstar today; she has the talent for it but perhaps not the temperament.

There are times when success comes too fast for an act. There are those who find themselves in the winner's circle before they know exactly where they are and know how to handle such sudden fame. Such an act was The Penguins, about whom Bobby tells the following story:

> These kids came in for a week, exactly five months after winning the Amateur Show. They were riding high on the crest of a record that wasn't merely a hit in the United States; it was a hit all over the world. It was called "Earth Angel." We felt a little insecure about their performing ability, so the night before the show

their manager, Ben Bart, brought them to the theater after the scenery had been hung. The idea was to rehearse their numbers on the stage so that they would be familiar with how it felt, where they were to take their positions, where the mikes would be located, and so on. When the rehearsal started, it became apparent that "Earth Angel" or no "Earth Angel" these kids were barely beyond the amateur stage. The truth of the matter is that they didn't really know how to get on and off the stage. Dad and Ben Bart spent half the night teaching them just that.

When the show went on the next day, they were scared to death, but they managed to get away with it because of their hit record. Two days later, one of them came up to me with a request. Could we cash a check for them? They had gotten their first royalty check from the record company and they wanted some cash. Of course we could cash the check for them. They brought it in, and I almost fell out of my chair. This five-month-old act, these nervous kids still wet behind the ears, handed me a check for sixty thousand dollars!

This points up a major problem in today's show business. The record business has made such success stories possible, and kids can achieve stardom without going through the long periods of preliminary training that were both offered and required in the old days when circuits consisting of dozens of theaters were interlaced with hundreds of small clubs and cafes all across the country. It was in those places where kids earned their spurs and learned their trade. They learned what they needed to do to get on and off the stage. (Doll Thomas once, quite correctly, said to me, "The most difficult thing for a performer to learn is the simple business of getting on and off the stage.") They learned which songs would work best with which audiences, which gags were funny and acceptable and where, when to sing the slow blues and how to pace their act for maximum reception. The *sudden* birth of stars "overnight" has been a myth that isn't really true.

I recall talking to Stephanie Mills in her Broadway dressing room when this nineteen-year-old youngster was starring in *The Wiz*. I said, "Honi Coles tells me that you won the Amateur Contest and four months later you landed this part on Broadway."

"Oh, that's really not true," she said. "After I won the Amateur Contest, I got a week at the Apollo with the Isley Brothers' show. At that time, I was eleven years old. I was sixteen before the Broadway role came along. There were parts in off-Broadway shows and lots of bit parts before I got to Broadway."

Leslie Uggams won her first Amateur Contest and an engagement at the Apollo when she was eight. Her mother continued the story for me. "Leslie worked on and off for a number of years at various places, learning her trade. She was a teen-ager when she hit the summer circuit, playing in the mountains with people like Buddy Hackett, Red Buttons, and Joey Bishop. She was twenty-three when she burst on the Broadway scene in the hit musical *Hallelujah Baby,* and she is in her early thirties today."

That's not exactly an instant success—sixteen years of training between her first contest win and the Broadway scene. Once in a great while it may be true, as one song has it, "next night on your dressing room they hang a star," but there are usually years of preparation and hard work before stardom arrives.

For everyone who makes it as a star there are hundreds who never do. For every active performer who manages to make a living at a difficult and demanding trade, there are hundreds who fall by the wayside, who drop out and give up. Every year, the pros of Broadway produce shows that die in Philly, are abandoned after Boston and even after tryouts, often flunk out on Broadway.

Every year there are kids who try out for shows, for night clubs, for theaters, and for amateur contests who simply don't have it. Ever wonder why those with seemingly obvious lack of talent try it anyway? Are they trying to climb out of the ghetto and figure what have they to lose? Is it a pure ego trip? Do they do it as a gag, on a dare? I asked a cross-section of people with long experience in the theater and got, surprisingly enough, one answer: They really think they can make it; they really think they have it.

Said veteran Doll Thomas: "Whoever they have in mind they would like to sound like, that's how they sound to themselves! They think that all they need is an audience to spread their talent before, and they'll be great. Everybody in the world sees himself as a certain kind of performer and he can't see himself any differently."

Former dancer, producer and Apollo manager Honi Coles put it this way: "Look, you go to a party and a cat will come up and say, 'Man! I want you to hear this girl sing.' He thinks she can sing—and she can't. She's positively horrible but someone will say, 'You sound just like Sarah Vaughan' and she believes it. It's pathetic."

Hans Nielsen, our stage manager for many years, put it this way: "I don't think any of the amateurs who came to the Amateur Show had any idea they were going to be shot off. They *all* thought they were going to make it." Except for David McCarthy, the last of our managers. Laughed David, "One of my proudest moments was being on the Amateur Show and *not* being shot off." David was the only person I know except George Plimpton who expected to lose.

The question of why the losers went on the Amateur Show, why they didn't know they were going to lose brings up another question of even deeper import. Why do people become performers in the first place? Again, Doll Thomas supplies the most interesting reason. "Back in the old days [Doll is ninety] there was nothing for you [a black man] to do outside of working in the white folks' kitchen. That was the whole thing in a nutshell. They just didn't want to be a servant or even a high-class slave letting 'massa' take care of you. This was a way for you to have a certain amount of freedom. For a while you were king. There were lots of youngsters who had a voice or a natural sense of rhythm."

The opportunities for black men and women were almost as circumscribed as for medieval peasants. If a boy could sing or dance or play a musical instrument, he *might* be able to carve out a career. As I've said in another context, we Americans put performers in strange places. Other societies have royalty; we have our artists.

Honi Coles was a veteran of hundreds of Amateur Nights. He emceed them, rehearsed them, staged them. He nursed the amateurs, listened to them cry, and sometimes watched careers begin. Said Honi: "Amateur Night was a very peculiar night. It was a highly technical night because people spent hours and days and weeks, making all sorts of preparations just to be on the Amateur Show. They'd come in with costumes and dances set with their particular music and it was a revelation to see the trouble they went through just in order to perform. And there was no other place in the United States or Europe for them. They wanted only to be on the Apollo stage. They wanted the Apollo because that's where it was at."

In 1977, the Apollo had been closed for over a year. Charlie Worrell was one of several people whom we hired to guard the place, to keep it secure, but Charlie had once been in charge of signing up the amateurs. "They still come around all the time," Charlie said with a somewhat bewildered shake of his head. "We've been closed all this time and still they come. Why last week, a station wagon pulled up in front of the theater and a pile of kids came out. They were all dressed in uniforms. They had instruments with them, they had driven all the way from Connecticut, and all they wanted to know was where they had to go to sign up for the Amateur Show and to be auditioned. We'd been closed for a year; we hadn't had an Amateur Show for at least that long, maybe longer. But those kids were ready to go on. They had rehearsed and they had planned, and it was the Apollo that they turned to. They just *knew* that if they could make it there, they'd be on their way!"

In February 1984, the Apollo Amateur Hour, emceed by Ralph Cooper, was launched once more in the newly refurbished theater.

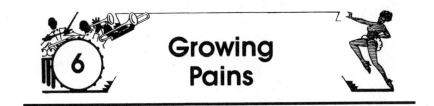

6

Growing Pains

"Jelly Jelly"

For a nation of so-called realists, we are still people who treasure our myths. Nowhere does this show up more graphically than in the world of entertainment. Not only do we lionize our entertainers and put them on absurd and precarious perches, we insist on treating them virtually as gods. In our mythology they needn't struggle, needn't err, needn't even bleed. No! Suddenly, overnight, at the blink of an eye, one of them is elevated to stardom; then another and another. Just like that! Bah! Humbug!

We may be fooled by such notions but *they* are not. Young or old, children or adults, they know what they had to do to get there and what is required of them to stay. The line that separates the superstars from the lesser stars and the also-rans is sometimes so thin that it is invisible—and often it is mysterious. Show-business history is loaded with talented people who almost made it to the top but who had to be satisfied with a bit less. Occasionally there is an artist who is hard to classify.

Jackie "Moms" Mabley labored long and hard from the twenties. Time and time again we would use her in the difficult next-to-closing spot, the one usually reserved for the main headliner, and yet star billing was not quite hers. She was reliable; she always gave a strong performance, an explosive finale. When Moms came out on stage, with or without her store-bought teeth, clad in a gingham old-lady's dress of some sort, frequently wearing a nondescript hat on her head, always with the oversized, floppy shoes reserved from time immemorial for the clown, she was always greeted with laughter. Like a few assorted comics of her day—"Pigmeat," "Spider Bruce," Dusty Fletcher, for example—the audience didn't really *need* to have her say anything, they laughed before she began. They laughed when she just stood there, they laughed when she danced, they laughed when she sang or joked in her basso-profundo voice.

"Jelly Jelly" is in the classic mold of the blues, but it was best performed by a balladeer, Billy Eckstine. "B.'s" rendition in fact was an early record hit. Its plaintive theme, suggestive lyrics and musical structure typify the blues.

36a.

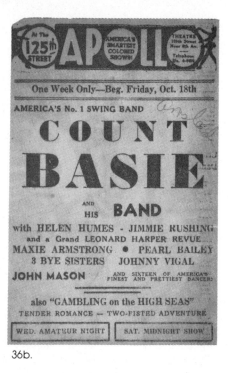

36b.

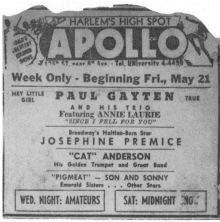

36c.

36d. Hazel Scott

Moms was funny, they knew she was going to be funny, and so they laughed when Moms appeared.

From the thirties until the sixties, she was a standby. Whenever we needed a strong act to close the show, Moms was there. Her salary varied little indeed. It rocked back and forth between 550 and 600 dollars per week, not a great deal for an entertainer who needs to pay transportation, hotel bills, and the like. And then something strange started happening; her popularity started to climb, a few records started to move, some national television shows came her way, and her salary started to edge upward. In 1961 we paid Moms 1000 dollars for one engagement, then 1500 dollars for another. In '62 she became a genuine headliner and by 1963 her salary had climbed to 5000 per week. In 1964 she graduated to the percentage-of-receipts class and in 1968, Jackie Mabley was worth every penny of 10,000 dollars per week. Moms had arrived, a long shot from the featured spot in the 1941 Count Basie show, whose ad is reproduced in Illustration 36b.

Moms was a bit rueful about it. She remarked to Dad one day, "Wouldn't you know it? By the time I finally arrived at the big money, I'm too old and sick to really enjoy it." It was no stage joke! At Dad's funeral, ailing Moms Mabley was one of the few performers in attendance.

Two other artists featured in the same Basie show, Helen Humes and Jimmie Rushing, were also great artists who "arrived" as singers but had to settle for something less than stardom. Whenever the history of the blues is written, "Mr. Five by Five," Jimmie Rushing, will always be included. Perhaps more than any blues singer, Jimmie's artistry helped move the blues back into national prominence in the fifties and sixties. For years, no Count Basie show was ever complete without a brace of numbers sung by Jimmie Rushing.

Although Helen Humes could handle blues with the best of them, her forte was pure and unadulterated jazz. Her musical imagination and inventiveness were a joy to the ear. But there was frustration in her voice during a conversation I had with her shortly before she died. "Gee," she said wistfully, "nobody ever has used me on a national television show. I sure would like to be on one, one of these days." She deserved it, too, for on anyone's list of first-rate jazz singers, the name Helen Humes should not be left out. Custom dictates that an artist must be "box office" to be worthy of a television appearance, and five-by-five Helen with a "following" only among a small coterie of jazz lovers didn't qualify.

In one of the very first shows I was involved in when I started working at the Apollo, an artist appeared whom I thought to be a supertalent. I still think so even though thirty-odd years have passed. She is Josephine Premice, and the show opened May 21, 1949. Just a few years ago, Josephine Premice along with Avon Long and Vivian Reed were Broadway smashes in *Bubbling Brown Sugar*. As far as I know, this was Josephine's first Broadway starring role since she appeared in *Jamaica* some years ago as less than a major headliner. Strange, because Josephine has everything a superstar needs for success. She is a show-woman to her fingertips, a superb dancer, great personality, and she has a voice that can handle songs in half-a-dozen languages effectively. She has the magic, I think, but it must be on a slightly different wavelength from her audience's.

I've often wondered why the late pianist Hazel Scott never became a superstar? Beautiful, intelligent, talented—how much more does an audience want? And yet, although we and others featured Hazel in many an exciting revue and she was always received with pleasure, she never quite lit those sparks. Illustration 36d is of Hazel at seventeen.

Billy Taylor, pianist, arranger, composer, told me a short anecdote about a guy who did light sparks.

Some years ago, in the days when demo [demonstration] records weren't made very often, I used to go down to Atlantic Records from time to time, and spend a few hours playing sheet music for them. The music would be left with them for their consideration by composers or agents and Ahmet Ertegun would sit and listen while I played it. One Saturday, I had played for a couple of hours, and we were taking a short break. Ahmet said, "Got an acetate [trial record] which I'd like you to hear. Tell me what you think." He played a disc featuring a pianist who was really good. I told him so. Ahmet then smiled and asked, "How do you like this one?"

"Pretty damned good," I said, becoming more excited. "In fact, awfully good. Say, what's the guy's name?"

"He's accompanying Dinah Washington now," he said. "Name is Ray Charles."

Known as "Mr. Blues," Wynonie Harris was what was known in the trade as a "blues shouter." Possessing a pair of tonsils tough as leather, Wynonie attacked the blues about as subtly as a player hitting O. J. Simpson coming around end. His approach was the opposite of Jimmie Rushing's, but it brought results in the form of audience reaction.

Another man we presented in 1950 was someone I always liked, respected, and could not help feeling sorry for: Mercer Ellington. Mercer had to buck a giant—his father, Duke. He is a fine musician, handling lots of chores for his father well. Mercer finally made it big when he arranged the music and conducted the hit show *Sophisticated Ladies*, whose original music was Duke's.

In Buddy Johnson's "knock-em-dead-and-stomp-em-in" band was a talent, Arthur Prysock, for years one of Buddy's two vocalists; the other was Buddy's sister, Ella. After he left the Johnson organization, Arthur made it part way up the ladder, a second magnitude albeit a genuine star. Arthur's major problem was that he sounded too much like his talented contemporary, Billy Eckstine.

At Broadway's Capital Theatre, at the celebrated nightclub known as the Copa, and in some of the classiest spots in the country, Billy Daniels, with a million bucks worth of sex appeal, warbled "That Ole Black Magic." He had talent, charm, and charisma, and he made it big for a short while. Billy belongs to that small category of stars who go on and on and on.

37a. Billy Daniels

37b.

37c.

Another singer whose popularity swept the nation all too briefly was Maxine Sullivan, whose lilting version of "Loch Lomond" had a popular run that topped everything in its day. Nor was Maxine's one well-known record the end of her talent. She appeared on Broadway once or twice, the most memorable occasion being a show called *Swingin' the Dream*, a musical version of Shakespeare's *Midsummer Night's Dream*. In it, Maxine was the fairy queen and Louis Armstrong was Puck. Maxine was a lissome, boyish-looking, utterly delightful Titania; Louis was a veritable sprite, with unbelievable mischief in his sly smile! In the early eighties Maxine Sullivan's soft, inventive style of jazz is still much in evidence at Newport and other cool jazz festivals.

Christopher Columbus was one of the best show drummers I ever knew. One of his legacies comes to us in his son, Sonny Payne, a jazz drummer par excellence. As for Chris, only drummer Jimmy Crawford had a smile that sparkled as much as his.

There was a cult around Josh White among the intelligentsia. His name out front in the Greenwich Village clubs was a guarantee of standing-room only. He was talented, serious, intense, and interesting, and yet Josh White was never more than a passing curiosity in the larger world of show business. I do not mean to give the Josh Whites of the world short shrift; I am merely pointing out that there are hundreds of first-rate performers who achieve popularity, sometimes even "cult status" in our society, and yet they never attract hordes of followers. But they bring pleasure, even inspiration to some people across the country.

Earlier I pointed out some of the myths with which we surround our performers. Have you ever considered how we regard their work? When we see them, they are performing for *our* pleasure. They sing, they dance, they tell jokes, or play music; in short, they are doing those things we associate with fun. Somehow, I think we come to the erroneous conclusion, therefore, that they are not really working, unless, that is, we see them sweating. Ladies and gentlemen, in case you have any doubts about it, please believe me when I insist that performing is labor of the most difficult order. Honi Coles, in talking about the young Leslie Uggams of more than twenty years ago, said, "The commonest sight on Broadway was Leslie and her manager Leroy Collins, making the daily trek from one agency to another, from one producer to the next." And Juanita Uggams, Leslie's mother, added, "When Leslie was a youngster, my husband had three jobs at once in order to make enough money to pay for all the lessons Leslie had to take. Leslie is always taking lessons. When she is home even today, there are dancing lessons, exercise classes, dramatic lessons. Look, she even studied dramatics for a long time with Stella Adler. How else do you think she learned enough about acting to do the job she did in *Roots*?"

I had a conversation with my arranger friend, Frankie Owens. "How much time and effort usually goes into making, rehearsing and presenting a number?" I asked. He replied, "We once worked out a tune called 'Could This Be Magic?' It became one of Petula's [Clark] biggest numbers. First we put our heads

38a. Josh White

38b.

together to discuss it. She usually had a pretty good idea of what she wanted. This one was to be very elaborate, with a sort of Bach fugue at the end and a "swingle-singers" style motif in the middle. It was loaded with brass and trumpets. Believe it or not, we worked out the *guts* of that number in only an hour and a half. But then," continued Frankie, "the work really began. There was the full arrangement to be made, the parts to be written and copied; but even that was hardly all of it. When we were doing a show for the first time, we averaged two days of band rehearsals during which time the lights were set, the sound was arranged, and then the music itself was rehearsed!" It added up to many days of work on one number and *that* is about par for the course.

Flip Wilson once told me that he wrote, rewrote, changed, and presented a single routine on and off, over a seven-year period before he was satisfied with it! And there never was an Apollo show in which the musical rehearsal alone ran less than four hours, and frequently a second rehearsal was required after the first show had been presented.

We see them on stage, those glittering, shimmering, polished stars, and in our imaginations we endow them with superhuman characteristics, like great confidence, wit, and presence of mind. Listen to another Frank Owens monologue and learn the sometimes sad truth.

> Petula came to me in Vegas in tears, one day. She had an arrangement for a number called "Who Am I!" which she had had made in England, and she hated that arrangement. It just didn't make it with her and she was beside herself. "What am I going to do? What am I going to do?" she kept repeating.
>
> "The first thing," I told her, "is to calm down. Now, let's look at the number and see what can be done." I talked about doing a grandiose Roman opening with her singing offstage; then I suggested she do the first part ad lib. I just kept talking and talking, trying to calm her down. I think by the time we were done, I could have given her "Twinkle, Twinkle, Little Star" and she would have accepted it. She just had gotten herself all upset.
>
> And mind you, Petula was really good at indicating just what she wanted in her arrangements although she usually gave me a reasonable amount of leeway. One time, I recall, she needed an up-tempo number for an opener and she was in Europe. We actually worked out the guts of the arrangement over the telephone. She'd give me an idea and I'd ask, "O.K., what's the opening chord?" She'd tell me right off the bat! She was musician enough for that. Sometimes she would make up something on a cassette and mail it to me and I'd take it from there.

Take Frankie's explanation of his work with Pet Clark, multiply it times the number of tunes you see and hear on a single television program in a single evening, and you begin to get the idea.

Illustration 38a is a handbill announcing a show we played in October 1942. Cootie Williams, for years one of the stalwart trumpeters with Duke Ellington, left Duke once or twice, formed his own band, played around and then returned to the fold. Others in the band, like Cat Anderson, Johnny Hodges, and even

Duke's son, Mercer, did likewise. But just run your eye down the list of entertainers. Down near the bottom, billed as "singer and dancer" is the now familiar name of Pearl Bailey, once known as Pearlie Mae. Few entertainers I know worked harder at her trade than did Pearl. She *started* as a singer and ended as an entertainer, but even in the forties there were few female singers who could best Pearl at just plain singing. The comedy, the thousand-and-one tricks of the trade that became her specialty were added later, bit by bit, piece by piece, by trial and error. They were added as an encore here, an afterthought there, added perhaps as an experiment or as a kind of tryout during a show or two. They were altered, honed, dressed up or dressed down, treated to a hundred nuances and shadings until the final product was arrived at, refined, polished— the thing you see on television or watch in a theater or club.

Recently Billy Taylor was playing an engagement in Orlando, Florida, at Disney's Village Lounge. Several times during this gig we talked, had a drink, broke bread together. "How do you like it here?" I asked Billy.

He leaned back and looked off into space. "You know, this has been an interesting gig for me. It's kind of like a glorified rehearsal. I mean, I've been trying out new things, new musical ideas, experimenting all week long. In most places, I come in with a fairly set routine, but this had been exciting. It's allowed me to try out a whole lot of new stuff."

I consider myself a fairly sophisticated listener. After all, I've been exposed to the greatest jazz musicians virtually all my life. I never would have guessed that Billy was doing anything less than presenting a studied, polished routine. In the truest jazz terms, even a studied routine is flexible; it must allow room for the improvisation that characterizes jazz. But Billy was saying something else. He was abandoning a preset musical routine altogether, taking a few basic themes, and allowing his creative imagination to work them over even as he played. That is the height of musical creativity, and the audience, without knowing it, was being treated to an act of original creation. It is, of course, the thing that distinguishes jazz from other musical forms.

To blues lovers the world over, Eddie Vinson was usually known as "Mr. Cleanhead." Vinson would have been unrecognizable with hair growing on his head or without the ever-present alto sax dangling round his neck. There was something a little droll in his manner, and the squeak he coaxed into his voice while intoning the lyrics to "Cherry Red" was unique. We always hit Eddie with a red spotlight when the lyrics asserted that he was about to perform "Cherry Red," but spotlight or no spotlight, he was all blues!

With Vinson's nickname, I am reminded of the dozens of colorful and varied sobriquets that dot show business—and jazz in particular. There are too many to mention, but a few will illustrate the point.

"Satch" or "Satchmo," the usual nickname for Louis Armstrong, was of course, a shortening of *satchelmouth*, but there was also a succession of cats named "Gatemouth" and "Dippermouth," all celebrating the oversized maw. Digging back a bit into early New Orleans history you will find records of piano

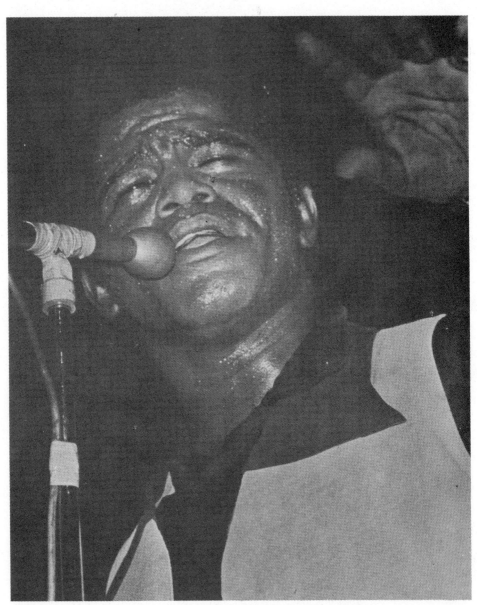

39. James Brown

players named Drag Nasty, Black Pete, and even Sore Dick! Don't forget too, the early jazzmaster Jelly Roll Morton. *Jelly roll* is a term that has well known sexual connotations, and it is an historical fact that many of the early jazzmen did more than a little pimping on the side, Jelly Roll Morton included. Jelly roll itself is celebrated in such songs as Lonnie Johnson's "She's a Jelly Roll Baker" ("she bakes the best jelly roll in town!"), and in one of his earliest hit records Billy Eckstine intoned:

> Jelly Roll killed my Momma,
> and ran my Daddy stone blind!

Early New Orleans is famous not only for its jazz and brothels, but for a number of cabarets with colorful names. How does Drag Nasty Hall grab you? Or would you prefer the Come Clean Hall, Big Easy Hall, Fewclothes, or perhaps (my favorite) the Funky Butt Hall?

Performers are human, of course, and they all have nerves; some are more uptight before a performance than others. Ernestine Allen laughingly recalled her first appearance at the Apollo. "I was standing in the wings when Lucky [Millinder] introduced me, and I just froze. I mean, I just refused to walk out—or maybe my legs did the refusing. Pigmeat Markham was standing there; he turned to me and asked, 'Ain't that your music?' I couldn't talk. I could only nod—and gulp. All Pigmeat did was turn around and give me a shove. I mean he pushed me out on the stage and Lucky caught me. He took my arm and led me to the mike. Don't ask me how it happened but Slim and Slam were the stars of that show and yet I stopped it cold. Your father came back after the show and moved me down." (Moving an artist down is about the highest compliment you can pay him or her, for the closer to the end of the show, the higher the degree of talent as a rule. Although there are often good acts early in the show, to get it moving, the spots closest to the headliner, who is almost always at the end of the bill, represent the better performers.)

Ernestine was certainly not the only artist who was nervous the first time out. What is amazing, however, is the number of artists who are always nervous before they go out on the stage. Nat "King" Cole, for one, confided to me one day: "I'm always nérvous until I get out and start singing. Once I'm out there and in my act, I'm okay, but until then, I die!" And even her adoring audiences recognize that Ella Fitzgerald is always frightened until about her fourth number.

The sweat on James Brown's face in Illustration 39 is no put-on. I don't think we have ever had an artist who worked harder than James did, and certainly we had few who had the impact or who managed to sustain his popularity as long. He generated an excitement few artists were ever able to match, and he did it over and over again, year after year after year. One amusing part of James' story is really a joke on us. In going over our files, I came across an early notation on his card. After a 1960 engagement, there was a note reading: "Good, but with limited box-office appeal." It shows how we could be wrong on occasion because in Apollo history James Brown ranks with the best.

I recall, in that connection, a conversation I had with my brother after we left the Apollo. We were discussing some of the black artists who had made it big, and whether or not we could have guessed their future success when we first saw them. On one we both agreed: we never would have guessed superstardom for James Brown. The reason has nothing whatever to do with James' considerable talent. Had he come up ten years earlier, he would probably have been successful *only* in the world of black show business, we felt, because white theatergoers wouldn't have understood his presentation. James Brown's superstardom is a part of the evolutionary process that permitted his success in black *and* white America, and it is perhaps a symbol of the amount of cultural integration that took place in recent decades.

I have been convinced, for example, that had he been born white or had he come up twenty years later, comedian Dewey Markham, with his talent, would have rivaled such international stars as Marcel Marceau and Jimmy Savo. Pigmeat was a consummate artist, a near-genius at pantomime but he was a little too early.

Had they been ten years earlier, I doubt that such singing stars as Diana Ross and the Supremes, Smokey Robinson and the Miracles—in fact *all* the Motown stars—would have achieved the kind of universal acceptance that they did. More than likely they would have remained in the rarefied world of black entertainment and "race" records. The path had to be paved for them by a whole generation of earlier singers, the way had to be prepared, white America's ear had to become attuned.

Our history, like most, is a series of adjustments and acceptances of the new and the different. The different is always frightening and challenging, and the fear has to be subdued before the challenges can be accepted. In a very real sense, the development and acceptance of black talent parallels the acceptance of black Americans into our society. Seen in these terms, the history of show business becomes a graphic illustration of integration at work. Indeed, the appeal of black artistry was perhaps one of the strongest spurs to integration and acceptance of black Americans by whites. Without the presence of black entertainers, greater acceptance by white Americans might have only come years later. The black artist, with his talent, style, songs, music, comedy, and dance may have done as much to advance acceptance of his brethren as did Martin Luther King and other integration leaders.

If we guessed wrong on James Brown's future, it wasn't the only time we did so. For instance, we labelled Brenda and the Tabulations, one of the super-acts of the James Brown era, as "just so-so" and then watched them become a major Apollo attraction. And we laughingly and shamefacedly point the file card on the Isley Brothers, which noted that they were "not a star act." But then, we were not the only ones to pass over some super talent.

40a.

40b.

I recall a *Variety* review of a Louis Prima show that said a lot about Louis and about an act called The Three Blazers; but although the reviewer treated the Will Mastin Trio with Sammy Davis, Jr., kindly, one would hardly guess that the act—and Sammy in particular—would become one of the biggest names in the history of show business.

For a graphic illustration of musical evolution in progress, consider the ad in Illustration 40a. It is for a show featuring Earl Hines and his band in 1941. The sharp reader will have noticed, I'm sure, that Billy Eckstine then spelled his name *Ekstein*. (Billy used to kid audiences, when it was appropriate, about being Jewish.) He was the featured male vocalist along with the beautiful and talented Madeline Green. When Madeline left the band, it was Billy who called Sarah Vaughan to Earl's attention. Sarah had won the Apollo's Amateur Contest and started one of the most glorious careers in modern show business. She joined Earl in 1941. It is worth mentioning that John Mason, known to Apollo audiences as "Spider Bruce," is billed over dancer Avon Long and, in fact, over the rest of the cast. But then, comedians were always among the most popular of all artists at the Apollo, and John was one of the best.

To further illustrate the growth of a group with talent, take an act like Martha and the Vandellas. In August 1963, they were paid 1500 dollars a week and went over "nicely." But in '64 they had two records, "Quicksand" and "Heatwave." Now a 2000-dollar-per-week act, they were off and flying. In '66 they earned 4000 dollars in one engagement and 4500 dollars in the next. And in September of 1967 Martha and her gals earned a nifty 6500 dollars.

The Temptations first appeared on the Apollo's stage in 1963 for 900 dollars. (900 dollars for an act with six men plus costumes plus music really is low.) In '64 they had gotten up to 2750 dollars; and a few years later, they racked up the highest box-office gross in the history of the Apollo Theatre until that date. It was, of course, reflected in their percentage.

For those interested in artistic evolution, consider the career of Esther Mae Jones. In the fifties, she was billed as "Little Esther" while touring with Johnny Otis' Band, and brothers and sisters, this kid was good! She was about thirteen years old, and with records like "Misery" and "Double Crossing Blues" she became an Apollo favorite. She played the Apollo several times, and then her childish appearance started to wear thin, the records started to play out, Johnny Otis and his troupe disappeared, and along with them, Little Esther. She played in May of 1964 in a Jackie Wilson show as a single, and had a few desultory appearances at salaries in the hundreds during the late sixties. And then, as though out of a fog, she reappeared as Esther Phillips; backed by a couple of hard-driving record albums she drove toward the top of the field. Esther Phillips may never achieve superstardom, but by sheer talent, drive, and energy, she rescued a career that was all but dead. My hat's off to her! It's off, too, to Johnny Otis. No other white man did more in a mostly black world, winning for himself the title "Godfather of Rhythm and Blues."

The Impressions included Curtis Mayfield, Samuel Gooden, and Fred

Cash. Singing together from 1958, their first record was with Jerry Butler. It was titled "For Your Precious Love" and brought them nationwide fame. Jerry Butler later went on as a single, one of the most successful in the business, and Curtis Mayfield, song writer par excellence, wrote all the Impressions' songs.

Part of the evolutionary process was the gradual emergence of "singles" from the vocal groups of the fifties and sixties. The Orioles, as I mentioned earlier, were the spark that lit up the careers of the new groups, such as The Five Keys, The Dominoes, The Drifters, The Clovers, the Moonglows, The Solitaires, and The Diamonds. There had been vocal groups in the past, of course, starting way back with the Mills Brothers, but The Orioles gave them a new dimension and a new life. Then out of many of these groups emerged such singles as Jackie Wilson, Clyde McPhatter, Sonny Til, and Jerry Butler. Succeeding the vocal groups, they completed the evolution.

The story continues, sometimes dramatically. In 1957 we played a gimmicky young man named Solomon Burke. He was sixteen years old and he was "closed out" after two nights. Being closed out (cancelled out of the show) can be the end of a career, but it wasn't with Solomon. In 1968, for 3000 dollars, Solomon Burke played a successful week. On his card was imprinted: "Quite a change. Cooperative, fairly clean, fine singer who takes care of business." Solomon Burke had evolved from an unsuccessful "drag" to a headliner.

At about the same time, we paid 3000 dollars for "a hot little artist, record-wise." He was used in the Motortown Revue and our card on him notes: "Plays harmonica very well. Worthwhile playing." In June 1966 this same artist earned 5000 dollars plus 1835 dollars in percentages and the card now read: "Very good; audiences loved him. A very talented kid." His name? Stevie Wonder.

In 1963 we played three girls, paid them 900 dollars, watched them go over quite well, and labeled them "good." In 1965 at 5000 dollars, they were "the hit of the show—the lead singer steals the show" said our card. The act was called The Supremes, and the show stealer was a "chick" named Diana Ross.

Reading the cast lists of some of the shows of the sixties when some of these artists were still "on the way up," gives a clue to the pace-making leadership that black artistry and the Apollo Theatre were providing the music industry.

January 19, 1962: Flip Wilson, Gladys Knight and the Pips.

December 12, 1962: The Barry Gordy (Motown) package consisted of Smokey Robinson and the Miracles, Mary Wells, The Marvelettes, Marie Johnson, The Contours, Marvin Gaye, The Supremes, and Stevie Wonder.

February 15, 1963: The B. B. King Show, Dione Warwick.

May 31, 1963: Smokey Robinson and the Miracles, Marvin Gaye, Little Stevie Wonder, The Marvelettes, Martha and the Vandellas and others.

41a. B. B. King

41b. Martha Reeves and the Vandellas

41c. Marvin Gaye

42a. Smokey Robinson and the Miracles

42b. Gladys Knight and the Pips*

February 28, 1964: Chuck Jackson, Ruby and the Romantics, The Sapphires, and Dionne Warwick.

September 25, 1964: Marvin Gaye, The Spinners, Martha and the Vandellas, Joe Tex, and Bo Diddley.

One can't help but be impressed, looking at these shows from today's vantage point, with the sheer number of acts on the bill. Most of them were new, and the format of the shows was revolutionary. Stevie Wonder, Dionne Warwick, Diana Ross, Marvin Gaye and the like were young, fresh, and still struggling; none of those artists had yet reached the astronomical salaries they command today. There is no present-day promoter who could afford shows with some of the cats listed above. But consider: in 1963 and 1964, the *total* salary expenses of some of those weeks was *less* than some of the acts alone today for a single engagement.

Who had the foresight and the courage to put such lineups on the stage? We did. It was my father's and brother's pioneering vision that put the shows together. Some of them made what I considered to be boring entertainment. But the audiences that flocked to the theater didn't think so. In the middle sixties, while black artists were beginning to establish themselves as major headliners all over the country and while Harlem was becoming an increasingly ingrown, embittered ghetto, the Apollo Theatre prospered as it had never prospered before. Whether that type of show, with its huge lineup of singers (groups and singles) was good showmanship or good for the entertainment business, is debatable. That it generated an excited, sometimes frenetic audience reponse is undeniable; scarcely any period generated more audience response that did that one.

In the long run, our job was to present entertainers; their job was to perform. Without their entertainment genius and without the will, the drive, the ambition to "make it," nothing we did could have been effective. In the last analysis, it is always the artist upon whose shoulders success or failure rests. It's a strange, exciting and demanding business. The musicians suffer growing pains all their lives—or they don't grow at all. A career, after all, is one long rehearsal followed by dozens of tryouts, followed by a few one-night stands.

The Supernovae

7

"Unforgettable"

They come in all shapes and guises, the heroes and heroines of the world of entertainment. Some flash across the horizon with a sudden and fierce light, then disappear. Some hover over us for years, satisfying if not inspiring, exciting if not electrifying. And then there are those who burst upon the scene, staggering, even shattering us. They are the supernovae, the superstars. It isn't only that a superstar's talents transcend the boundaries of race, color, even language. There is more to them than that, for theirs is the secret ingredient that inhabits the seer, the prophet, the magician. The supernova has that something special that marks him as an artist, flaws and all. He stirs us, moves us, excites us, and we're not quite certain why. Nor do we care. A star may sometimes sing off key, miss a step, even hit a sour note, and still generate a reaction that lifts us out of the commonplace.

No performer was ever more entitled to the much overworked term *glamorous* than Josephine Baker, for from the time she first capered before a bewitched Broadway audience at the tail end of the chorus line in *Shuffle Along,* Josephine was *always* creating excitement. In that 1921 production she made her first sizable splash on the stage. A couple of years later she appeared in the line at the Cotton Club, where the made an even bigger splash. In 1936 she was on Broadway again in *The Ziegfeld Follies*, where she was only a hair short of real triumph, and then she headed for Paris. If Broadway had been bewitched, Paris was totally entranced when tall, lithe, brown-skinned Josephine did a seminude dance at the Follies Bergere. From that year La Baker was the toast not only of Paris but of the entire European continent. While the war clouds were gathering, she remained in Paris and was trapped when the fighting started

---

A superstar is superior to others, above them in talent and in that appeal we label "box office." Accordingly, one can hardly say that an individual superstar is greater than another. But one can single out a few and say they are more beloved by the public. Such a one was the late Nat "King" Cole, who remains a superstar today, more than seventeen years after his untimely death. It seems fitting, therefore, that the themesong for this chapter is his hit record "Unforgettable."

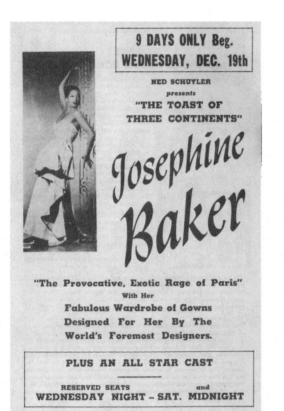

9 DAYS ONLY Beg.
WEDNESDAY, DEC. 19th

NED SCHUYLER

presents

"THE TOAST OF
THREE CONTINENTS"

Josephine
Baker

"The Provocative, Exotic Rage of Paris"

With Her

Fabulous Wardrobe of Gowns
Designed For Her By The
World's Foremost Designers.

PLUS AN ALL STAR CAST

RESERVED SEATS and
WEDNESDAY NIGHT – SAT. MIDNIGHT

43a.

43b.

and Paris fell to the Nazis. It wasn't until the war was over that she returned to the States, a decorated heroine of the French Resistance; she returned in 1950 to the homage and plaudits of her native countrymen. During that postwar visit, she played an S.R.O. engagement at Broadway's Strand Theatre and then toured the country in triumph, returning to New York and the first of two Apollo engagements.

Josephine sang in half a dozen languages, danced with an exotic and provocative ease, as limber at fifty as she had been at twenty. She had every audience eating out of her hand, but for nine solid days she gave me one royal pain! I must admit, however, that I was the only one at the Apollo who was relieved when her first engagement was over.

It may not have been entirely her fault. After all, she was engaged in a pair of lawsuits against Walter Winchell, the Broadway columnist who accused her of collaborating with the Germans during the war; it was an accusation she fought with great passion.

We cheerfully gave her the three dressing rooms she required (one for her gowns, one in the wings for quick changes, and one for socializing), but we struggled nervously through scheduling problems. "I'm simply too old to be at the theater *that* early," she said. "Early" was 1:00 PM, a half-hour *after* our customary first show time.

But that was the least of it: She walked off stage in the middle of a matinee performance, stalked out the stage door, and casually flung "I've got a meeting and I'm not sure just when I'll be back" over one svelte shoulder as she climbed into a waiting cab. All I had to do was explain her sudden disappearance to *that* audience and then worry about the reserved-seat, sellout crowd later that evening, who would lynch me, I was sure, if she didn't show up. She did return, in the nick of time, and the show went on!

Nevertheless, Josephine was glamour personified, and temperamental as she was, I could only stand in awe at her masterful performances. She covered the stage with all the agility of a cat and the ease of a seal in water. The audience adored her as she brought children up on stage to dance with her, adults up to talk to her. She appealed to young and old alike. Not once, but six or eight times per performance she swirled off stage while the orchestra vamped, returning in various outrageous costumes: enormous hats with fruit and flowers on them, gowns that ranged from Arabian striped affairs to furling, sequined gowns sparkling under the spots. She was, to put it in today's parlance, something else! She sang in French, she sang in Italian; she could have sung in Hindustani and that Harlem crowd would have stood up and cheered. I never saw the likes of her before or since! When my father visited her backstage at the Follies in Paris several years later, she greeted him as an old friend. Their acquaintance went back to *Shuffle Along, Chocolate Dandies*, and the chorus lines at the old Lafayette Theatre.

Nat Cole broke into the big-time in the mid-forties, leading a group called the King Cole Trio, thus launching one of the most fabulous careers in modern

44a.

Apollo, N. Y.

Nat "King" Cole & Trio (4); Sy Oliver Orch (12), Timmie Rogers, Conway & Parks, The Fontaines (3), Peggy Thomas; "Follow Me Quietly" (RKO).

With Nat "King" Cole and his trio topping the bill, current Apollo vaude fare shapes up into a palatable session for the stubholders. Recording star, who's grooved in the closing niche, does a half-dozen numbers for a rousing finale. Sy Oliver's crew, comprising four reed, three rhythm and five brass, gets the layout off to a snappy start with a noisy instrumental, "House Party," to pave the way for comic Timmie Rogers. Latter, who also emcees the bill, is an affable lad with a good sense of timing. Unfortunately, much of his material is somewhat mossy.

Introed as "back from entertaining in Korea," Conway & Parks register mildly with songs and patter, but pick up plaudits with some comedy hoofing on their exit.

Only ofay in the lineup, the Fontaines, score handily with their acro routines. Two men and a girl move through assorted feats with unerring finesse. Informal touch is lent when they prevail upon emcee Rogers to participate in one routine. It nets hefty guffaws.

Cole, backed by his customary piano (self-accomped), bongos, bass and guitar, runs through a batch of tunes and garners most palming on his current fave, "Unforgettable." His warbling, per usual, is showmanly and his entire time onstage bespeaks top musical proficiency in the pop idiom.

Sentimental touch is provided at the curtain-lowering when Cole joins Rogers to carol the latter's own dittty, "It's Crazy." A catchy tune in its own right, it added up to neat peg on which to hang the finale.　　　　Gilb.

44b.

Apollo, N. Y.

Ethel Waters, Dizzy Gillespie Orch (12) with Joe Carroll, Manny (Tables) Gates, Dusty Rhodes & Co. (3), Jean Dawn, Leon Collins; "The Sword of Monte Cristo" (20th).

Frank Schiffman, who's been getting into somewhat of a rut via the booking of latter-day topliners to his Negro vaude flagship, has one of his brightest marquee draws this sesh in a vet name, Ethel Waters. For her return to the Apollo after years in legit and films, Schiffman has surrounded her with a topflight bill which rounds out one of the house's best layouts in months.

A seasoned trouper, Miss Waters compensates for a weakening voice with warm projection and effective stage demeanor that win aud affection and response from outset. Excellently coiffed and garbed, Miss Waters takes hold from the moment she walks on and never lets go. It's an exciting sesh for those who remember her from her musicomedy and cabaret days, but it's also clicko with the younger set. She's solid in an 18-minuter that augurs vaude and nitery followups.

Songalog, which Miss Waters delivers without a break, opens with a trifle tagged "I Ain't Got No More." She builds steadily thereafter with a good special material tune, "Move It Where You Had It

Last Night" and "Frankie and Johnny." Gets biggest reception for the oldie faves in her repertoire, "Dinah," "Stormy Weather" and "Cabin in the Sky." She delivers tender praise, in windup, for the supporting turns with a special bow to comedian Dusty Rhodes and house comic, George Wiltshire, with whom she worked 25 years ago.

44c.

Dizzy Gillespie's orch, which supplies an outstanding backing during the singer's stint (with her own accompanist, Reginald Bean, at the 88), opens show with a fast and brassy workover of "Russian Lullaby." Band is reduced from 12 instrumentalists (including the maestro) to three rhythm, one reed and leader's trumpet for a zany musical set. With Joe Carroll on the vocals, combo whips out such items as "Bluest Blues," "Swing Low Sweet Cadillac," "Oo Shoody Dooby" and "School Days." It's familiar Gillespie stuff but it goes over big. Group also clicks with a straight instrumental rendition of "Alone Together" in which Gillespie's trumpet licks are standout.

Manny (Tables) Gates wins good reaction with his teeth-gripping stint. Builds from a single chair, which he lifts with his choppers, to hoisting six tables and a chair via the molars. Leon Collins packs a wallop in his terping route. Nifty turns, slides and spins keep aud's mitts warm. Jean Dawn, acrocontortionist, is reviewed under New Acts.

Standard house comedics are handled by Rhodes with a capable assist from Wiltshire and Edna Mae Harris.　　　　Gros.

show business. But in the beginning, in the very early days, we sometimes wondered who it was the unbelievable crowds came to see or hear. Among his musicians was a handsome man named Oscar Moore, his guitarist, and the female voices that jammed our switchboard were mostly directed to him. But as time passed, there was no doubt as to who was the real star of the act.

A more deserving gentleman never existed. Nat Cole was a pleasure to work with. He had always considered himself primarily a musician, a pianist cast in the mold of Earl Hines, in fact. No one was more surprised than he when his vocals caught on and zoomed him into the super big-time. Today of course, years after his lamentably early demise, they are still being heard.

The tradition of Nat "King" Cole is currently being continued in the person of his charming and talented daughter, Natalie. There is only one thing about her career and the attending publicity that puzzles me. I wonder why the publicity people never mention her mother, Maria Ellington, one of a trio of talented gals who at one time sang with Duke Ellington's Band (no relation).

Unfortunately, our 1952 show with the great Ethel Waters was not one of our more sucessful offerings, but its headliner, even at that late date was still a magnificent performer. The name, Ethel Waters, probably conjures up images of a ponderous woman who played serious dramatic roles in Hollywood and on Broadway. But Ethel had started as a singer, and in the history of jazz she was a performer of considerable stature. In this engagement both she and the theater suffered the fate that frequently comes when aging artists are on the bill and nostalgia the foremost appeal. It rarely works, and the results of the attempt often bring bitterness in their wake. Ethel Waters didn't need any help in feeling bitter; in her last years, before she died in 1977, she felt that the world had unjustly abandoned her.

My father was an ardent admirer of Ethel. I'm sure that that fact took precedence over his better judgment in presenting this show. The difficulty of finding headline talent for forty or more shows a year probably also had something to do with it. Here are his comments on the show: "Her first appearance here in years. Miss Waters had a fine, well-coordinated repertoire. Depsite her weight, she looked well. She was heartily applauded. She is indeed one of the greatest performers on the American stage. But she has been typed only with dramas and pictures in the last few years and had no appeal to the younger element."

When he was an infant, they changed his diapers in the dressing room. When he was a young kid he ran around backstage, occasionally being brought out to face the audience. And when he grew up, Sammy Davis, Jr., "born in a trunk," became one of the superstars of modern time. In a 1958 engagement at the Apollo, Sammy made one of his last appearances as part of the Will Mastin Trio. It included his father, Sammy Davis, Sr., and his uncle, Will Mastin, about whom Sammy said, "He taught me everything I know about show business." Uncle Will was one of the last of a vanishing breed, a remnant of the early days of the traveling minstrel shows and the TOBA. The act began with

45a.

45b.

45c.

45d.

the three men doing an opening song-and-dance routine cut out of the tradition of the thirties. Even though Sammy, Sr. and Uncle Will were no longer spring chickens, they could still dance, but it was Sammy with his energy, youth, and talent who carried the act. As a dancer he was among the greatest; as a mimic only George Kirby could touch him; as a singer, he was already one of the top recording artists in show business. He was always a showman to his fingertips; and he never let the audience down. I recall one engagement in which to get near him was almost to feel scorched. You could feel his fever radiate out into the room. But he never missed a note, let alone a show.

There was another occasion when he not only missed a show, he missed two days of shows—and he wasn't even sick. It started with a telephone call to Dad from Nat Kalcheim, at that time one of the top bananas at the William Morris Agency, Sammy's booking agents. "Sammy has noticed," Nat said, "that his upcoming engagement at the Apollo comes at the time of the Jewish High Holy Days, and since he is Jewish, he wants you to know that he will not perform on those days. He wants me to tell you that if you want to cancel the engagement, he is willing to let you do so."

Dad's response was a sputter and then a gasp, for the High Holy Days in New York City are like a full-fledged holiday. Since so many businesses in New York are owned by Jews and since the High Holy Days are observed even by the only casually observant, many businesses simply close until the holiday is over. During this time off, the theater business usually prospers. It presented us with a neat problem: give up Sammy Davis, Jr., at so late a date and you give up the biggest attraction in show business without knowing when you'll ever get him back again. Keep the engagement, and you miss two of the best days in the entire engagement.

Dad tried everything. He spoke again with Kalcheim; he even called Sammy at home, trying to convince him to play on at least part of the holiday. No deal. And so, on the mornings of the High Holy Days, the Apollo Theatre that year remained shut, a large sign out front telling prospective patrons that the star wouldn't appear because of the religious holiday. Moreover, at the Free Synagogue of Westchester, the Temple's president, Mr. Frank Schiffman, escorted into the temple an honored guest, Mr. Sammy Davis, Jr.

In 1949, we played one of the most exciting groups to appear at the Apollo in years. The Ravens were a male vocal quartet, but one with a difference. Instead of the usual tenor as lead singer, this one featured Jimmy Ricks, a bass. When Jimmy reached down into his swinging lower register for a deep note, the audience went wild. On the same bill was Dinah Washington, who had been popular for a number of years. With her hit record, "It's Too Soon to Know," she began to come into her own as a full-fledged star. That number was used in the show's finale, and it was performed by Dinah and the Ravens to ecstatic applause by our audiences. Ricky looked down on short, plump Dinah with what appeared to be great affection; she gazed up at him and fluttered her eyelids. It must have seemed idyllic and loving to the audience. But had anyone come backstage that week, he would have seen another scene entirely. Throughout the years I was at the theater, I never saw a rivalry quite so bitter and intense as theirs.

What was the focus of their rivalry? Why who got No. #6, the largest of the dressing rooms, of course. Now what would you do when you assigned rooms to these two stars? Give it to the lady, of course. But you wouldn't have reckoned with the temperament and the sensitivities of James Ricks. The matter was eventually resolved with the promise that on the next engagement they each would occupy No. 6, meaning that never again would we play Dinah Washington and the Ravens on the same bill. It was either separate them or build two new dressing rooms and number each one 6.

One could examine the entire history of Harlem and never find a more beloved figure than the "Brown Bomber," Joe Louis. Even when he was a fading champion, people swarmed around him like bees near the hive, as he walked up the street. They didn't need to talk to him or even touch him; being within hailing distance of the great one was enough for almost anyone. And when Joe finally did hang up his gloves, we brought him in to do several shows, the first of which opened April 10, 1953. The character leaning against Joe in Illustration 45c is Leonard Reed. Comic, performer, producer (he produced one of the Cotton Club shows when the club was downtown on Broadway), Leonard remained to the end one of Joe's closest friends. He wrote, staged, and worked out the details of this act with Joe, and everything in it was designed to present Joe as entertainingly as possible. As for the audience, they ate it up. It was only a short time later that we brought the Joe Louis show back for a repeat, one of those cases where the expression "brought back by popular demand" was literally true.

In 1953 we presented Sugar Ray Robinson, in his day the only man in the ring who could comapre in stature with Joe. As different as were their styles in the ring were their styles on the stage. Sugar Ray, light on his feet, as suave and smooth onstage as he'd been quick in the ring, was an accomplished dancer, and where we relied on Leonard Reed's clever comic antics to enhance Joe's appearance, Sugar Ray did his act virtually alone. I would sum up the difference in audience reactions to this boxing pair like this: Sugar Ray was respected for his undeniable talents in and out of the ring; Joe Louis was, quite simply, loved! In Sugar Ray's show was little Thelma Carpenter, a singer of considerable talent, an Amateur Contest winner some years before, a young lady who should have reached superstardom and had to be content with being merely a star! Early in her career, she was befriended by and appeared with Eddie Cantor.

In November 1949, Harry Belafonte made his last regular appearance at the Apollo while he was relatively unknown; he was the featured vocalist with Andy Kirk's band. In one of those lightning-in-a-bottle affairs that occasionally electrify show business, Harry was an international star a year or two later. But if 1949 was the last time Harry Belafonte worked at the Apollo, it wasn't the last time he had a part in our operations. A little-known fact about him is the interest he has shown in new talent, and the help he has offered them. Through scholarships, personal intercession, money and interest, he has been instrumental in bringing some great talent to the American stage.

For instance, Miriam Makeba first came to the United States largely through the help and encouragement he offered her. This particular show (see 46b) was presented in 1967, but by that time Miriam Makeba was an established star, one who had delighted our audiences with her native African songs and her warm personality.

If anything is obvious, it is that the only thing you can expect in the theater is the unexpected. The star of today is often forgotten tomorrow; today's unknown sometimes reaches the ultimate in popularity. Such is certainly the case with one of the participants in Miriam's show. For today, some seventeen years later, Richard Pryor is better known than everyone else in this particular presentation; indeed, he is the most popular and highly paid black star in the world. With good reason, for there seems to be no limit to his versatility and talent.

A few years later, Belafonte was instrumental in bringing another African singer to us. Had she been here first, Letta M'Bulu could easily have been the Miriam Makeba of her day. But Miriam and Letta weren't the last of Harry Belafonte's gifts to the Apollo and the United States. Another was a super-musician, trumpeter, and composer whose full name is Hugh Ramapolo wa xa Masakela, known more popularly among jazz lovers as Hugh Masakela.

Johnny Mathis appeared at the Apollo about fifteen years ago as a nervous up-and-coming record star who earned a mere 350 dollars for his first week's engagement and who cancelled out with laryngitis after the first show. Two months later, Johnny Mathis reappeared at a salary of 1500 dollars, a big jump so early in his career but mere petty cash today. His career has been one of the most notable in show business, for more than anyone I can think of, Johnny Mathis' appeal cuts across the generation gap that has separated adults and their children. Usually a singer is popular with younger *or* older people, and as the young ones grow up, their kids do not go along with ancient choices. Johnny Mathis is the exception to the rules of history, for he is immensely popular with today's kids and the adults—after fifteen years of stardom!

Fats Domino is all rock and roll. But the fans of that medium are as numerous as the grains of sand on a beach, at least to judge by the box office appeal of Fats. He was an established star in 1958 when we featured him during a glorious Easter week. As he has pointed out, rock and roll was merely another name for rhythm-and-blues, a musical form that had been around for a long time. By the middle fifties, the "new" rock-show format was in vogue. Five vocal groups plus three more singing combinations joined Fats and the Reuben Phillips Band in presenting a show that rattled the old rafters from start to finish.

They were true superstars during the fifties, and so The Platters headlined an Apollo show that opened September 21, 1956. "The Great Pretender" and

46a. Harry Belafonte

46b.

46c. Johnny Mathis

"My Prayer" were heard not only up and down 125th Street; but they were heard on every main street in the entire forty-eight states plus a lot of the rest of the world. As is often the way, some names in the supporting cast offer more than casual interest: Bill Bailey, Pearl's brother, was one of the top tapsters in show business; Earl Warren, an alto saxophonist of jazz repute, had long been one of Basie's key sidemen, about whom Buddy Tate tells the following story:

> The band was traveling through the South in the depressing days when blacks were barely even second-class citizens. But Earl has no single feature that is characteristic of blacks. His skin is fair, his features acquiline. And so, in the interests of a decent meal, Earl snuck away from the rest of the musicians and headed for a restaurant. There he was, sitting at the counter and eating. I wanted some of that good food, so, along with another member of the band, I walked in and sat down at the counter. Earl turned his head to one side, pretending that he'd never seen us before in his life. The waitress turned around and said, "I'm sorry, we don't serve Negroes here." She used the word *Negroes*, I recall. Guess she was trying to be nice about it. Well, we stared at her and then I pointed at Earl and said, "Well, you're serving him." Earl looked at us and we'd have both been dead if looks could kill. Then he paid the bill and walked out.

Ray Charles headlined an Apollo show in 1969. It was neither the first nor the last time his name stretched across the marquee in sixteen-inch letters, for among the supernovae in Apollo history, the name Ray Charles rests secure. There have been few talents on our stage that could measure up to his. On the index card that encapsulates the considerable span of Ray Charles' Apollo appearances is scrawled, "Genius! genius! genius!" It was the enthusiastic comment made by Dad or my brother Bobby or Honi Coles—or perhaps all three. It doesn't overstate anything. For whether his offering was purely instrumental or one of his stirring blues numbers; whether it was drawn from his country and western repertoire or from the infinitely clever songs he composed, the appeal of Ray Charles is always universal.

I can never hear a number like his "Georgia on My Mind" without recalling an incident Dad was fond of recounting. The daughter of a close friend of his had come with a small group to hear Ray Charles. They were deposited in the "A" box right behind the door leading to the stage. During the show Dad went backstage on some errand; he came back during Ray's act and noticed the young lady in tears. Thinking that perhaps something upsetting had occurred, he rushed to her side and asked, "What's wrong, dear?" She shook her tear-stained head and murmured, "I can't listen to him sing the blues without crying. He just moves me that way." The eternal theme of the blues is heard in Ray's trenchant lyric, "If I didn't have any bad luck, I wouldn't have any luck at all."

There's not the slightest doubt about it; the first black superstar was Bill "Bojangles" Robinson. At Harlem's white Cotton Club or the Apollo, at Broadway's fabled Palace Theatre, or on Hollywood's silver screen, Bill's infectious smile and rhythmic dancing were instantly recognized. There were other dancers

ONE "NEVER-TO-BE FORGOTTEN" WEEK BEGINNING FRIDAY, JULY 4th

THE
RAY CHARLES
SHOW - '69
★
With A Cast Of 35
Including
THE RAELETS
BILLY WALLACE
THE
LON FONTAINE DANCERS

47a. Ray Charles

Dr. Jive, Ray Charles Head Apollo Revue

Rock 'n roll exponent Tommy "Dr. Jive" Smalls brings another stellar show into the Apollo Friday for a one week stand.

It headlines Ray "Yes Indeed" Charles, the Drifters "Down on My Knees," the Cadillacs "Speedo," the Crowns and the Cookies. Singles include songstress Ann Cole, Tiny Topsy, Mary Ann Fisher, and Solomon Burke.

Dr. Jive is holder of one of the record week's Apollo attendance mark.

For years, Ray Charles has been considered without equal when it comes to singing the blues. Show folk say his singing comes from the heart and that his sincerity cannot be questioned. He had his own private cult of fans for years before the miracle fo records gave him to the nation.

RAY CHARLES

47b.

who could do things with their feet that Bill couldn't or perhaps didn't do, but you would have to look far and wide to find another showman who was his equal. Said Honi Coles, "There were more versatile dancers than Bill, but no one had better dancing precision than he." My father always claimed that the only other entertainer who could match him as Al Jolson. As for me, I would have added Danny Kaye and Sammy Davis, Jr., to that list.

Certainly there were other black stars with great talent and immense popularity in the twenties and thirties: Bert Williams, "Bricktop," Florence Mills, Cab Calloway, Louis Armstrong, and Duke Ellington, for instance, but none of them ever quite reached the apex of their popularity with whites and blacks at the same time. When Louis was "hot" in Harlem, he was known only to a small coterie of jazz buffs whose skins were white. Duke gained enormous prestige among whites, but although he was popular among his black confreres, he never was a gate-crusher in Harlem after the very early days. Indeed, it sometimes seems that when black artists saw their popularity in the white world rise, it fell in the black.

If you look back at history with a philosophic eye, it seems that certain adjustments had to be made by white society in order to accept black entertainers' offerings. Indeed, the history of black entertainers and their acceptance by our total society parallels almost exactly the advances they made in other areas of American life, social, economic, and political. Trying to discover whether the acceptance of entertainers came *before* or *after* their acceptance elsewhere is a bit like trying to solve the riddle of the chicken and the egg. But there seems little doubt that black entertainers had a material effect in gaining black acceptance in areas far beyond the entertainment business.

Not only did white society have to prepare itself to accept blacks in general, they had to train their ears to accept the new sounds that emanated from them musically, for jazz, gospel, and the blues were not within the musical framework white society knew. White America first started to hear black jazzmen, for example, when Benny Goodman, at the urging of his brother-in-law, John Hammond, brought pianist Teddy Wilson and vibraphonist Lionel Hampton into the Goodman Band. Although Lionel and Teddy both became household names among jazz buffs and later among swing lovers, they were part of the Goodman organization and not individual stars who would attract large audiences on their own. The same was true of another Goodman alumnus, Charlie Christian. But as they played before the gyrating, swaying kids who danced in the aisles in the Paramount Theatre or congregated before the bandstands at the Larchmont Casino or the Meadowbrook, American ears were being trained to hear a new sound.

In the last analysis, however, it was the impact of World War II, which for all time changed the American scene and permitted the increasing introduction of black artists. For during the war both ends of the racial equation were exposed to a shocking new world. White Americans, some for the first time, discovered that be his skin black, tan, or brown, the color of the man's blood was red, the same as his own. Black Americans discovered that they weren't the only victims of discrimination. They also learned that there were even some white men with good will toward them. Like President Franklin D. Roosevelt.

In all of American history there was no more beloved white figure in the black world than that of F.D.R., including President Lincoln. You may recall the picture of a weeping black man standing on a street corner as Roosevelt's funeral cortege passed by. It was a scene repeated a thousand times wherever black men congregated. For in black eyes, F.D.R. became the voice, perhaps the conscience of white America speaking to him. He said that in response to black effort and sacrifice in the war, America was, at long last, offering the promise of equality. I do not mean to be simplistic. No man, white or black, expected the gates of brotherly love to suddenly swing open when the war ended. What was possible to believe was that a promise was being made *and* that its fulfillment could be demanded. It was, at any rate, a beginning, a hope, a prayer. There are those, of course, who deny that the promise has been kept or even that a start has been made toward keeping it. In recognition that full equality has not yet arrived, that black Americans have ample and frequent reasons to be frustrated, it does, however, seem obvious that there have been accomplishments.

When the war ended, the first new star in an entertainment revolution arrived in the person of handsome, talented Billy Eckstine. Although not a new performer, "Mr. B" became the first true postwar superstar. He was, in truth, a one-man revolution in more senses than one. Musically, for example, he is an important figure in the history of jazz. I have already spoken of some of his contributions as a band leader, his espousal of bop, his encouragement of the new young musicians on the way up. Vocally, nothing was ever quite the same after his "Caravan," "I Apologize," and other hit records smashed the sound barriers. He ended his songs on notes which no one expected, hanging as they did in musical midair, up a half tone here, down a whole tone there. And the harmonies and changes of key he injected in unexpected places made every other singer sit up and take notice. For example, few Sarah Vaughan numbers, even today, are minus the musical debt she owes her friend Billy Eckstine.

But if musical innovativeness was important in Billy's career, he wittingly or unwittingly added a revolutionary something else that left its mark on entertainment history for all time. Billy Eckstine became the first black entertainer whose immense sex appeal got across to white America. It came not only because of his extreme good looks, but because it was really a part of his musicality, showmanship, and personality. The screaming, bouncing bobby-soxers, *white and black,* testified to the fact that the message was getting across. And if you doubted that, a quick visit to see the bedlam at every stagedoor when Billy was starring would have convinced you. The scene, of course, would be repeated time and again for Frank Sinatra, Vic Damone, and scores of other singers, but they were there for the first time on behalf of a singer who was black! The acceptance of Billy Eckstine, sex appeal and all, by whites is, to me, an important symbol, for it puts him on the same human scale as other male

48a. Billy Eckstine

Apollo, N. Y.

Billy Eckstine, Dizzy Gillespie and (13), 3 Berry Bros., China Doll & Calypso Boys, "Pigmeat" Markham & Co. (3); "50 Years Before Your Eyes' (WB).

The Apollo hits a new high in budgetary outlay on this stanza with perhaps the sockiest layout the Harlem vauder has ever projected. After a seasonal shutdown and recent reopening it looks like the management is shooting the works on top talent to lure back the vacationing audiences.

From a booker's viewpoint, it would seem that Billy Eckstine would be sufficient to lure 'em in. However, despite the pull of the M-G-M recording star, management tosses in Dizzy Gillespie's solid bop combo and the Three Berry Bros. for a triple threat lure —and it's paying off at the wickets.

Eckstine, long a fave at this house through previous appearances, has come a long way since his last appearance there, three years ago. Consequently, he is given a reception that rocks the house. With slick delivery and sock arrangements he baritones his way to top results and is held on for over 25 minutes of the hour-long bill. It's strategic that he's spotted in closing slot, since nothing could have followed him.

Gillespie's crack combo, comprising three rhythm, four reeds and six brass, is another solid factor. Aside from backing the other acts, with exception of Eckstine, group gives out on its own with a solid bop session, with the maestro alternating between zany stuff and hot trumpeting. This, too, rates high applause. Three Berry Bros. are sock as usual with their slick hoofery and comedics, with cane dance the topper.

Rounding out the bill are the China Doll and Calypso Boys, also playing a repeat here, in a neat song and dance session, and "Pigmeat" Markham & Co. house nics, in a comedy bit that goes neatly. *Edba.*

48b.

singers, some with great sex appeal, some with little, as a human being rather than a racial symbol, accepted (or rejected) on the same terms as any other artist.

Although he was far from handsome in the stereotyped sense of the word, there is no denying that Nat "King" Cole also projected an image laden with sex appeal. He was, after all, a singer of romantic ballads, "Nature Boy," "Unforgettable," "Darling, Je Vous Aime Beaucoup," "Sweet Lorraine."

Then there is the case of Lena Horne. You can hardly mention the term *sex appeal* and leave Lena Horne out, for she is truly one of the most beautiful women of our time. And yet white America's attitude toward beautiful black women has always been discriminatory. They have been regarded as "fair game" or sex *objects*, and that fact has been deeply and correctly resented by generations of blacks, male and female. Lena played the Apollo and other black spots early in her career, and played mostly white-oriented spots later on, shunning the black ones. It is a shame, too, for there are few more dedicated and sincere workers on behalf of racial justice and equality than she. Our own feeling was that she was afraid of being rejected by her own people, probably because she was married to Lenny Hayton, a white man. It is a real tragedy, for in a deep sense, Lena was probably bringing rejection on herself. We always believed that she would have received joyful and sincere accolades from black audiences had she appeared before them. And no one would have deserved them any more than she.

There appears to be a strange anomaly present when one considers the fate of black performers in relation to their own people. Time after time we have seen it: a black artist makes it big before white audiences, his records catch on, the number of white engagements increases, and suddenly he has lost his appeal to blacks. In black entertainment circles, such artists become known as "white entertainers," meaning that that is where their appeal lies. Do black audiences spurn them because they feel betrayed, because the black artist is now identified with "whitey"? In all honesty, I think the answer is probably "yes." I say probably, because I have some reservations. We have also seen it happen that *some* of these performers either retain their popularity among blacks or return to popularity later on. Sammy Davis, Jr., is probably about as popular with black audiences today as he ever was. Stevie wonder is, without question, an international superstar. The same can be said for Aretha Franklin, Marvin Gaye, Roberta Flack, and others.

On the other hand, the likelihood is that if Cab Calloway headlined an Apollo show today, his drawing power would be limited. At least a part of the answer seems to rest with the artists themselves. If they continue to be dynamic in their work, if their musical offerings are fresh and innovative, they are likely to maintain their appeal. The black audience, it has been noted time and time again by both artists and critics, is about the most sophisticated, responsive, and critical audience one can find. Or, as one superstar once remarked to me, "You can't kid *that* audience, man! They know what they want and what they like."

Part of the black rejection of black artists is a quirk of human nature. In racial terms it is as though black audiences are saying they want an exclusive on their own stars! The strangest anomaly is to be found in today's *total scene*. Black artists have never been more popular, more in demand than they are today. At the same time, there has never been more overt and obvious racial tension and animosity than there is at this very moment. How can we explain this apparent contradiction? The popularity is the easiest part of the conundrum to understand. Black artists are popular quite simply because they are so good! They are popular because they bring an exciting and dynamic art to the live theater. The overt interracial hostility exists because the underlying resentments have been permitted to become externalized. At long last, black people feel strong enough and protected enough to give vent to the frustrations that have been abuilding for two hundred years. Some whites, now frustrated at their loss of power, react in anger. In the truest sense, nothing could be healthier than the mutual ability to experess the deep resentments the two races feel toward each other.

I have heard white and black musicians alike express resentments toward each other. "That white honkey," said one black man about a celebrated white saxophonist. "Who needs all that hate?" said a white bass player in talking about an eminent black one. And yet, in most cases, the white and the black musician would admit their admiration for the other's musicianship. Resolving the simultaneous admiration and anger is a problem that transcends logic. For its root causes are emotional and the resolutions must come in the same genre. I cannot suggest the solution, only the direction from which it must come. It is a tragic waste that will only be solved with the passage of time and the appearance of several new generations that can view each other from a new base.

And after that long aside, I shall return to the summer of 1969 and a couple of shows that indicate the taste of Apollo audiences at the time. They included The Delfonics, The Intruders, and Sly and the Family Stone. We were hard into the rock business, hard in the midst of the "group" popularity. Many of the headliners are still at or near the top of the entertainment heap. Some of the artists were, to put it mildly, troublesome. On the other hand, my brother Bobby always has a single comment for Gladys Knight, who along with her Pips and The Marvelettes, headlined a 1967 show: "She's a sweetheart."

Rock and roll, rhythm and blues, funky shows, sexy shows—they could all come and go, but the world of jazz was never forgotten at the Apollo. There were times when its followers dwindled in numbers, especially in favor of some current passion, but they were always there, and a 1961 show proved it. Carmen McRae wasn't new at the Apollo; she had appeared on and off since she was first brought to us by Oscar Cohen (now president of the late Joe Glaser's company, Associated Booking Corporation). But at the time of the Apollo appearance, her career had been rescued from oblivion by a combination of new records, higher evaluation, and a sudden burgeoning popularity.

In the world of jazz, both Carmen and Joe Williams are important figures.

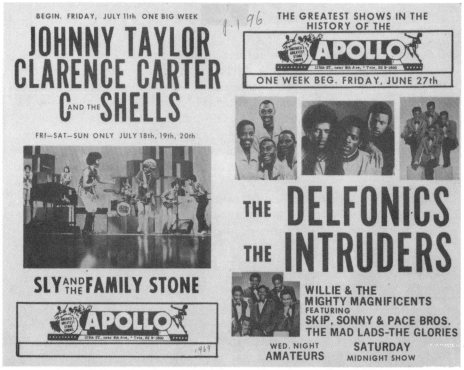

BEGIN. FRIDAY, JULY 11th ONE BIG WEEK

JOHNNY TAYLOR
CLARENCE CARTER
C AND THE SHELLS

FRI—SAT—SUN ONLY JULY 18th, 19th, 20th

SLY AND THE FAMILY STONE

APOLLO
America's Greatest Stage Shows
125th ST, near 8th Ave. • Tele. RI 9-1800

1969

THE GREATEST SHOWS IN THE
HISTORY OF THE

APOLLO
America's Greatest Stage Shows
125th ST, near 8th Ave. • Tele. RI 9-1800

ONE WEEK BEG. FRIDAY, JUNE 27th

THE DELFONICS
THE INTRUDERS

WILLIE & THE
MIGHTY MAGNIFICENTS
FEATURING
SKIP, SONNY & PACE BROS.
THE MAD LADS-THE GLORIES

WED. NIGHT
AMATEURS

SATURDAY
MIDNIGHT SHOW

49a.

Beg. Fri.
OCT. 27

★ WORLD-FAMOUS ★
APOLLO
America's Greatest Stage Shows
125th St. near 8th Ave. • Tel. RI 9-1800

ROCKY G Presents

THE MARVELETTES
GLADYS THE
KNIGHT & PIPS

LAURA LEE — THE WEBS

THE MILLIONAIRES

FANTASTIC JOHNNY C

FRANKIE CROCKER

49b.

There are those who feel that imaginative Joe Williams is the best male jazz singer around today; I will not quarrel with them. I have always had an especially warm feeling for Joe Williams since the night when, at a testimonial dinner to my father he murmured to me, "I always loved the Apollo. They let you do your thing. They don't bug you." As for Carmen, she is more than a female singer; she is one of jazzdom's greats. In that same show, worthy of special note were Harry "Sweets" Edison, one of the great trumpeters of the Roy Eldridge school, and Eddie "Lockjaw" Davis, a driving tenor saxman.

Sam Cooke, in Illustration 50a, recorded "You Send Me," which sent him into a worldwide orbit that he didn't come down from until his tragic, early death. Since I discuss gospel singers in Chapter 9, "Soul Food," I will have more to say there about Aretha Franklin, Della Reese, and Marvin Gaye. Along with Sam Cooke, there are no singers on the present scene whose debt to gospel music is deeper than theirs. Suffice it to note that none of them would scarcely be able to sing a bar were their gospel background expunged.

Smokey Robinson is a superstar in the firmament of show business. But he is a great deal more than that because of the influence he has had on the course of music in the last fifteen years or so. During that period there arose a group of artists—Diana Ross and the Supremes, Gladys Knight and the Pips, The Temptations, Stevie Wonder, and Martha Reeves and the Vandellas, for example—all of whom had a special sound. They all recorded for the Motown Record Company and the sound that was so characteristic was probably inspired by Smokey Robinson more than of anyone else. That the "Motown Sound" changed the whole direction of our popular music in the sixties is historically evident; that Smokey Robinson's name must be written large should be acknowledged. Incidentally, it must be pointed out that another revolution came out of Motown. With Diana Ross and the Supremes, the first all-girl vocal group hit the big-time. They were the leaders in an exciting parade which followed them.

Otis Redding deserves a whole chapter, for he stood supreme for a time in the world of entertainment excitement. His career was shortened by a tragic plane crash.

On December 4, 1960, the *Jewel Box Revue* opened at the Apollo. There are those who would object to a show made up of men impersonating women. Indeed, there were people in Harlem who objected—strongly enough so that we eventually cancelled what had become an annual engagement. The *Jewel Box Revue*, however, was *not* a raunchy show that glorified the male homosexual. On the contrary, it was a dignified, artistic, and altogether "proper" show to which you could have taken your grandchild or mother without shame or embarassment. We were always astounded at the audience responses we got when the *Jewel Box Revue* was playing. It was the first show in the Apollo's history which had a three-week engagement, and year after year, each week was a commercial as well as an artistic success.

In 1968 two of the most beautiful, talented, and charming headliners we ever played came to town to tear it up. Of Nancy Wilson, Honi Coles once

50a. Sam Cooke

50b.

51a. Della Reese

51b. Otis Redding

wrote, "What can you say about an angel with Soul?" For in the Apollo's entire history it would be hard to find an artist who inspired the kind of adoring respect that Nancy Wilson did—unless you were to turn to another beauteous lady named Dionne Warwick. Along with Nancy, the late alto saxophonist, jazz intellectual, and musical genius Cannonball Adderly appeared, as well as Flip Wilson in one of his last Apollo appearances. With Dionne and her talented sister, Dee Dee Warwick, another modern-day show-biz miracle, Redd Foxx, appeared.

In 1969, when his name was emblazoned across the Apollo's marquee, Lou Rawls was a star. Today, he is one of the superstars of show business. In this show, by the way, was the African singer, Letta M'Bulu, and a master musician, Mongo Santamaria.

They were lively, they were talented. They could swing, they could sing. Back in the late sixties and the early seventies, there were few headliners who created more excitement than did the Jackson Five. For a time, they vied with another swinging family act called the Five Stairsteps, but going down the stretch it was the Jackson Five by a few noses. Today, that adorable kid now grown, Michael Jackson is the greatest and most versatile superstar of all. He swept the Grammy Awards in 1984 with eight trophies. His producer is the enduring and talented Quincy Jones.

When I first started working on this chapter, I made a list of artists whose names I thought belonged in it. The list, like Topsy, just kept growing and growing. I kept adding names to it, kept trying to subtract them just to make the list a bit shorter. There were some, I thought, who either were in other chapters or who belonged there. For instance, how can you write about super-stars and leave out Ella Fitzgerald, Sarah Vaughan, the Mills Brothers or The Ink Spots? They are all treated at length elsewhere in this book. And how can one write a chapter and leave out the name B. B. King? His name will appear in another chapter along with other singers of blues. Or, for that matter, how could I leave out a name like Brook Benton? Or for historical purposes, our own Ruth Brown? How about Peaches and Herb, Joe Tex, The Spinners, Eartha Kitt or Ike and Tina Turner? You can't, so here they are. There are probably more, and without exception, they all walked out onto the Apollo's stage at one time or another.

52a.

52c.

52b.

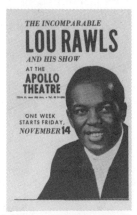

52d.

52e. The Jackson Five

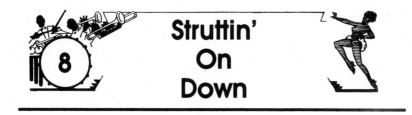

Struttin'
On
Down

"Charleston"

Of the many and varied forms entertainment has taken, none can match the dance for sheer exuberant joy. In its evolution from highly stylized ballet and various folk and ethnic dances onto today's Broadway stage, no other dance form has the elements of spontaneity contained in the dancing that evolved around jazz.

The names of the older jazz dances seem exotic today: the Charleston, Black Bottom, Cake Walk, Suzie Que, Truckin', Peckin', the Lindy Hop. The names of more recent entries are more unique than romantic: the Frug, Monkey, Jerk, Twist, Reggae, and Disco. In the history of popular dance one can cull out scores of dance routines, all linked together in "parlays"—leaning, borrowing, and influencing each other as their fans pranced them into varying degrees of popularity, ranging from mild public interest to national "crazes." The Camel Walk, the Bugaloo, Bunny Hop, Heebie Jeebies, Eagle Hop, Scronch, Skate, Shuffle, Snake Hips, and Waddle—the names are often humorous, sometimes even bizarre, especially if you consider the Break-A-Leg, Buzzard Glide, Ditty Bop Walk, Shoot the Pistol, or Shorty George.

Perhaps this is the place to explain which dance it is that this chapter will deal with. We emphatically are not talking about ballet or even what has become known as "modern dance." Nor are we talking about the dances associated with religious rites, voodoo or other exotica. No, we are talking about what Jean and Marshall Stearns called jazz dance in their marvelous book by that title. It is the dance whose basis is the swinging jazz music that characterizes the period I have called the Heyday Years. Without denigrating the more classical or popular dances of our day, I suggest that the jazz dance exemplifies several generations in their most vigorous expression of humor, joy, individual-

---

Of the many dances which ranged in popularity from national crazes to passing fads, none became more famous than the Charleston. Like the Black Bottom, it had a special song with which it was identified. The song was written by one of the towering figures in the world of jazz, James "Pete" Johnson, Fats Waller's teacher and a master of the stride piano.

161

ity, and freedom.

There have been many major white contributors to the history of jazz dancing, of course. Fred Astaire, Gene Kelly, Ray Bolger, and James Barton are prime examples. The movies would never have been the same without the first two; the Broadway stage without Bolger would have been like eggs without salt. As for Barton, although he may be remembered by many readers as the star of Broadway's long-lived play, *Tobacco Road*, his more enduring contributions to the theater probably lie in the innovative dances he left behind him. There have been other white contributors to the dance, especially as they relate to the Broadway stage, but as with jazz itself, each major white dancer in the jazz-oriented school can be matched by at least a dozen black ones. The jazz dance like jazz itself, has been held in relatively low esteem by our society until recently, despite its being more spontaneous and freer than any other style.

The scarcity of books on the jazz dance is astonishing, especially when one considers how widespread has been its popularity. Its aficionados are, I'm certain, more numerous than those who choose ballet. The followers of reggae, and disco dancing are obvious testimony to the continuing and considerable popularity of jazz dance and its descendants. The black dancers not "put down" by white society are Katherine Dunham, Pearl Primus, Bill Robinson, and Geoffrey Holder. Of these, Bojangles Robinson was as much an entertainer as a dancer, and the other three found more acceptance because their dancing was thrust into the broad category labeled "cultural."

These are few serious references in the brief literature on the dance to John Bubbles and Avon Long, despite the fact that they both portrayed Sportin' Life in the premiere of George Gershwin's *Porgy and Bess*. Nor do you find reference to Babe Lawrence and Bunny Briggs, both of whom danced in the extraordinarily well-received sacred-music concerts of Duke Ellington. And except for devotees of the Heyday Years, who knows about the marvelous efforts of such dancers as Eddie Rector, Derby Wilson, Bill Bailey, or Mae Barnes? Honi Coles must have almost given up hope of recognition before he was "discovered" by Broadway in the eighties.

Ask the average middle-aged American who the greatest tap-dancer was, and I'll wager he'll answer Bill "Bojangles" Robinson. About Bill, Honi Coles said, "He was perhaps the most precise of the tap-dancers, but certainly there were better dancers around than Bill." Even the famous up-and-down-the-stairs dance he did was not only relatively simple, but it wasn't original with him. It was "borrowed" from King "Rastus" Brown, who had, of course, borrowed it from someone else. Its origin is lost to history. No, Bill was an excellent dancer, but his real claim to fame lies in his overall skill as an entertainer. Like many of the early dancers, he began his career as a "pic"; he began at the age of sixteen when, at a salary of fifty cents per night, he danced in a company headed by Mayme Remington. In her company were two other dancers of considerable accomplishment: Eddie Rector and Dewey Weinglass.

Pic, short for *pickaninny*, is a highly offensive term to most black people.

Its derivation, according to Marshall and Jean Stearns, probably comes from the Portuguese word *pegueno,* meaning "little one." These young and talented black dancers were usually mere kids who were added to mostly white acts to liven things up with their "cuteness" and their extraordinary, dextrous dancing. They were never given a "billing," of course; they were merely adjuncts to the stars' act, even though they frequently could dance rings around their white elders!

Of all the dances in the broad category labeled jazz dance, none has endured longer or become better know that the tap dance. In the eighties the tap dance has been resurrected and is enjoying a renaissance in the United States. As with many jazz forms, the tap dance's origins are largely African. Tap probably did not originate with the Irish jig, as some claim but in the sliding, dragging, shuffling steps that sprang from the African dancer's barefooted crouch, the barefoot stance requiring him to stay close to the ground. The tap was the key ingredient added when civilization caught up with the dancer and forced him to wear shoes. Never mind that discomfort; the tap enabled him to add the one embellishment needed to move the dance from the veldt to the stage: the emphatic *sound* of rhythm. Sometimes syncopated, sometimes eccentric, always rhythmic, the tapping was dramatic. "Dancers are percussionists," says Honi Coles. Tapsters, wittingly or unwittingly, were melding the rhythms and movements of their forebears into the dextrous dances we still see today.

Back in the early minstrel days, a black dancer named William Henry Lane, probably one of the all-time great dancers, did a dance called the Juba, in which rhythmic accompaniment was supplied by other dancers clapping their hands. Clapping was done in place of drumming since drumming was outlawed by white masters out of fear that it might be used either to send signals or stir passions. That clapping survived in the dance routines of such acts as the Step Brothers, for it had the double effect of adding an exciting sound to their routines and avoiding the hiring of an extra man, a drummer.

The Juba also played a significant role in another dance with an African background, one of the earliest dances to fall into the category of a national craze. One of that dance's practitioners was billed as the "Queen of Charleston," for the Charleston was the name of the dance. The queen was a gal named Ginger Rogers. Another Charleston dancer who did the dance in a film called *Our Dancing Daughters* was Joan Crawford.

In the road-show company of *Shuffle Along* the Charleston was performed by a lady who is one of the most enduring performers on the stage. Today she is a singer of world-weary sophisticated songs and a mime of class and talent. But back in the twenties Mae Barnes was a dancer, one who ranks with the greatest of all female dancers. Another dancer in that same road company was pantomimist Johnny Hudgins. The Charleston itself was superseded in the twenties by the Black Bottom, but it returned to popularity many times in the ensuing years. With due respect for Ginger Rogers and the late Joan Crawford, the dances which their agents claimed for them as originators, had long been performed by black dancers.

Then there was the Cake Walk. It was introduced on the Broadway stage by Bert Williams and George Walker in a show called *In Dahomey* in 1902. But the Cake Walk had very early origins. Its African roots go back to the ring shout, in which a dancing group formed a counterclockwise moving circle around the principal dancers, but the Cake Walk itself was really a sly take-off on the stuffy manners of white Americans. The main ingredient of the Cake Walk was the "strut," in which the dancer danced a preening, puffed-up poulter-pigeon routine of mockery, which went straight over the heads of white society, its real target. The strut became part and parcel of other dances, its greatest practitioner probably being Ananias Berry of the Berry Brothers.

When you begin to visualize the innovations that were gradually being added to the dance through routines like the Charleston, the Black Bottom, and the Cake Walk, the ensuing dances become more meaningful. And there were more innovations to come. The Shimmy added hesitation, the Itch (also known as the Heebie Jeebies) was an eccentric dance in which the dancer performed spasmodic hand, arm, and leg movements as though he was trying to scratch a series of itches that jumped from one part of his body to another. It was a particular favorite of Jodie Edwards, better known as Butterbeans of Butterbeans and Susie, but Rubberlegs Williams also frequently included it in his routines.

Nor can you forget dances like Ballin' the Jack (*The Jack* was the locomotive in black jargon; *ballin'* or *high ballin'* was the fist-clenched signal to start the train, a signal adopted by Black Power advocates), the Sand Dance, Walkin' the Dog, the Fanny Bump, Grind, Squat, Mooche, or the Funky Butt!

And then there was a little item called Truckin', which became a nation-wide craze for a while. Introduced in the old Cotton Club by Cora LaRedd, Truckin' was the invention of a comic named Bilo, who did his routine with another comic who went by the name of Ashes. Leonard Reed described it: "Bilo would start his truckin' routine to the accompanying roars of laughter which an appreciative audience supplied, and as he danced Ashes would demand, 'Where ya goin', Son?' The reply was, 'Goin' to the fertilize factory.' Ashes would shake his head and say, 'No wonder you're putting' it on so strong.' It never failed to bring a yock."

Dancers are numbered among the supporting acts of show business. With rare exceptions, dancers don't become headliners, don't receive the tremendous salaries that go to the singers and sometimes the musicians of the day. Why and how do they get into show biz in the first place?

Says Honi Coles: "In my neighborhood in Philadelphia, the only form of recreation was dancing. Everyone I knew could dance. We used to dance on street corners at night, and then we'd start going to the various neighborhood houses and amateur contests. First I won a few prizes here and there, and then I got together with other prizewinners and we formed little trios or quartets of dancers. Finally, George and Danny Miller and I formed an act we called the Miller Brothers. We rehearsed every day and every night." Laughed Honi with obvious pleasure at the recollection, "We even broke into the community center off Ridge Avenue to rehearse. The cops found out that we were breaking in, but after they were satisfied that it was legit, they used to come around at night and watch us!"

Honi continued, "In my day, I don't know anyone who went to school to learn show business or dancing. You learned it by osmosis, as you were exposed to it. The Miller Brothers and I used to walk out on the boulevard and into various places to dance. We'd dance on street corners for whatever coins people would throw us; that was our pay for the night. We'd dance in amateur contests, which we sometimes didn't win; then we had nothing but some applause for our efforts. But dancing was all we knew. I guess it was all we wanted to know."

Like the cutting contests I described earlier involving jazz musicians, there were "challenge contests" among the dancers. At the Hoofers Club in New York a rich protocol of customs was observed, including the maxim that newcomers would play it "cool" (quiet, show no emotion, and never ask for help or advice) *and* that they would never copy someone else's steps. Out of the Hoofers Club emerged such greats as John "Bubber" Sublett, who was laughed out of the club his first time there, but who, as part of the immortal team of Buck and Bubbles (he was the latter) made dancing history, as well as Honi Coles, Eddie Rector, "Slappy" Wallace, and "Baby" Lawrence, who is probably to tap dancing what John Coltrane was to the saxophone (the end of the line, the tail of the parley).

In speaking of his own career, Honi Coles said, "When I was with the Miller Brothers, we were a sensational act, but we were really a bunch of dumb kids. Hell! We didn't even know enough to get ourselves an agent, and, brother, things were tough in those days. It was before Equity, the Union, came in and we had no protection at all." A somewhat bitter laugh, "For one show in particular, I recall, we had to rehearse every day. They gave us ten cents a day for carfare—period!"

"What were you supposed to live on?" I asked.

"They really didn't care about that; it wasn't their concern. We had to scuffle for food; that's all there was to it. And making a living as a dancer was tough. Later on, I rehearsed my own act for one solid year before I took my first job as a single, and after the job finally came through, it was catch as catch can. You'd work one week and lay off for six. But you kept going because you loved your work. It was pure devotion, I guess; and anyway, there was no other place to go. You wanted to be the best-looking act around, the best-dressed guy in the crowd—and anyway, I had no other trade. I was a dancer and that was that."

Later Honi added, "When I was doing a single, I joined Pop Foster as part of his act. It consisted of Baby Lawrence, who was then a boy soprano—it was long before he became a dancer; a guy named Smiley, who was a comic; and I was the dancer. Pop Foster was the master of ceremonies and Billie Holiday was the singer. That was about 1934. We'd finish our act with a fast Shim-Sham, everyone joining in!"

Then there was a covey of sisters who made show-business history. They were four of the most formidable females in the world of the theater; theirs was the highest paid troupe on the old TOBA circuit, and they literally put dancers on the map. They were the Whitman Sisters: Essie, Alberta (Bert), Alice, and Mabel (Mae, the leader of the troupe). The Whitman Sisters pioneered in the teens and twenties, and well into the thirties they were the first to feature dancers, and not just also-rans on their show. Alice was billed as the "Queen of Taps," and such show-business experts as Leonard Reed and Willie Bryant (who worked with the troupe) claimed she was the greatest female tap-dancer. When you consider that she was competing with Louise Madison, Cora LaRedd, Mae Barnes, and her sister Bert, it was high compliment indeed.

Along with her straight tap dances, Alice danced such routines as Ballin' the Jack, the Dog, the Sand Dance, and as a favorite show-stopper, the Shim-Sham. Probably only Earl "Snakehips" Tucker could wiggle more individual parts of his anatomy than Alice. Said Alice, "I could sure wiggle a mean ———— around," and she'd whistle to let your imagination fill in the blank.

For over twenty years the Whitman women dominated black show business and our showplace was proud to present some of their talent. "Mae Whitman's Juvenile Wonders—POPS AND LOUIS," for instance, consisted of one Louis Williams and Alice Whitman's dancing son who went under the name "Pops." Pops and Louis became major headliners in the twenties and thirties, working with some of the great swing bands, and then later in Hollywood. Historically, acrobatic dancing wasn't strong among most black dancers, but there were two exceptions: Pops was one of them, and an act known as The Crackerjacks was the other. Separately or together, they could have burned up anyone's stage and probably the Ringling Brothers Circus to boot.

Dancing was not all the Whitman Sisters offered. Essie, for example, sang. Said Leonard Reed, "In those days of stage shows without microphones, Essie could sing "Some of These Days" in a contralto so powerful that she would have made Sophie Tucker seem anemic." Leonard was not the only one to have made such a claim for Essie. Essie, by the way, said that their father claimed to have been a first cousin of the American poet Walt Whitman. And since the girls were fair-skinned and blond, though always identifying themselves as black, that is entirely possible.

As part of their act in the twenties, the sisters added a talented midget who went under the stage name "Princess Wee Wee." She did a dance with Willie Bryant that was a show-stopper. Willie was over six feet tall and very skinny; Princess Wee Wee, of course, looked miniscule standing beside him. She would sing a song in her cute, high-pitched voice, and then dance all over the stage, skipping in between Willie's legs. A show-stopper of another variety took place one day backstage. Leonard Reed supplied the details, laughing at the memory:

> They had an act called the Five Spirits of Rhythm, and Mae found out that one of them, a chap called Leo, was screwing Princess Wee Wee. So she went to Leo's room and literally kicked the door open. Just as she arrived there, Leo was coming

out of the bathroom and he didn't have a stitch of clothing on. Mae, who was very strait-laced, had a cane in her hand, and she started hitting him with it. He jumped on the bed, and, man, she hit him everywhere! In the meanwhile, the entire cast of the show crowded in through the doorway and, along with her other sisters, offered Mae ample advice as to where and how to hit poor old Leo. I mean, she hit him everywhere she could until he finally caught the cane and stopped the act. He didn't show up for the next several days. He was black, I mean, *really black*—and that was probably a good thing because otherwise you could have seen him blushing for weeks!

Every era and every art has its unsung heroes. In the dance, one such hero was Eddie Rector. I last saw Eddie in the late fifties, almost a decade before he died in 1962. He was as lean, lithe, and limber then, I suspect, as when he was a chorus boy in J. Lubrie Hul's *Darktown Follies* in 1916, or when he danced a lead in *Shuffle Along* in 1921. Whether he was dancing his classic soft-shoe routines, the Cake Walk, Charleston, Waltz Clog, or his famous Sand Dance (he would sprinkle sand on the stage and the sound of his gliding feet on it was hypnotic), Eddie had that something called "class." He was also a dance innovator, whose style still affects dancing, more than a half century after he first glided across the Broadway stage flashing his smile, twirling his tails! For Eddie "traveled" across the stage with uncommon grace, and traveling was something new at that time. *Twirling* is too simple a term for what Eddie did; his movement was partly floating, partly gliding, partly what would almost pass for levitation. No one before or since has bettered the peerless grace of Eddie Rector. Said Honi, "He was one of the real greats."

Only a few years before he died, Eddie was rehearsing for a downtown show. At the request of the director, he quietly walked on stage, took out a container, and sprinkled sand on the stage. The younger dancers smiled knowingly and silently, demanding to know just what this old-timer was going to show them. Their smirks turned to looks of disbelief as the "king of class" did a soft-shoe Sand Dance routine, the likes of which they had never seen or imagined before. There were others who did that dance from time to time, but no one ever did it with quite the style of Eddie Rector. Sandman Sims is not quite an Eddie Rector, but his Sand Dance is good enough and he is one of the few dancers around still doing it.

In *Darktown Follies,* a dance called the Texas Tommy was performed. It was the earliest precursor of the Lindy Hop, replete with female partners flying through the air, double and triple steps, and it was the first dance in which the dancers separated. That element, known as the "break," added a new dimension in freedom and individual expression to the dance; it has stayed with it ever since. Almost without exception, the jazz-dance routines of today evolved out of the Lindy Hop, and the beginning of that parlay was the old Texas Tommy.

Florence Ziegfeld, Broadway producer extraordinaire, was so impressed by a number titled "At the Ball" in *Darktown Follies* that he purchased it for his *Follies*. It was performed on Broadway hundreds of times as part of that show, but *never* did the program give a single word of credit to its first producer, J. Lubrie Hul! Similarly, the Black Bottom was "introduced" on Broadway by Anne Pennington in George White's *Scandals of 1926,* introduced as a new and "original" dance. How misleading! Such dancers as Rubberlegs Williams and Butterbeans had performed it as far back as 1915. It was, as some of the old-timers claimed, "as old as the hills."

If Eddie Rector is an unsung hero of the dance, James Barton is almost totally unknown as far as dance is concerned. And yet this star of the famed *Tobacco Road* of a later era was a supreme dancer. Indeed, the great Bill Robinson claimed that Barton had taught him how to dance, but since Bill's dancing went back to his early days as a "pic" and to appearances in such shows as Lew Leslie's *Blackbirds,* his statement is some sort of a lapse for which he is to be forgiven. But James Barton did make innumerable appearances at the old Cotton Club with both Bill Robinson and Eddie Rector. Some of those appearances created a unique brand of excitement even for the Cotton Club.

Another of the stars of *Blackbirds* was Earl "Snakehips" Tucker. Henry Frankel says, "Snakehips was one mean guy and he was ugly to boot, but for some reason he always had a couple of good-lookin' chicks on his arm." But then, remembering the soft cries of "Honey, you can park your shoes under my bed any night" that frequently greeted his performances, perhaps that is understandable.

Dad told me about an incident in a show in which Snakehips was involved, which really scared him. The show starred Ethel Waters, and on Thursday afternoon the money for the show had been paid over to Ethel's manager and a receipt signed. But when night descended on the Apollo, neither manager nor money were to be found. In something of a panic Dad called the entire cast together to explain the circumstances—but not before he had obtained the services of two plainclothesmen who "stood by." In truth, Dad was afraid of Snakehips' reaction to all this, for he was known to carry a switchblade. Patiently, Dad explained to the cast that the theater had lived up to its end of the bargain, that the show had been paid off, and a receipt obtained. It was not his fault that the money had "flown the coop." All eyes turned to Snakehips, the two plainclothesmen nervously fingered their service revolvers, but everyone heaved a sigh of relief when Tucker shrugged his shoulders, acknowledged that the theater was not to blame, and vowed to "get that son of a bitch." The "son of a bitch" was from that day on, called "Mr. Danger" by Ethel Waters.

As for Tucker, everyone who ever saw him dance was incredulous at the extent and variety of his movements. Said Henry Frankel, a former hoofer himself, "that man moved every muscle in his body, and he seemed to move every one of them at the same time. I mean, when Snakehips danced, *everything* moved. He used to wear a silk shirt with ruffled sleeves and shoulders, and the movements of his body made them flutter and quiver as though a wind was blowing right through him." Added Duke Ellington, who hired Tucker to work for him, "I think he came from Tidewater, Maryland, one of those primitive lost colonies where they practice pagan rituals and their dancing styles evolved from religious seizures."

Legend has it that back in the teens Snakehips showed up backstage at the old Lafayette Theatre while producer Irvin C. Miller was holding tryouts for a show. Finally Miller noticed him and asked what he could do. In his hoarse whisper Snakehips allowed as how "I'm a dancer and if I don't stop the show you can fire me." Impressed, after an audition, Miller hired him. No one, but *no one*, ever fired Earl Tucker, the "mean s.o.b. who could move it all."

In 1932, a couple of years before Frank Schiffman moved his operations from the Lafayette Theater to the Harlem Opera House on 125th Street, he put two youngsters into a Lafayette show. One of them was fourteen years old and the other was eight. They took the place by storm. The two were Fayard and Harold Nicholas, billed as the Nicholas Kids, and they set the entire world of entertainment afire. Shortly after their initial Lafayette appearance, they moved into the Cotton Club, where they starred for two years. In 1936 they closed in on Broadway as part of the *Ziegfield Follies*. They literally stopped the show cold, a feat they continued in Lew Leslie's *Blackbirds* and in an assortment of movies including *The Big Broadcast of 1936*. Harold and Fayard could do anything— tap, acrobatics, songs. They had class to spare, and for sheer terpsichorean excitement there was only one act that could even approach them. That act was made up of three brothers, Ananias, Jimmy, and young Warren Berry. They were known, of course, as the Berry Brothers, and it's a tossup as to which was the better group. Having seen both of them in action, you'll excuse me if I bow out of the betting.

The Berry Brothers did what is known in the trade as a "flash act," and there is no better term to explain or describe the four and a half minutes of dancing dynamite those boys spliced together. Ananias and Jimmy had been in the *Blackbirds* in 1932, but when they added their "little" brother, the act really took off. Ananias had what one professional dancer called "the greatest strut on the stage"; it showed to best advantage when he fused the Cake Walk with a rapid-fire acrobatic dance routine. Theirs was an act in which not merely every stop but every movement was perfectly timed. It was split-second timing at that, with syncopated steps followed hard by flying leaps and acrobatics. As the finale approached, young Warren retreated to one end of the stage, turned, ran, and leapt, twisting around in mid-air. He wrapped his legs around Jimmy's neck while Jimmy went into a fast airplane spin, twirling Warren about as though he were a rag doll. Talk about excitement! The explosive finish of their act rarely failed to bring the audience to its feet.

In 1937, the late Herman Stark, manager of the Cotton Club and also the Nicholas Brothers' manager, put the Nicholas and the Berry Brothers into the same Cotton Club show. To counterbalance the superlative finish of the Berry Brothers' act, Harold and Fayard Nicholas dashed to the wings, climbed two steps up the side of the proscenium, and then back-flipped (no hands) into a

53a. Eddie Hector

53b. The Nicholas Brothers

split! Probably the last word in the great debate about the merits of each group is contained in these remarks by Cholly Atkins: "The Nicholas Brothers sang, tapped, and did acrobatics. They were the best all-around talent. The Berry Brothers did not tap, and their singing was only fair, but they were the greatest flash act of them all." The only thing one could safely say about the Nicholas and Berry Brothers is that between the five of them was an agglomeration of the most exciting dancing talent on the stage at that time. Quite likely they have never been matched. Unfortunately, Ananias died in 1951. Otherwise the Berry Brothers might still be doing a four-and-a-half minute flash act, leaving dancers, singers, and musicians gasping on the stage as audiences roared.

Their real names were John Sublett and Ford Lee Washington; they became the toast of Broadway, the rage of Hollywood, the favorites of Harlem; and, according to some, one of them was the greatest dancer of all. Their stage name, of course, was Buck and Bubbles, and they played them all, from the *Ziegfield Follies* through *Blackbirds,* from the old Palace Theatre, the Lafayette, the Harlem Opera House, to the Apollo. Dancer Honi Coles states his opinion clearly enough: "In my book, John Bubbles was the greatest dancer of them all. He could do anything and do it with an ease that none of us could even approach." However, debating who is the greatest dancer is probably a lot like deciding whether Joe Louis, Jack Dempsey, or Mohammed Ali was the greatest heavyweight of them all. Since John Bubbles was past his prime when Teddy Hale and Baby Lawrence were in theirs, there is hardly any way to compare them. But no matter what your bias is, none can deny that John Bubbles was one of a handful of truly great dancers and that with his piano-playing partner, Buck, they were among the stage's finest entertainers.

John Bubbles' influence on the dance is deep and abiding. Such dancing greats as Coles and Atkins, Pete Nugent, Derby Wilson and Ralph Brown, all tipped their hats in his direction. In 1922, while at the Palace, he was seen by Fred Astaire. In a recent conversation, the Apollo's one-time manager, David McCarthy, told me he heard Astaire claim that he became interested in tap-dancing only *after* he saw Bubbles perform. He was, by all accounts, the ad lib dancer supreme. Honi commented, "No one could ever steal John Bubbles' material because it was never the same two times in a row." His trick of accentuating the beat with unusual heel-and-toe combinations is one of Bubbles' enduring contributions to the jazz dance.

John was ten and Buck was six when they formed their act; they danced together until Buck died in 1955, but Bubbles continued singing and dancing for years thereafter, piling triumph on top of triumph. But there was glory enough in the history of Buck and Bubbles. None of it surpassed their triumph in the *Ziegfield Follies of 1931.* In rehearsal they got, as was the frequent wont of the day, "the racial treatment," being cut (that is, the time of their next act shortened), shifted, slighted, even stuck in a dressing room in the basement. But on opening night they had to be rushed back onstage from their basement dressing room, because the audience wouldn't stop applauding. Then, the act that had stopped the show cold, was shifted around from one spot to another, ending in the only logical spot for a showstopper: next to closing.

More than one tap-dancer claimed the great Bill Robinson as his mentor, inspiration, or leader. It was sort of like touching the Blarney stone to claim descendency from Bill; perhaps his magic would rub off on you. But of all the claimants, Bill Bailey was by far the most legitimate. And yet Bill, who bears no relation to the man in the song "Bill Bailey, Won't You Please Come Home" but who was Pearl's brother, was a distinctive and distinguished tapster on his own. Bill and Pearl's father was a preacher in a Holy Roller church. You can feel that influence in Pearl's singing, and Bill himself claimed that his dancing began while he sat tapping his feet to the shouting excitement that went on Sunday mornings and evenings. Back some thirty-odd years ago, while Bill was at the height of his popularity as a dancer, he received the "call" of the Lord, left the stage, and entered the ministry.

It was at the time that Daddy Grace was at the height of his popularity. He had a temple at the corner of 125th Street and Eighth Avenue, diagonally across the street from the Apollo. On Sunday nights, with loudspeakers piped into the street to bring the message outside, Grace's congregation sounded similar to an old Holy Roller service. I was told that along with the singing was dancing of an order that any Holy Roller would have been proud of. And leading the dancers was Reverend William Bailey, who, according to the letter he sent Dad in 1949 inviting him to a benefit at the old Golden Gate Arena, was known as the "Former World's Greatest Tap Dancer." Having witnessed Bill Bailey in his heyday, I am not inclined to argue with his own description of himself.

If you had followed the black dancing of the Heyday Years, you would know of Willie Covan, part of an act called the Covan Brothers. He is entitled to be included in anyone's list of great tapsters. If you are scratching your head wondering about Willie Covan's credentials, let me list a few of the Hollywood stars who took lessons and were coached by him: Eleanor Powell, Signe Hasso, Polly Bergen, Pier Angeli, Jeanette McDonald, Mickey Rooney, Robert Taylor, Kirk Douglas, Gregory Peck, Mary Tyler Moore, and Dick Van Dyke. Need I say more?

Dancers, dancers, dancers—the Heyday Years saw them come and go by the dozens, beating out the rhythms of the day, performing the gymnastics, meeting the jazz beat with simultaneous and contrapuntal beats emanating from tapping feet and swaying bodies. It was as though sparks from their flashing feet lit up the firmament as they pranced out on the Apollo's stage. Dewey Weinglass, whom I knew as a booking agent in the fifties, performed "Russian dancing" in his earlier days. I knew him as a genial little man with a wide smile; Dad knew him as a dancer of the highest caliber.

Derby Wilson first hit town with a bang in a show called *Bamboola,* presented in 1929; in the fifties and sixties, Derby was still charming audiences with his light-as-a-feather dexterity and a personality as warm and pleasing as any on the stage. Derby used to say in his soft tones, "I'm just tryin' to get

54a. Derby Wilson

54b. Chorus line

where Bill [Robinson] was. Now wait a minute; I ain't tryin' to get where he *is,* jest where he *was.* So I want you to notice how light I am on my feetses—and when I finish my routine, jest lay it [the applause] on me. I promise you, if I get where Bill was, I won't forget you." The audiences always loved Derby, no matter how often they had heard him or watched him dance. He was a great little dancer.

Audiences loved Avon Long, who charmed Broadway audiences in the long-lived revue *Bubbling Brown Sugar,* but they had loved him since he succeeded John Bubbles in *Porgy and Bess.* (He died just as this book was going to press, in February, 1984.)

Dancers were always popular at the Apollo; there never was an Apollo show without them. Even the rock shows of a decade ago had dancing integrated into the singing routines of the various vocal groups. In an earlier time, the Apollo had even presented the likes of dear old Pat Rooney, Sr.! When he was a spry eighty, we put Pat into one Apollo show, and soft shoe, strutting, corny songs and all, he brought down the house.

I would be doing an injustice to my friend Honi Coles if I didn't add a few words about his dancing. For by any standard, Honi belongs in the top rank. He is lean to the point of being too thin. There is an angularity in his dancing. There is also a grace, the kind of dexterity that immediately labels him as a "class" act. In an age that saw gradual if painful transitions for black artists from "race" spots to Broadway, Honi was a classical and classy tapster. It would be hard to imagine, much less find, a spot in which he didn't fit. Nor was class his sole claim to fame. There is hardly a step he doesn't own, and all are done with an ease that is almost careless. "The man never seems to exert himself," breathed one aficionado watching Honi dance. That, perhaps, is the supreme accolade for any artist.

It would be hard to rank many of the other dancers who strutted on the Apollo's stage. They included Pete Nugent, Peaches, Herb and Duke, the Miller Brothers and Lois, Rubberlegs Williams, the Four Step Brothers, Tip, Tap & Toe, and Sammy Davis, Jr. Most of them were tapsters. Why? One of them put it neatly enough, put it in a single word: *rhythm.* He continued: "Swing, jazz music—it's the rhythm that counts, and when we danced, all we wanted to do was pick up that beat, play around with it, and ride it on out!" Maybe, as some have suggested, the tap-dancer's message was the modern-day recapitulation of the tropical-forest drum message. Always, running through the dance, was that surging rhythm.

In the early days there was Raymond Winfield in an act called Tip, Tap & Toe. On a five-foot-long, two-and-a-half-foot-wide raised platform they danced Over the Top, Through the Trenches, Falling off a Log, Off to Buffalo, and Wings—in short, all the dance steps performed by the master dancers of the time. Raymond was the heart of the act. Tragically, he was an addict. He would stand in the wings while the act was being announced, nodding. As they were introduced and the band struck up their music, someone would push Raymond on stage with the other two men. Instantly, he would be transformed into a smiling, dextrous, personable dancer. Atop that narrow platform, Raymond could do every step, every roll, every precision move without missing a beat, and with the ease of dancing genius. But when the music was over, the applause registered, and the platform "struck," Raymond Winfield would be standing back in the wings, nodding—back into his own private world, alone.

It would be hard to choose between Al Williams, Maceo Anderson, Prince Spencer, or Flash McDonald, members of the last group known as the Four Step Brothers (there had been others in the act); they were a quartet of dancing demons. Maceo was as much a comic as a dancer (although an excellent one), and Al Williams was the assumed leader of the troupe. The younger members of the act—Prince and McDonald—each in his own way would have been able to challenge any dancer in excellence. Prince had an uncanny speed afoot, and McDonald had a trick of bouncing up and down while seeming to turn his legs into rubber that I never saw another dancer duplicate.

There were other dancers of great stature, but sooner or later we come down to a handful—four, to be precise. To some of the older experts, John Bubbles was the greatest. But you can't finish the debate without bringing up a few challengers—like Bunny Briggs, Teddy Hale, and Baby Lawrence. I am somewhat younger than Honi Coles (a partisan of John Bubbles) so my bias, perhaps, lies with the last three.

Bunny Briggs is a quiet, modest, almost painfully shy dancer. One night a friend of mine turned to me while Bunny was in the middle of his act and asked, "Is he really making those sounds with his *feet?*" It was not a foolish question, for Bunny dances with his feet barely an inch off the floor, and the staccato rhythm of his taps come out so rapidly, so firmly, so all together, that it is hard to believe that that cacophony of sound could possibly have been made by a mere pair of feet. But at the old Ubangi Club, when they were both kids, Bunny Briggs had been "cut" by the wizardry of Baby Lawrence, and although they became fast friends, Bunny always said that Baby was the greater of the two. Only a few years before Duke Ellington died, Bunny danced his "David Danced before the Lord with All His Might" in Ellington's *Concert of Sacred Music,* to universal critical acclaim.

In other performances of Duke's *Sacred Music,* Geoffrey Holder and Baby Lawrence also performed. "Tap dancing is very much like jazz music," said Baby Lawrence. "The dancer improvises his own solo and expresses himself." That about sums it up for the truly creative dancer. In the late forties, Baby Lawrence had been "separated from society" for a while, narcotics being the problem. In the spring of 1950, word was whispered around Harlem, "Baby Lawrence is out, and I hear he's created some new routines that are out of sight." Baby appeared at our office, requested a week and some money for clothes and food. Fearfully, we complied. But out of that period of separation had sprung a tap-dance routine that quite defies description. Every step in the book was blended into that routine, linked together in machine-gun rapidity,

55a. Bunny Briggs

55b. Four Step Brothers

delivered without strain, without a pant, delivered with a flawless ease, the kind one would expect from the practitioner of a relaxed art, rather than one of the most strenuous in the books. Baby started out as a boy soprano, and in 1932 he was a vocalist with Don Redman's band. Leonard Reed once helped him put a dance routine together. Baby studied the dancing of Pete Nugent, Peaches and Duke, Bill Bailey, and Derby Wilson. He danced with Basie, Woody Herman, and Duke Ellington. In 1938, he was half of a now-legendary "challenge contest" with Freddie James, then a lead dancer with the Four Step Brothers.

But it isn't only in the flawless and exciting execution of steps that Baby Lawrence shone so brightly. He sang with the great Art Tatum, he studied the music of Charlie "Bird" Parker, and he claimed that both of them influenced his dancing. Once, while doing an especially difficult routine at the Apollo, a wag in the audience yelled, "Showoff!" Baby smiled, barely pausing in his routine and said, "You're only saying that because it's true." But he wasn't a showoff; he was merely currently the most innovative dancer of them all, with one possible exception. His aim and accomplishment was to blend his dancing with the jazz music of the day.

To my way of thinking, only Teddy Hale was in the same league with Baby Lawrence. With due respect to John Bubbles and with respect and affection for Bunny Briggs, Hale was one of the most tragic yet heroic figures in show business. Teddy started at the age of five in 1931, when he was Ted Lewis' shadow. He died in his early thirties, a genius lost in the world of narcotics. Of him, his manager and a former performer himself, Nat Nazarro once said, "He dances as though his ankles were made of bananas."

One of Teddy's tour de forces was "Begin the Beguine." Not only did he hit every single beat with either heel or toe, but it seemed as though he added new dimensions to the tune as he went along. And as if that weren't enough, he would then bring a chair out to stage center, seat himself, and go into a five-minute tap routine, an innocent smile playing on his face as he beat out one rhythm, changed it, speeded it up and slowed it down, doing the impossible while your legs fairly ached with sympathetic pain. Now tap-dancing is difficult enough, but to perform an intricate routine like that while seated is almost impossible—for anyone but Teddy Hale.

But tap, except to Willie Covan, wasn't the only dance form of consequence. There was the dancing of Katherine Dunham, for instance. Dunham's work cannot be classified as jazz dance; it is rooted in the traditions of the West Indies and in various folk dances. Illustration 56a is an ad for her 1958 appearance at the Apollo. Her troupe was a sensation. So too were the African-rooted routines of the exotic and exciting Pearl Primus. Nor can one forget the compelling, magnetic Geoffrey Holder. When Holder first leapt out onto the Apollo stage, he was greeted with a gasp, then a shout, then wild applause. He deserved every bit of it, for Holder is one of the great creative forces in the dance world.

For sheer excitement through the dance, no Apollo show will ever surpass, I believe, the *African Holiday* show that was arranged by Pete Long. It came in

'African Holiday' At Apollo On 26th

...CAN HOLIDAY," an authentic African song and dance ...gramed by Peter Long, will be presented for a lim... ...ment at the Apollo Theatre on Friday morning, ... Headlining the extravaganza of 30 top notch African dancers, singers, drummers and specialty performers are Michael Olatunji, the Nigerian drummer and folklore artist, and Gus Dinizulu and his dancers and singers. Also to be featured in cast are Lucinda Ransom, Jerome Jeffrey, Alice Dinzulu, Sandra Busch, Alverta La Palla and Zebedee Colins.

56a.

56b.

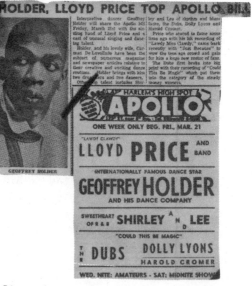

56c.

1960 at a time when black Americans were becoming increasingly aware of their African heritage and increasingly anxious to see examples of it. It was a strange and exotic blend—those French-speaking Africans doing wild dances on the Apollo's stage to deliriously happy audiences, many of whom were proudly getting their first visual taste of their own cultural heritage.

Novelty dancers, comedy dancers, singing dancers—the list is endless. One dancer, Jimmy Smith, danced on a homemade xylophone, playing tunes with his feet as his top hat and tail-clad figure contracted itself to hit the proper notes. A succession of dancers like "Tables" Davis "danced" while holding a pyramid of tables and chairs in their teeth. It may not have qualified as dancing in the strictest sense, but you couldn't help wondering how they could do any steps at all without spilling teeth all over the stage. The efforts of Harold King were delightful. He danced on roller skates—tap-danced, that is—and he managed to inject more than one tricky and imaginative step into his routine while swirling about on those skates. For finishers, he blindfolded himself and did a tap-dance routine on skates on a table that was three-and-a-half-feet square.

Comedians and the dance are like Siamese twins; you can't separate them from each other. At least this was true on the black stage. Pigmeat Markham, for instance, did about every hep dance from the Suzie Que through Truckin', and Jackie Mabley never finished her routine with anything but a dance, even when she was growing old and feeble. The Three Chocolateers was an act known in the trade as a "knockabout comedy act." Among their dance routines they introduced a dance called Peckin', which became a nationwide rage for a brief time. The dance was done with head and neck movements imitative of a rooster as it walked around the barnyard, head and neck bobbing back and forth as if just about to dart for a worm. But even Peckin' couldn't obscure the fact that the Three Chocolateers were dancers of more than passing talent. Their leader Paul Black, for instance, could only be described as chubby. Solid as a wall, Paul executed a Chinese split, then walked almost the full length of the stage in the split position! Albert Gibson, another partner, was a tapster of more than pedestrian talents, and partner number three, Eddie West, was an acrobat.

Truckin' had its origins in a dance that was introduced in the 1820s by Tom Rice, a famous name in minstrelsy. Rice copied and developed the dance from watching an old crippled slave who sang a little ditty, then did a little dance. The slave's song contained the words "Jump Jim Crow" (the slave's name), and Tom Rice made his name and fortune by imitating the dance, developing it, and, in blackface, performing it all over the world. Descriptions of the dance confirm that it had all the elements of the dance craze of the thirties and forties known as Truckin'. It was used by almost every comic and a lot of straight professional dancers including Rubberlegs Williams and Cora LaRedd.

Other comedy teams developed their own distinctive brand of dancing, which they used as adjuncts and closings for their acts. Cook and Brown, Moke and Poke, Chuck and Chuckles are a few of them who endured and were featured at the Apollo for years. I have already referred to Jodie Edwards, otherwise known as Butterbeans, whose dance, the Heebie Jeebies or the Itch, was used as a closing for his act. One of the finest of the comedy-dance teams was Stump and Stumpy. They were James Cross and Harold Cromer (although Harold wasn't the only Stump in history), and a funnier, faster-moving team didn't exist. So good were Cross and Cromer that in more than one Apollo show they took over the next-to-closing spot, Harold playing straight man to Jimmy's comedy routine.

Not to be omitted is the extraordinary group of handicapped dancers who were able to do more with damaged bodies or missing limbs than most dancers could manage with two good arms and leg. Take for instance Peg Leg Bates. He rose to stardom in Lew Leslie's *Blackbirds* and was featured at the old Cotton Club. As the result of an accident, one leg had been severed below the knee. On it he strapped a wooden leg, of which he had an assortment in colors matching the suit and hat he was wearing for each show. One dancer said, "Peg could do taps on his peg leg which many dancers couldn't do at all." And Honi Coles adds, "There were times when Peg would sit in his dressing room and literally cry with the pain he experienced from his dance routines, but it never stopped him from performing them."

The supreme test of his skill and endurance came at the end of his act when Peg performed the step he called Jet Plane. A running leap halfway across the stage, a brief flight through the air, and he landed full force on the peg leg, then hopped off backwards while the band hit a chord to accompany each hop! He performed it for years, at what cost in pain only Peg himself could tell you. When he returned for his bow, Peg's speech always was the same. I have no doubt that it was sincere. "Ladies and gentlemen," he'd say, "you have made a certain one-legged dancer very very happy. From the bottom of my heart I thank you."

He was short, a little mean in spirit, but with his handicap, why not? His name was Jesse James and he could barely walk, let alone dance! Both Jesse's legs had been badly crippled by polio, but he was a dancer nevertheless. One leg was usable, the other dragged behind him as Jesse swung out on stage aided by a pair of crutches. On his "good" leg he tapped, using his crutches to supplement the sound of only one good leg. He was incredible. So was another handicapped dancer called "Big Time Crip," who never let his handicap interfere with either his dancing or his disposition.

And then there was a pair of dancers who to my way of thinking were the most astonishing of all, for both of them were missing one arm and one leg. Leroy Strange and "Crip" Heard could do the Hucklebuck, the Suzie Que, Truckin', indeed, most of the dances of the day. They made you ashamed, they made you proud. Ashamed that you could complain about your situation at all; proud that a couple of men were courageous and skillful enough to go beyond the normal demands of the human spirit.

When we look back on the period before and after the Heyday Years, it seems the scene was dominated by one dance or another. Truckin' was once the

57a. Jesse James

57b. Harold "Rhythm" King

57c. Peg Leg Bates

rage, followed by Peckin'. The Big Apple was so all-pervading as to have been a national craze bordering on obsession; for one brief period, a mere dance possessed the entire country. At one time the Lindy Hop was another hysteria, and most of my readers will happily recall when the Twist was the rage. Each decade, indeed almost every year, has been characterized by at least one dance.

The Cake Walk, as we mentioned earlier, was first and foremost a subtle way for black dancers to poke fun at white pomposity. It was also a much-needed emotional release for the dancers themselves. Slowly the dance became freer and looser. The Charleston, the Black Bottom, the tap dance evolved, as well as scores of minor ones. But the biggest revolution came when the Lindy Hop, or Jitterbug, emerged and with it "the break," allowing dance partners to separate, perform their own individualized steps, then rejoin. A dancing couple, sometimes two of them, would suddenly leap out onto stage or dance floor. Their feet were shod in sneakers, their torsos in fancy, polka-dotted silk shirts; white slacks or short white skirts completed the costume, permitting maximum freedom of movement. The Lindy was performed at high speed, a full routine rarely lasting more than four or five minutes (even the vigor of youth had its physical limits). They danced in unison, knees high, bodies rising and falling to a lightning beat. Suddenly, up over the boy's head the girl flew, thrown five feet above the stage! Returning to earth she never lost the beat as she turned and boosted *him* skyward! It was mayhem, karate, judo and levitation all rolled up into one and even the best of show drummers worked like mad to keep their sticks flying in tempo with those dancing feet.

Each year during the thirties and forties the Harvest Moon Dance Contest was held in New York's Madison Square Garden. The waltz, stately and elegant, the tango, insinuating and gliding, the fox trot and rhumba—all were won by white couples, who hardly sweated while performing their suave and elegant routines. But it was the jitterbuggers everyone was waiting for; with their bound-less energy they made everything that preceded them boring by comparison.

It was Herbert White, ex-fighter, ex-bouncer at the Savoy and Alhambra Ballrooms, who put the Lindy on the show-biz map. White helped choreograph the Lindy-hoppers' routines; then he put together some seventy-odd dancers in various teams and troupes. They crisscrossed the country, bringing the Lindy with them. Whitey's Lindy Hoppers, the Jive-a-Dears, Whitey's Truckin' Maniacs, Whitey's Champion Jitterbugs—all graced the Apollo Theater stage. Virtually without exception, all the modern dances of the past few decades—the Frug, the Monkey, the Suzie Que, the Jerk, and even disco dancing—sprang from the seeds spread around the country by the jitterbug.

As with all developments in show business, the audience played a significant supporting role. And from the jitterbug to the Frug, from tap-dancing to Truckin', the Harlem audience's role was doubly significant. John Bubbles, comparing audience reactions while playing, at the same time, the Lafayette Theater in Harlem and in *The Ziegfield Follies* on Broadway, said: "I was doing the same steps at both places, but with a different feeling. Downtown it was a battle between the acts; uptown, between the dancer and the audience. In Harlem the audience practically dared you to dance and you had to swing. Downtown they just watched and you couldn't fail. I danced loose and rhythmic uptown, simple and distinct downtown."

What John Bubbles seems to be saying is that the Broadway audience sat back ready to enjoy the fruits of the dancers' labors, while the Harlem audience *demanded* a higher level of performance. But there was more to it than that. The Harlem audience, of course, accepted black offerings without question, and alas, nothing like such acceptance was forthcoming downtown, especially by the management or the other performers. On the contrary, a super performance on Broadway by a black act was a one-way ticket to trouble, rejection and oblivion. The tap-dance team of Covan and Ruffin, for example, played the Palace Theater on Broadway during the thirties. They were good; in fact, they stopped the show. Their reward? They were shifted about in the show's lineup because none of the white acts wanted to follow them. Ultimately, they were fired. In turn, they were hired by the Hippodrome Theater and put into their review. Poetic justice? Hardly! They were accorded exactly the same treatment there and were fired within three days. They were, to put it bluntly, just too good!

One can make an interesting comparison between the reception Buck and Bubbles were accorded in the early days with that of Ben Vereen. A lifetime has passed between the two of them, but Ben is the first black dancing star to have been accorded superstardom since the days of Bill "Bojangles" Robinson. Part of the reason lies in his versatility, for Ben's acting ability makes him more than just a dancer. But the larger reason lies in the changed attitudes toward black artists in general. As for his dancing, Ben's style belongs more to Broadway than to the variety theater. It wasn't until *Uptown* was taped that Ben even attempted tap-dancing. It is worth noting that since that show about the early thirties, he has been taking tap-dancing lessons from Sandman Sims and others. During the taping of *Uptown* I said to Ben, "I know you never played the Apollo, but my father would have loved your style." His reply: "I dreamed of dancing there when I was a kid." He laughed. "Guess I was born a little too late." With his great talent for dancing, I hate to sell Ben Vereen short. I wish him well as a tapster, but my guess is that he would be better served to stick to his own genre, modern dancing. Somehow, Ben's style doesn't seem well suited to tap.

If jazz is an invention primarily of the black world, so too is the jazz dance. Musicians and dancers have always stimulated each other. Legendary among show-biz folk are the stories about Dizzy Gillespie while he was trumpeting with the old Luis Russell Band. Dizzy would shout out a "crazy" riff while someone was dancing, and, like a gauntlet thrown down, the challenge would be picked up, resulting in an equally "crazy" step interpolated into his dance routine. Or, as John Bubbles put it, the audience made him "swing." And *that* is the point of the whole story; evolution and development occur when creative artists have the courage, the grace, the talent, and the strength to depart from the norm and reach out and up to another level. For the dancer this has

58a.

58c. Iron Jaw Wilson

58b.

meant being able to express his exuberance in his own special way. Removed, albeit momentarily, from the harsh world that was into the freer world of a new unfettered moment, he could "travel" in ways beyond even Eddie Rector's airy glidings. He could travel, that is, into a sphere of his own choosing.

What I am talking about is evolution, not necessarily excellence. One would be hard pressed to say that the dancing of today is better than that of two, three, five decades ago. One could hardly say that cool jazz is *better* than Dixieland merely because it came years later. What you have is evolutionary change, the pyramiding of one influence on another, building, adding, altering, reinterpreting, that is, the continuing exploration and development of the creative spirit reaching further and further beyond itself.

I would be guilty of ignoring history as well as evolution if I failed to mention the influence of Latin-American dances on the innovations of the past twenty-odd years. For just as Latin musical rhythms influenced jazz, so did the rhumba, tango, and meringe have an impact on the dance scene. I am not talking about pure Latin dancing, but about the insinuating movements that intruded into other dance steps, leaving a permanent Latin American imprint. In the midst of a routine, Sammy Davis, Jr., would insert the sinuous movements of the bullfighter. In the midst of a torrid tap, Teddy Hale would slide into a graceful, backward series of interlocking, rhumba-inspired steps. And Moms Mabley slid toward the wings at the end of her comedy routine doing a peculiar, side-stepping Latin routine, an obvious cousin of the meringe. If someone had shouted "Ole!" everyone in the house would have recognized the allusion.

I have alluded to the fact that, like jazz, the jazz dance was once held in rather low esteem, especially among the sophisticates in our society and in spite of the fact that its offspring became overwhelmingly popular. Why was this true?

Richard Lockridge, writing in the *New York Times* in 1929, probably supplied a good part of the answer. After seeing an exhibition of black dancing, Lockridge commented: "Men and women who dance like that have the strength for violence." His words fairly quiver with fear. It is fear born of the knowledge that the black man has just cause for anger and the physical strength to go with it. It is the age-old fear of violence, revolution; it is even the ambivalent fear of sex. From ballet to modern dance and certainly in all the many forms the jazz dance has taken, sex is more than present; it is an integral part of the message. At best, there is only the thinnest of scrims separating the overt sexuality of the dancers from the audience. As always, the fear is a compound of aversion and attraction, simultaneously pulling the viewer now in one direction, now in another.

Soul Food

9

"Swing Lo, Sweet Chariot"

It is a commonplace fact that gospel and blues are inseparable. They spring from the same emotional and historical roots; they express both need and mood in a people's soul. The gospel song rises in exultation; the blues are mood songs ranging from despair to earthy humor. Gospel offers the hope which can ward off despair; blues offers a catharsis to keep faltering spirits from withering on the vine. Blues are an invention for the preservation of sanity; gospel is the expression of the how, the why and the where of salvation.

Logically speaking, gospel should never have been, for the Christian message was brought to black men and women by their tormentors. Obviously, this message was attractive enough to overcome the reluctance they may have felt in accepting anything offered by the whites. The heart and soul of gospel is to be found in the black churches. But there is more to gospel than song; there is the message, the spelling out of which, like the confessional, permits an emotional unburdening tantamount to lifting a weight from troubled souls. The gospel sounds set a unique pattern in vocalizing that is an integral part of *all* popular singing today, white or black. There is the soaring tone, the dipping, wavering, burgeoning sound that undulates its way up and down the scale, forming musical patterns of immense variety and intensity. It is hard to separate the gospel sound from today's singing; among the black singers of the past thirty or forty years I can scarcely think of a single one whose musical debt is not to be found in gospel.

As for the blues, there are those like LeRoi Jones (as set forth in his strong and compelling book *Blues People*) to whom that musical idiom forms the heart of modern black music—jazz, vocal, instrumental, the works. In the history of blues, there is only one white singer who has been credited by black musicians

---

No gospel song is better known than "Swing Lo, Sweet Chariot." It has been sung with verve and passion by every gospel singer from Rosetta Tharpe to Mahalia Jackon. Audiences have been seen to weep upon hearing an especially touching rendition of it. At the Apollo, no shows engendered more emotional responses than the gospel ones; no artist ever sang "Swing Lo, Sweet Chariot" to more enthusiastic response than Christine Clark.

with even *knowing* the blues; he was the trombonist Jack Teagarden. If there are white musicians who claim the blues as part of their musical equipment, it would be true only to the degree that they had absorbed a strictly black musical expression by osmosis, by imitation, or perhaps some other mysterious legerdemain. For blues can *only* be regarded as the "turf" of black musicians and singers. Probably only the cantor's wail in the synogogues can begin to approach the blues in intensity and spirit. The blues are more than a peripheral part of the black individual's existence. He doesn't merely hear or sing them, he lives them. From the earliest days, the songs of such artists as Bessie Smith, Ida Cox, Victoria Spivey, Blind Lemon Jefferson, Leadbelly, and Son House were accepted musical fare on the black scene. And yet with few exceptions—Bessie being the principal one—blues singers were never major headliners in Harlem. Indeed, it wasn't until the late sixties, with the ascendancy of such an artist as B. B. King, that blues became nationally popular. Even then the blues singers' major successes were among white intellectuals and college kids.

We had always played blues singers at the Apollo, the Lafayette, and the Harlem Opera House in the late thirties, forties, and fifties. Joe Turner, T Bone Walker, Wynonie "Mr. Blues" Harris, Jimmie Rushing, Eddie "Mr. Cleanhead" Vinson, Leadbelly, Lonnie Johnson—all of them were accepted, even popular uptown. But major attractions? Hardly! It may be claimed that Dinah Washington was a blues singer—she was—but Dinah's major success came as a pop singer rather than as a blues artist.

Yes, the blues were almost a way of life among black people in the United States, and that fact may explain why blues were always accepted but never sought after at the box office. People probably didn't want to be reminded of the melancholy that is part and parcel of the blues; their daily lives were reminder enough. And so the blues were looked upon as one would look at a wayward child: put indulgently in a corner, watched with care, and hauled out for company from time to time.

Both gospel and blues had to struggle hard for commercial success and economic survival. For years we played a selected handful of gospel singers: Sister Rosetta Tharpe, the Deep River Boys, and a few others. But although they always "went over" well, they never became box-office attractions. It took an idea and a great deal of initiative to bring the all-gospel show to life and get the public to accept it. In the process, the hard-and-fast gospel-oriented churchgoers were angered at the gospelers and never really forgave them. There are some first-rate gospel groups today that stuggle constantly against the taboo devout churchgoers have placed on purely theatrical appearances. We had many discussions with the great Mahalia Jackson in a futile attempt to convince her that an Apollo appearance would not be sacrilegious.

THE GOSPEL TRUTH

In the long history of the Apollo Theater many shows created a great deal of excitement. One Lionel Hampton show of the forties literally swayed the second balcony. Various shows headlining The Tempations, James Brown, Billy Eckstine, or Aretha Franklin were equally exciting, and virtually every major name in black show business contributed to the excitement at one time or another. But none of them produced the electric audience responses we experienced during the heyday of the gospel shows. There is really only one word to describe the audience reaction: *hysterical.*

"When we played a gospel show," said my brother Bobby, "we had to employ an army of nurses to take care of the weeping, shouting, almost possessed patrons." When the "Holy Spirit" arrived, which it regularly did, anything could happen—and it usually did. The performers sometimes acted as though in a trance, and the nurses had to work overtime, just tending to the needs of patrons.

"There were times," Bobby continued, "when we were actually frightened at the reactions of audience and patrons alike. Sometimes, the arrival of the Holy Spirit had its comic overtones. I remember one show that was running so long we were having trouble keeping a schedule. Leonard Reed talked to the headliner to try to convince him that he must stick to his alloted time span. 'But,' asked the singer, 'what if the Holy Spirit arrives in the middle of our performance?' 'Just make sure he doesn't stay longer than your twelve minutes' was Leonard's laconic reply."

In addition to the frequent arrival of the Holy Spirit, there was another intruder on the gospel scene. It was the "Holy Dance," a special dance, part jig, part jump, part sliding wiggle. Performed by virtually all the gospel singers, it added one more element of excitement to the gospel shows. The Holy Dance was performed on stage, out in the aisles among the audience, everywhere where gravity and human dexterity permitted. If it weren't for gravity, it probably would have been performed on the ceiling!

The history of gospel singing is ancient, but its history in the theater is short and intense. Indeed, the heyday of the all-gospel show was over almost as quickly as it began, but during that brief span, utter bedlam ensued.

Outstanding among the earlier gospel singers of the early thirties and forties was Sister Rosetta Tharpe. Sister Tharpe was a veteran of the Cotton Club and the old variety theater. She was a solid guitarist and a rousing house-rocker with her vocals. Once, in 1948 she was teamed at the Apollo with another great showman, Lucky Millinder, whose style dovetailed neatly with gospel. Still, Sister Tharpe's best efforts ended sadly, for she was one of the earliest targets of the churchy set, who virtually shunned her because she dared sing gospel music in places other than churches.

Sister Tharpe wasn't the only early gospeler; there was, for instance, the lovely Madame Marie Knight. Her performances were only slightly less electric than Sister Tharpe's, with whom she frequently appeared. The Deep River Boys, the Golden Gate Quartet, and The Charioteers also played the Apollo. In the fifties, the first all-gospel show appeared, patterned after the rock and roll shows that were then very popular. All-gospel shows were the brain child of Thurman Ruth, a gospel disc jockey on New York's radio station WOV. Thurman came to us with a gospel show using the rock and roll formula.

In the rock and roll show, the usual variety show format had been virtually abandoned. Gone were the comedy acts, the dancing, and novelty performers who added variety. In their place was a procession of singing acts following one after the other. As Bobby put it, "They sounded so much alike that you could have had them change clothes, come out and sing another couple of songs, and no one would have known the difference."

The gospel show story for the Apollo began in the midst of the rock and roll craze when a young girl appeared on the Wednesday Night Amateur Contest and won it week after week. She won it singing "Swing Lo, Sweet Chariot." She was not especially pretty; she did not radiate the kind of sex appeal that showed up later among many of the gospelers. She was not a great showman or a compelling personality, but she could *sing!* Despite the fact that she came up right in the middle of rock and roll's heyday, she beat the best of those rock-singing youngsters week after week. Her name was Christine Clark, a name that belongs in show-biz history, for only Mahalia Jackson could stir an audience and touch people's souls as Christine could. Said one hardened stagehand, "I can't help it. When that girl sings that song, I start crying whether I want to or not."

And when Thurman Ruth heard her and saw the audience response, he put Christine and rock and roll together in his imagination and came up with a new format: the all-gospel show. But in order to put his idea in motion, more than merely booking such a show was required. The matter of getting public and artistic acceptance proved a formidable job.

It was Dad who hatched up the idea that enabled us to put it all together. He did it in his usual direct and logical way—by calling a meeting of local ministers and laying the idea before them. Dad could be a spellbinder, and it required all his powers of persuasion to win this one. But when he finished explaining the idea ("We'll make the theater look as little like a theater as possible, do away with the band and other acts and concentrate on the vocal gospel message, pure and simple. We intend to put on the most dignified show you can imagine."), he'd won his battle. One minister banged his hand on the desk enthusiastically and declared, "You can preach the Gospel of Jesus anywhere." That was a message which Clara Ward and others later repeated at virtually each and every performance.

Said Bobby, "We changed everything. We even changed the appearance of the theater, decorating it with stained-glass window panels and the like. Usually we'd line the entire cast up in the rear of the theater and march them down the aisles, sometimes holding candles as they marched and sang. Once on stage they would form a big cross, we'd turn down the houselights, and all you could see was that cross and those candles. It was really impressive."

Leonard Reed, who helped stage some of the gospel shows, added, "We'd

ONE WEEK ONLY
Beginning
FRIDAY, SEPTEMBER 26

HARLEM'S HIGH SPOT
APOLLO
WORLD'S GREATEST COLORED SHOWS
125ᵗʰ ST. near 8ᵗʰ Ave. · Tel. UNiversity 4-4490

1941

SHE'LL RAISE YOUR SPIRITS—
SHE'LL STEAL YOUR HEART

SISTER THARPE

APPEARING WITH

LUCKY MILLINDER and BAND

with Trevor Bacon and a Great Cast, Including
McCAIN & ROSS — FREDDIE & FLO
BURNHAM HARRIS & SCOTT - DEMAY, MOORE & MARTIN

59a.

59b. Christine Clark

seat the entire cast on the stage, like in a minstrel show. They'd all stay there from the beginning of the show 'till the end. Then each act would come down to stage center to perform its specialty, while the rest of the cast backed them up with songs, clapping, and general enthusiasm." The gospel show is built on exhortation—exhortation of the self by each act and exhortation of the other acts by the remainder of the cast. (The exhortation by the way, is the extension of the age-old African system of call and response. It is to be found in such rituals as responsive reading and throughout the services in most black churches; enthusiastic comments by individual members of the congregation are called out as responses to the appeal of the minister.)

Later, in the interest of heightened drama, we added a few musical instruments. "We started out with only an organ," said Bobby, "and then Thurman and Big Dan [another producer] suggested more. So we added a drum and then a guitar, but those were the only three instruments we ever used in a gospel show." In the last analysis, of course, the final enthusiasm-creating instrument was the audience itself, for their spontaneous reactions raised the level of excitement to pitches that sometimes astonished even the performers themselves. "Bobby!" a wide-eyed and ecstatic Christine said after one show, "I finally got the Holy Spirit!" Several members of an all-girl group commented, "We get enthusiastic audience responses in many places, but this audience lifts us ten feet into the air!"

The gospel show brought a new dimension and spirit into the religious arena. Our society has always tended to treat religious practices with great solemnity, even to the point of restraining enthusiasm. But this is not true among blacks. Not in the gospel shows! They traced the essentially religious songs as an expression of sheer exuberance. There are no dirges in gospel; there *is* an earthiness, even a sexuality. Indeed, you can really sum up gospel's basic spirit with one word: hallelujah! Gospel carries a yea-saying, a "Thank you, Lord!" message. It is a release from tension; it expresses a love of Jesus and an ecstacy in the message of redemption. Its participants, audiences and artists alike, are bathed in an aura of joy.

When is a quartet not a quartet? When it is a gospel quartet, of course. Because in gospel, a quartet is a group of male singers which may number four, five or more, and still be called a quartet. Any of these groups, The Mighty Clouds of Joy, The Soul Stirrers, The Pilgrim Travelers, and The Five Blind Boys of Mississippi, would be called quartets in the rarefied world of gospel. As you can see, their numbers do not always add up to four. They are usually clad in street clothes when they sing, but their connection with the street ceases then and there. Each of these groups has seen many changes of personnel over the years, and some of them have spawned singers who later went on to considerable fame in the pop field. Such stars as Isaac Hayes, Sam Cooke, and Lou Rawls appeared in gospel quartets at one time or another and then left to become major pop stars.

Some think of gospel as a field dominated by women. I do not wholly

60a. Gospel Group

60b. The Pilgrim Travelers

agree for although many of the enduring names in gospel belong to females, there are far too many men. Still, Mahalia Jackson, Clara Ward, Roberta Martin, Sallie Martin, Willie Mae Ford Smith, Marion Williams, Dorothy Love Coates, Inez Andrews, Shirley Caesar—the list of women gospelers goes on and on. The women nearly always dressed in church gowns, for as one of them put it backstage at the Apollo, "It lets us sweat easier that way." And sweat they did, sometimes from other causes than their gowns; there was no way that a mere gown was going to desex some of those women. Clara Ward's group, for example, wore high and exotic wigs, and their lavish theatrical makeup was hardly that of cloistered women. But they were not the only gospelers who did little to hide their sexuality. Sex, after all, became a part of the gospelers' exuberant message dedicated to life!

We were never privileged to play her at the Apollo but, by all odds, the most famous gospeler of them all was Mahalia Jackson. She was a woman of prodigious talents and dynamic personality, which she used in projecting her musical message. Her idol, so history tells us, was the blues-singing queen, Bessie Smith. Mahalia Jackson's most enduring contribution to gospel was that she blended gospel's unique sounds with the blues she had absorbed from early listening to Bessie.

If sex was a portion of the gospel-singers message, that fact doesn't indicate any lack of sincerity on the gospeler's part. Still, there it was, backstage and on stage. Says Bobby, "They were an earthy bunch and the carryings-on backstage were as overt and blatant as you could find anywhere." Hans Nielson, our stage manager, was a little shocked. "I was brought up a Catholic and I always thought that religious people behaved in a very straight manner. Boy! Was I surprised when I saw how those gospel singers carried on backstage! I mean, I never expected anything like *that!*"

On stage, there was a forceful projection of sex appeal, but none projected it more dynamically than Sam Cooke, who left gospel later on to become one of the hottest pop singers until his tragic early death. Sam rose to fame as the lead singer with the Soul Stirrers, and when he switched to pop he took his own distinctive yodel with him. It fitted in pop as it had in gospel.

In many respects, the all-gospel show combines rare anomalies, and yet these shows were also a logical extension of the black church and its practices. In the rural South, for instance, virtually all social activity revolved about the local church. Its minister became a combination of unoffical mayor, judge, master of ceremonies, showman, and philosopher. In short, he was the leader around whose personality and wit the life of the community revolved. They were spellbinders in the pulpit; they were the centers of attention out of it. The mantle of those showmen-churchmen-leaders fell upon the shoulders of the leaders of the singing groups, some of whom actually were ministers, when they took their gospel songs into theaters. Alex Bradford, Clara Ward, James Cleveland, and the Reverend C. L. Franklin (Aretha's father) are but a few who carried on the traditions that were part of their own cultural heritage.

The first all-gospel show was presented at the Apollo in 1955. Its cast would be impossible to put together today, and even a relative newcomer to gospel would be amazed at the list of performers. It included Christine Clark, the Soul Stirrers (with Sam Cooke as its star), the Dixie Hummingbirds, the Suwannee Quartet, the Swan Silvertone Singers, the Five Blind Boys of Mississippi (only four, however were blind), the Caravans with Albertina Walker and Alex Bradford. The Dixie Hummingbirds became international celebrities, especially when they joined Paul Simon in recording "Loves Me Like a Rock," surely one of the greatest pop-gospel songs.

In the Swan Silvertone Singers was the Reverend Claude Jeter, about whom Bobby said, "In my opinion, Jeter is the greatest of all the male gospel singers!" The Reverend Alex Bradford was an earlier practitioner of the falsetto voice (as was Jeter and a whole coterie of modern "pop" singers, including Smokey Robinson). He used the falsetto in sudden elisions from his normal husky baritone voice. (The falsetto, it should be noted, has an African tradition and is sometimes traced to Islamic origins.) The genial Bradford started in vaudeville as a song and dance man, and to the fervor of his gospel songs he added the deft and sure showman's touch that only a born performer reared in vaudeville could bring. He was an economic success.

I would nominate James Cleveland as the preeminent male gospel figure. He wrote more than 275 gospel songs, but that isn't the prime reason. He helped teach Aretha Franklin to play the piano (he appeared to have copied Roberta Martin's style), he was sometimes called the "Louis Armstrong of Gospel" because his voice became so hoarse from shouting although more often he is called, simply, "King James." No, James Cleveland is important because he helped mold gospel and pop into a unique and unforgettable musical form.

In one Apollo show in 1956 still another innovation was successfully tried: a battle of gospel quartets. They were calculated to create an atmosphere of excitement, but hysteria was more the order of the day when the gospelers battled for supremacy.

Gospel singing is a family tradition in many American families, white and black. But no family that I know of was able to parlay that avocation into an exciting, world-renowned act with quite the success of the Staple Singers. Led by their guitar-playing father, Roebuck (whose musical roots go back to the legendary blues-singing guitarist Big Bill Broonzy), the Staples include Cleotha, Mavis, Yvonne, and Purvis. Some of Mavis' big, moving contralto renditions invaded the pop field and, as was the case with other artists, this created problems for them. Indeed, the Staples, along with other gospel singers like Sam Cooke, Al Green, Clara Ward, and Aretha Franklin, were rebuffed by some of their former followers. It was a painful experience for all of them. Sometimes one could slide from pop back to the gospel field, but a lot of forgiving had to be offered by the church set first.

There are those who consider Clara Ward the greatest female gospel singer, even surpassing such luminaries as Mahalia Jackson, Roberta Martin, or Willie

61a. The Mighty Clouds of Joy

61b. The Five Blind Boys

61c. The Soul Stirrers

62a. James Cleveland

62b.

62c. The Staple Singers

62d. Clara Ward and Her Gospel Singers

Mae Ford Smith. Certainly there is little question that the Clara Ward Singers rank among the most successful gospel groups. Clara was a first-rate pianist, a moaner as great as any, a musical innovator, and a marvelous artist; but those who knew the Ward Singers best acknowledged that Clara's mother, Mrs. Gertrude Mae Murphy Ward, who started the group when Clara was a child, was the driving force behind the Ward Singers' immense success. Their biggest recorded hit is titled "Surely." In their fancy wigs and colorful gowns, they made show-business history by adding a colorful dimension to gospel that it never had before. The conservative faction denied that such innovations represented progress (and indeed, some of them actually seemed ashamed of Clara and her singers), while show-business buffs could only admire them. Late in their career, the Clara Ward Singers invaded the night-club circuit and toward the end their popularity with the white Las Vegas crowd far surpassed their following among blacks.

Not among the least of Clara Ward's contributions was her presentation of Marion Williams as a member of the group; the fans of gospel acknowledged her as one of the most gifted gospel practitioners of them all. For a number of years, Marion was the mainstay and backbone of the Clara Ward Singers, but long before the group headed out on the nightclub trail, she and others had left. Her departure may have dented their style, but it didn't slow the group down. In Clara's last years, buoyed by Aretha Franklin's public acknowledgement of her debt to Clara, the Ward Singers continued until Clara died in 1973, survived by her reputation, her records, and her mother.

As with Aretha Franklin, who copied and built on Clara Ward's style, the influence of gospel singers on the pop and blues fields was profound. Sallie Martin, one of the early, legendary figures in gospel trained a piano-playing singer named Ruth Jones when the latter was a youngster. Ruth was the real name of Dinah Washington. Sam Cooke, who was the featured star with the Soul Stirrers before "going pop," was influenced in turn by that group's originator, A. H. Harris, who in turn acknowledged *his* debts to a legendary figure in blues, Blind Lemon Jefferson. Then here is Wilson Pickett, who leaned on the Reverend Julius Cheeks, leader of the immensely popular group called the Sensational Nightingales and later the Sensational Knights. B. B. King has patterned much of his style on the songs of Sam McCrary; Cissy Houston of the Drinkard Singers passed more than a few tips over to her manager's daughters, Dionne and Dee Dee Warwick; while the Meditation Singers included a unique stylist in Della Reese. The Dixie Nightingales included pop star David Ruffin; Marvin Gaye's early training was in a church whose minister was his father; Lou Rawls, of course, sprang from the Pilgrim Travelers, and Isaac Hayes has also acknowledged his debt to early training in gospel. Straddling the line between gospel and pop was Faye Adams, whose 1953 disc "Shake a Hand" shook a few rafters from coast to coast.

No one ever claimed that the entertainment business offers a sure-fire, easy road to riches. The truth is that for every fabulously successful artist, there are a thousand who barely survive. Among the performing artists I have known, few have had a tougher road to travel than the singers of gospel. Restricted for the most part to ill-paying church jobs, forced by their occupation to travel extensively through some of the poorer sections of the United States, the gospeler's life is nearly as hard as was the life of their Lord. One of our comedians, after a tough Sunday schedule, turned to my father and said, "This is sure a tough way to make an easy living!"

Listen to Lou Rawls reminisce about his early days: "You went from town to town in rickety old cars and you slept in church members' homes—if they opened them up to you. If not, you slept in your car. I was singing with a group called the Highway QCs and Sam Cooke was part of the group. The pay was pretty poor and there were times when we weren't paid at all." No wonder Sam, Lou, and others deserted the field of pure gospel for the lucrative world of pop.

Lou is currently the most successful refugee from the gospel. His rich baritone may sound like sermonizing, but the appeal is to earthbound ethics.

The hard-line gospel followers don't forget those who abandon gospel. They virtually shun those who try to straddle musical fields and combine gospel, pop, and soul. Rosetta Tharpe sang gospel in nightclubs, theaters, and arenas. To her sorrow, she became persona non grata among the gospel purists. Clara Ward, who never sang love songs, had only a slightly less traumatic experience. The masters of soul, the Staple Singers, consider themselves gospelers, but the conservatives have rejected them.

The most heart-breaking example of a former gospeler's treatment by his former followers was to be found late in Sam Cooke's career. It is described by Tony Heilbut in his book *The Gospel Sound.*

> There came a time in the mid-sixties when Cooke thought of returning to gospel. For about six weeks he managed to attend Soul Stirrer concerts, and, coincidentally, they always asked him to sing. But gospel followers are a hard, unforgiving lot, and the scheme didn't work. The saddest occasion was the Soul Stirrers' anniversary in Chicago. All the old members attended and Harris himself emceed. . . . While the Soul Stirrers were on stage, they called Sam up. I was the emcee but I didn't know nothing about it. Somehow when Sam hit the stage, the crowd went dead and stayed dead till Jimmy Outler and Paul Foster came back. Folks were hollering, 'Get that blues singer down. Get that no good so-and-so down. This is a *Christian* program. And it pierced me to my heart, it *shamed* me how he was rejected by the home people. He walked off the stage, tearin'. He was hurt badly."[1]

Why do men and women go into gospel? Why subject themselves to the trials and tribulations, the rejections and the ardent demands thrust upon them in that field? I think it is because gospel performs a function not only for its listeners but for the singers who are in it. One might say, for starters, that the blues tell it like it is, while gospel offers "saving Grace." Tony Heilbut has pointed out that most gospel singers are "depression children." Seen in this light, the *art* of gospel singing is designed simultaneously to lift the spirit and express the joy of Christianity's message. It is the ultimate answer to those who think that every aspect of religion must be clothed in solemnity, must be chanted in lugubrious tones. No! A good case can be made for the opposite. At last there is a message of relief, release and peace to a group of people whose lives really are a "vale of tears." Gospel is earthy, physical, and uplifting. It is an expression of the ultimate, soaring joy wrenched from the soul of people whose lives have seen precious little happiness.

BLUE NOTES

To Duke Ellington "blues are basic to all jazz"[2] and to LeRoi Jones "blues is the parent of all legitimate jazz."[3] Blues are constructed in twelve bars with the verses in an A A B pattern and they contain "blue notes," those flatted thirds, fifths, and sevenths.[4] To Samuel Charters blues contain the sounds of a special brand of lyric poetry,[5] and in Bruce Cook's lexicon they are the "fundamental American music."[6]

They are all correct; for the blues are more than mere music or poetry; they are more than a particular construction or even a special kind of sound. They are the stuff which, in a unique language and encompassing words and music, express to their authors and the world the special character found in the life of almost every black person in America.

In his book of reminiscences, *Night People,* the great jazz trombonist Dickie Wells explains the blues in the simplest of terms: "We all get the dumps some time, and then you've got the blues, nothing but, and when you start reciting your woes to yourself or another, then you're singing the blues. Maybe the melody isn't there, but it's the blues just the same. Our outlet for misery is the twelve-bar blues, and I guess we owe some thanks to the great W. C. Handy."[7]

Save for the restriction limiting them to "the twelve-bar blues," Wells' statement encapsulates the basics of the blues about as well as any statement I know of, for the blues are at least as much emotional as musical. They are a particularly American and a distinctively black mode.

The connection between gospel and blues is strong for, musically and emotionally, they are constructed of similar stuff. Many of the blues singers of renown sang gospel; some, like the legendary Son House, were ministers who suffered guilt because they sang the blues at all. Indeed, all of Son House's blues were strongly flavored with distinctive gospel sounds. Mamie Forehand and Blind Willie Johnson actually sang spirituals in the twelve-bar blues form, and Dinah Washington and Muddy Waters both sang gospel at one time or another.

In speaking of the strong kinship between blues and gospel, Duke Ellington had this to say:

The blues were wordy songs, but the gospel songs and spirituals of the black churches were also an important element from the beginning, for the way they

63a. Wynonie "Mr. Blues" Harris

63b. Joe Turner

63c.

were sung, the soulfulness and great enthusiasm, made an unforgettable impression on most jazz musicians when they were young. If you compare records by Bessie Smith and the great gospel singer Mahalia Jackson, you will see that despite the difference in *what* they sang, there is a similarity in the *way they sang, and that there is a joint relationship with early forms of jazz expression.*[8]

But in the world of church folk the blues were known as the "Devil's music," an acknowledgement that their wordy messages ran counter to the more rarified and exalted themes found in gospel. Indeed, a recent book by Giles Oakley is succinctly titled *The Devil's Music.* About the blues and the black church's attitude Oakley says: "For large portions of the community the blues was still the devil's music, the music of immorality, licentiousness, eroticism, whiskey-drinking, juke joints, low-life violence, a source of corruption, a harbinger of social disruption. And to many blacks salvation was to be found in ridding from the race its stereotyped image of irresponsibility and unreliability."[9]

Both blues and gospel music are based on the African ring-shout; it is in the subject matter of their lyrics that they go off in opposite directions, for if they both sing of love, their concept of it involves wholly disparate worlds. Put in the simplest of terms, the love found in the blues is physical, sexual, and utterly worldly. If it is exalted, it is so only through the highly charged exaltation which pain can bring. The pain found in promiscuity discovered, the pain found in infidelity inflicted, the pain set loose by rejection and frustration—those are the tortures inherent in blues' heady themes. Often a desire to escape is expressed:

> Feeling tomorrow like I feel today,
> If I feel tomorrow like I feel today,
> I'll pack my suitcase and make my getaway.

The common notion that the blues are solely about love and sex is untrue, for careful reading of blues lyrics reveals that their scope is as broad as the lives of the people who sing and write them. Some of their underpinning is to be found in the work songs, those musical concoctions that were part of earthly labors ranging from picking cotton to hauling timber and breaking up rocks on the chain gangs of the South. Their themes transcended mere love and its frustrations. They sang feelingly about their lot, about justice and injustice, about prison, the fear of it and the desire to leave it, about the world and its problems, about life. And if the loves of the black men and women who wrote and sang so feelingly were frustrating and melancholy, well then, they were hardly different from the experience of all of us.

Some blues lyrics tell a story, like Willie Newborn's

> Well, I left Margit, on the way back to
> Memphis, Tennessee.
> Well, I left Margit, on the way back to

Memphis, Tennessee.
No sooner I got at the bus station, Lord,
the police arrested poor me.

Lord the police arrest me, carried me before
the judge.
Police, 'rest me, take me 'fore the judge.
Well, the law talks so fast I didn't have
time to say nary a word.

Well, the lawyer plead and the judge he
wrote it down,
Lawyer plead and the judge he wrote it down.
Says I'll give you ten days, buddy, down in
little Shelby town.

Blind Willie McTell's verse merely evokes a mood:

Blues grabbed me at midnight, didn't turn me
loose 'til day,
Blues grabbed me at midnight, didn't turn me
loose 'til day,
I didn't have no mama to drive these blues
away.

While a humorous piece goes

You can always tell when your woman got
another man,
You can always tell when your woman got
another man,
Your meals ain't regular and your house
ain't never clean.

At and around the turn of the century, the blues singers of the deep South and in particular in the Mississippi Delta were a traveling lot. Indeed, traveling was the way in which they eked out a precarious living. They went from one small town to another, singing at barbeques, church picnics, dances, and similar occasions. Most of them sang gospel songs as well as blues. To me, they were a kind of latter-day troubador, a concept I think is helpful in understanding what the blues singers and shouters really were. Like the troubadors of old, they traveled; like them they usually carried and used a stringed instrument. They were the entertainers, the conscious and subconscious voices of their constituents. They even brought their listeners news, not the daily newspaper headlines but the news that they weren't totally alone. It was the news that in the melancholy character of their lives there was company aplenty and perhaps even a kind of forlorn hope of better times to come. The listeners' inchoate cries were echoed in the verbalized shouts and wails of the blues singer who, guitar or harmonica in hand, told all who would listen just how it was to be black in America.

Sometimes there was a note of protest:

> The nigger and the white man playing Seven-up,
> The nigger win the pot, but he's afraid to pick it up.

Son House's courageous shout told it "like it was":

> Down South when you do anything that's wrong,
> Down South when you do anything that's wrong,
> Down South when you do anything that's wrong,
> They'll sure put you down on the country farm.

Some of these troubadors composed the lyrics as they went along; indeed, many of the writers about the blues have pointed out that the repetition of the first two lines was probably for the dual purpose of adding drama through repetition and giving the singer time to think up the next line.

The blues have been divided into two broad categories: the urban and the country blues. Both forms have been called offspring of the Depression. It is because emotional depression is so human an experience that all of us, white or black, can hear the blues, hear them deep down, hear them where they grab us. (Ray Charles has said that if a white person could sing the blues, it would have to be a Jew.) It is not altogether surprising that a great number of blues singers have been blind. Perhaps the fact of their blindness gave them the deeper insights that enabled them to feel and speak of life's impact. Perhaps their affliction piled on top of normal burdens made their melancholy all the more poignant.

Blind Willie McTell sings of a love affair:

> The big star fallin', mama, 'taint long 'fo day,
> The big star fallin', mama, 'taint long 'fo day,
> Maybe the sunshine will drive these blues away.

Blind Boy Fuller was sometimes humorous:

> Little lean woman can't draw my pay.
> She haven't got a thing to drive my blues away.

Blind Lemon Jefferson, Blind Boy Fuller, Blind Willie McTell, Blind Blake, Blind Roosevelt Graves, Blind Willie Johnson, and Blind Joe Reynolds—to these sightless blues singers of a bygone age we must add two great names from today's scene: Al Hibbler, who for years sang with Duke Ellington and then went out to become a major star on his own, and, of course, the genius Ray Charles.

Of his blindness and his life, Ray had these telling observations to make in an interview in *Playboy:* "I learned how to handle my blindness pretty early in life, thanks to my mother and a little hard work . . . but because I'm a black man whatever affects my people affects me. This means that the greatest handicap I've had—and still have—is my color." [10] Imagine, my fellow white folks, imagine if you can how it must feel to acknowledge that your color is a worse trauma than blindness.

The first blues to be published was "The Memphis Blues," by W. C. Handy, the "father of the blues." The first blues to be recorded was called "Crazy Blues," sung by Mamie Smith in 1920. That record is notable more because it was the first than because it was the best. Although Mamie Smith (no relation to Bessie) was an able blues singer, the choice of "Crazy Blues" was made, it seems, not because it was a great song but because the studio people thought it would be acceptable to the public.

In the early days, before and around the turn of the century, the blues were called "the reel." One of the reel's greatest practitioners was Blind Lemon Jefferson. In true troubador fashion, Jefferson traveled throughout the South singing and later recording. He died in a Chicago snowstorm in 1929. Lemon combined the ancient African field-holler with the Texas "gang shout." He accompanied himself on the guitar with unpredictable improvisations and rhythms. At one time or another, he performed with Huddie "Leadbelly" Ledbetter and had a strong influence on him. Blind Lemon was able to impart an aura of loneliness to his songs; he sang everything, including hymns, in addition to the blues. A long list of blues singers and shouters sprang from the creative seeds dropped on the Southern landscape by Lemon. In addition to Leadbelly, there were Big Bill Broonzy, Robert Johnson, Son House, Booker White, Lightning Hopkins, Henry Townsend, Furry Lewis, Lonnie Johnson, and Bessie Smith.

Blind Lemon left a lot more songs than "Black Snake Moan" behind him, but this is one of my favorites:

Um-um, black snake crawling in my room.
Um-um, black snake crawling in my room.
Yes, some pretty mama better get this black snake soon.

Um-mm—what's the matter now?
Um-mm—what's the matter now?
Tell me what's the matter, baby? "I don't like no
     black snake nohow."

Well, I wonder where this black snake's gone.

I wonder where this black snake's gone.
Lord, that black snake, mama, done run my mama home.

There were many black women besides Bessie Smith who added their higher-pitched sounds to blues history. Since they were less mobile—the requirements of children and family keeping them closer to the hearth—they came along a bit later. Ma Rainey, Alberta Hunter, (who composed and sang and is still, at about age 88, singing), Clara Smith, Trixie Smith, Sarah Martin, Chippie Hill, Sippie Wallace, Ida Cox, and Victoria Spivey round out the list of blues-singing immortals.

Here is one of Ma Rainey's melancholy blues:

My man left this morning just about half past four.
My man left this morning just about half past four.
He left a note on the pillow saying he couldn't use me no more.

I grabbed a pillow, turned over in my bed.
I grabbed a pillow, turned over in my bed.
I cried about my daddy until my cheeks turned cherry red.

It's awful hard to take it, it was such a bitter pill.
It's awful hard to take it, it was such a bitter pill.
If the blues don't kill me that man's meanness will.

Of the men listed above, none ranks higher than the man known as Leadbelly, for this forbidding and unpredictable man not only sang the blues, he wrote them too. In addition to "Good Night, Irene," there were also "The Rock Island Line" and "Take This Hammer." Leadbelly was not regarded as an especially good musician or singer by many of his musical contemporaries. As with many of the modern-day blues singers, his popularity probably was greater with whites than blacks. Certainly, as the object of a cult Leadbelly has been placed there by whites, not blacks. Pops Foster, pioneering jazz bass player, in his book *Pops Foster, New Orleans Jazz Man* had this to say about Leadbelly: "Leadbelly didn't know which key he was going to play in. He'd play in all naturals and sharps. We'd listen to him and then search and search around to find the key." He wasn't the first celebrated musician, of course, with a limited knowledge of music. I recall my father expressing shock about Leadbelly's singing. "I thought he was awful," he said.

In 1949 we played another blues immortal, Lonnie Johnson, at the Apollo. He was a small man, a quiet man. He was also a contemplative man, and it is that quality which made him so outstanding in the field of urban blues. Lonnie Johnson was a keen observer of human beings, and since his own life was replete with tragedies, movement, and change, he was able to inject the knowledge he gained into the songs he sang and wrote. One of the greatest of all the blues guitarists, he also played piano, violin, mandolin, and at one time or another, he recorded with Louis Armstrong, Duke Ellington, Victoria Spivey, and others.

Lonnie said, "It [the blues] comes from my soul within. The heartaches and the things which have happened to me in my life—that's what makes a good blues singer."[11] Lonnie Johnson composed and sang sad songs, sweet songs, gay songs, bawdy songs. One of his hits spoke of the "jelly roll," a sexual allusion that crops up often in blues songs. Like the "black snake" and a man's "pay," the blacks were perhaps being careful to conceal from whites their sexuality, always a dangerous area in the South.

> She said, Mr. Jelly Roll Baker, let me be your slave.
> When Gabriel blows his trumpet then I'll rise from
>   my grave,
> For some of your good jelly roll,
> Yes, I love your jelly roll.
> It's good for the sick, yes,
> And it's good for the old!!
>
> She said, Can I put an order in, for two weeks ahead?
> I'd rather have your jelly roll than my home-cooked bread.
> I love your jelly roll,
> I love your good jelly roll.

Wynonie Harris, who appeared at the Apollo dozens of times during the forties and fifties, was known in the trade as a "shouter." The term means exactly what it says—a singer whose voice was registered more in decibels than in tone but who nevertheless was able to make a musical impact on audiences. You had only to hear Wynonie once to know why he fell into that category; his tonsils were probably made of leather, his larynx of steel, and his vocal chords of cat gut. Don't get the idea, though, that Wynonie was without talent. Shouting or not, he was singing the blues.

In a somewhat different tradition was Aaron "T-Bone" Walker, who added some spectacular guitaring to a quieter, mellower blues voice. T-Bone's guitar-playing was on the showy side; the instrument usually ended up behind his neck or back while he still strummed away, but if that seems a trifle bizarre, it didn't seem to interfere with the quality of his playing, which was of the first order. His singing voice was more like a balladeer's than a blues singer's because "that's the kind of blues I like," he said. His guitar playing was a decided and acknowledged influence on B. B. King's style. Followers of rock can add the name of Chuck Berry to those influenced by T-Bone.

Of a different order altogether was Eddie "Mr. Cleanhead" Vinson, who also popped up during that groovy period. Eddie got his nickname because his head was so devoid of hair that it shone. Whether that was so because he was totally bald or totally shaven I never did discover, but there was never any doubt that on alto sax or doing vocals, Eddie Vinson was a consumate bluesman.

Joe Turner is a large man, both in physique and blues stature. His billing line is "Boss of the Blues," and if Joe is not the absolute boss, he ranks high on the list. Sometimes Joe's efforts could be branded as "shouting," but he is also capable of singing the blues soft and mellow. He belongs to a small group of blues singers who transcended the forties and lasted into the fifties and beyond. He's still at it.

There is, for instance, the late Jimmie Rushing. For many years he was the vocalizing mainstay of the Count Basie Band. Of the Basie group, Dickie Wells wrote, "At its best the Basie rhythm section was nothing less than a Cadillac with the force of a Mack truck." If that is true, the driveshaft was often Jimmie Rushing, whose voice was as flexible as he was. (Despite his girth, Jimmy was quick and nimble on his feet.) Once you heard Jimmie you never could forget his "Goin' to Chicago / Sorry that I can't take you—oooh!"

Johnny Otis was sometimes called the "Godfather of the Blues." Actually Johnny was a kind of way station between pure blues and what came to be known as rhythm and blues. He will probably be best remembered for the people he brought along with him than for what he himself did. There was, for instance, Willie Mae "Big Mama" Thornton, who tore up many an Apollo show both with and without Johnny's performing troupe. She was, to put it kindly, a large woman, and her voice was exactly what you would have expected from a gal who probably tipped the scales at two hundred and forty or so. Like Wynonie Harris, Jimmie Rushing, and others, Big Mama was a shouter. Another of Johnny's performers was Marie Adams.

But the prize artist of them all showed up one day when she was a mere fourteen years old. She was short and dark, not exactly the glamor-girl type, but when she started to sing, strange things happened, for this kid had one of the most intuitively unique styles and voices we had ever heard. Back in the early fifties, she went under the name "Little Esther," and in her initial appearances she was a smash. Her career, however, spans a number of years, for it went into a total eclipse until the seventies, when Little Esther resurfaced as Esther Phillips and launched a new career that is still going strong. Esther Phillips is not a standard blues singer; she is that rare performer who defies classification.

There were those who thought that when Jimmie Rushing tired of the road and retired from the Basie Band (but not from singing) that organization would never be the same. They reckoned without Joe Williams, who succeeded Jimmie and remained with the Basie organization for some years. Basie calls him his "number one son." Joe Williams can sing blues, ballads, and jazz, and is an another artist whom it is hard to classify. But he has a rare ability to handle the blues. When Joe left Basie, he was succeeded by O. C. Smith, no mean blues singer himself.

And then we come to Ray Charles, a chapter, a book, an epoch all by himself. There is no way to classify the man; he remains one of the transcending geniuses of the jazz age. Ray can do ballads and novelty songs; he even did some great country and western albums. (Country and western is first cousin to the country blues, having sprung from them.) One need only listen to his classic "Georgia on My Mind" to know that Ray Charles is master of the blues. I do not exaggerate when I say that I have seen grown men cry while listening to Ray do that song. The blues touch and transform absolutely everything Ray Charles does.

What are the influences that helped shape his artistry? For starters, you have to go back to Nat "King" Cole. Ray talked often about how he'd listen to Nat, then try to sound as much like him as possible. And also Charles Brown, the man who recorded "Driftin' Blues" in the fifties and who is suddenly enjoying a renaissance in popularity. Charles and the Three Blazers were one of our major attractions back in those days, and our switchboard lights kept flickering on and off with calls for the tall, handsome singer all during his engagements. Ray has also talked of the influence of Art Tatum on his musical style, even though their pianos don't sound like each other. Musical influences are often so subtle that it takes a keen ear to pick up the nuances, but they are there nevertheless. The musicians involved know them even if you and I don't.

The blues parlay, which spanned five decades at least, went something like this: blues to rhythm-and-blues to rock and roll to soul. The fifties was the transitional period when emphasis and support in the black audience shifted from pure blues to rhythm-and-blues. Joe Turner was one of those able to make the shift, for "Shake, Rattle and Roll" jumped from pure blues to rock blues in one gigantic leap. Joe was a shouter in his days as a pure blues stylist; he remained a shouter in rhythm-and-blues. (Rhythm-and-blues, it should be noted, is broader, less rigid, less countrified than pure blues; it includes blues shouting, blues ballads, blues that jump, even elements of gospel.) Roy Brown followed with "Trouble at Midnight" and then "Good Rockin' Tonight" (also recorded successfully by Wynonie Harris).

A host of singers, male and female, followed to end the popular era of pure blues and bring on its successors, rhythm-and-blues and rock. There was Ruth Brown, an ex-Apollo amateur who could handle everything from slow blues to fast rock, and Big Maybelle, as big in stature as she was in voice. Out of the tradition of the talented Lil Green of the forties ("In the Dark" was her smash hit) rose, for instance, a gal like Lavern Baker, whose throaty voice shook the old Apollo rafters on many a memorable occasion.

Joe Liggins and his Honeydrippers, Roy Milton and his Solid Senders, guitar-playing and singing Pee Wee Crayton, Jimmy Witherspoon, Nappy Brown, Amos Milburn—one after another they paraded their talents, issued their records, rose to stardom. Some became more than casual stars. Like Fats Domino, for instance. He was a major Apollo headliner for several years and is still a rock star of formidable talents. Nor can I forget Bo Diddley and Louis Jordan, who was not purely a rhythm-and-blues artist; he was too much of an entertainer to be confined. He wanted to make you laugh, and he did, but his alto saxophoning was serious.

There are more. There was John Lee Hooker, for instance, a man who first recorded back in 1948, a chap who learned the guitar from his father, who, in turn, had learned from Charley Patton, Blind Blake and Lemon Jefferson. Nor can I leave out Ivory Joe Hunter, Percy Mayfield, and Johnny Ace.

Why was there a shift, a sudden movement away from pure blues? That fact is a matter of regret, concern, and frustration to some of the blues artists themselves. B. B. King, for instance, mentioned his frustration at not being accepted in the sixties by the white college kids who were accepting other blues artists, but his deeper concern was that blues itself was being rejected by black people everywhere. Why?

The traditional explanation has been that they didn't want to be reminded of the humiliating, segregated, disaster-ridden past, whose cry from the heart was inherent in classical blues. But while this is probably true, it doesn't suffice entirely to explain the move away from the blues. The shift in emphasis and interest lies in a restless surging toward new and more exciting forms. It was tied to the restlessness of the times; even more so it was tied to the eager searching of the youth of the day. They wanted to strike out on their own; they really weren't interested in following the lead and dictates of their parents; they wanted a sound in which they had a personal and a creative stake! In the postwar era there was, it seems to me, more hope, a thrusting forward of selves, a need to be part of a dynamic new dimension. And so, during the fifties, it was rhythm-and-blues, then rock, and then, in the sixties and seventies, soul. But all of them, it must be remembered, are extensions built on the solid foundations of the twelve-bar blues!

Thus, if the up-and-coming young musicians rejected the pure blues as "old-fashioned," they nevertheless saw to the bending and altering of those same blues into the various shapes that culminated in soul. Charles Keil, in his interesting and provocative book, *Urban Blues,* has literally page upon page defining the music known as soul,[12] but in my judgment, soul boils down to the old blues blended with the old gospel sound and combined creatively in a newer, more vibrant guise. Soul became the latest in a dazzling series of blues innovations culminating in the exciting work of "Soul Brother Number," "The Godfather of Soul," or whatever title you wish to bestow upon James Brown.

In this acquisitive society of ours, of course, money is a motivating factor of surpassing force. The big money, after all, has always been pop music rather than in such forms as blues. And pop was a field long denied black performers until the arrival of Billy Eckstine and Nat "King" Cole. They saw to it that the black man, as a singer of romantic ballads, was no longer persona non grata in the white world of Tin Pan Alley. Following their success, some black artists cast longing and covetous glances at the pop field, even as they were still singing the blues.

One such was the late Dinah Washington. Now Dinah was basically a blues singer, a blues singer of inordinate talent. In my judgment she should have stayed there. Still, one can hardly fault her for wanting a shot at something bigger, and so she swung out into the pop field. Nor was her foray without success. "It's Too Soon to Know," "This Bitter Earth," and other songs were recorded with considerable success, and yet their success was still primarily restricted to the black audiences who were already fans of hers. Even so, you can't listen to any of Dinah's discs without recognizing that here was essentially a singer of blues, first, last, and always.

Earlier, I pointed out that in the sixties and early seventies there was a renaissance of interest in the blues, but the interest was evinced primarily by the white college students and other white intellectuals. Why was this so? One must remember that the blues were new to them; they had never experienced the miseries of life in the Mississippi Delta or other deep South areas during the Depression era. The bitter associations that burned deeply into black memories were totally absent among these new listeners. To them it could become an intellectual experience, even an emotional one.

There remain a handful of blues artists who achieved stardom in the fifties, sixties, and seventies. Some of them are still performing today; some have died. They deserve to be recognized; in some cases their careers or contributions should be detailed. There was, for instance, a chap named Chester Burnett, who performed as the "Howling Wolf." A large man, an energetic man, Wolf played the Apollo and other selected spots, bringing his Mississippi Delta blues style plus a soulful harmonica. He played with reckless abandon, presenting a blasting series of seering and moaning songs that electrified audiences wherever he went. I do not know if Wolf eventually burned out, but he died in 1976.

And then there was McKinley Morganfield, better known as Muddy Waters. Muddy Waters specialized in what might be called the up-dated Delta blues; he was the inheritor of the traditions of Son House and Robert Johnson. Helped by Big Bill Broonzy, another imposing figure in blues history, Muddy Waters recorded "I Can't Be Satisfied" in 1948 and then went on to become one of the towering figures in modern-day blues. Not the least of his contributions was the gift of two musicians who played with him. Although Waters himself was a first-rate guitar player, his group was augmented by Jimmy Rogers' guitar. Of perhaps even more importance was the harmonica playing of Little Walter, who became a major figure on his own.

The harmonica is a natural adjunct to the blues. It has an inherently mournful sound that fits in with the blues mood. In the hands of Little Walter, the "harp" became an instrument of musical movement, as well as torture— torture to the listener's nerves, torture in the positive sense that it stretched the listener's reactions almost to the breaking point. In 1952, Little Walter recorded "Juke" while with Muddy. He then left to become a star in his own right, a star whose career, eclipsed somewhat in the sixties as were the careers of most blues artists, continued on its frustrated and fitful course until his death in 1968.

Jimmy Reed looked like a one-man band, harmonica strapped around his neck, guitar over his shoulder. He played them simultaneously in the subtle manner popularized in the deep South as "swamp blues." For a while in the fifties and sixties, some of his discs hit the pop charts, and he even had a hit in 1974. Another favorite at the Apollo was Little Johnny Taylor, a blues singer who ranks with the best.

Bobby Bland is at the apex of blues, gospel, and soul. Indicative of that is the fact that he once called himself Bobby "Blue" Bland, although he later eliminated "Blue." That, I hasten to add, is not because he cannot or does not sing the blues. No, it is a gesture to announce himself as more than a blues singer. Bobby started singing in a church choir, a point of origin that does not render him unique. But with his smooth and mellow style, he skillfully blends the musical thrust of gospel with his blues renditions. And he does something else; a soupçon of sex appeal is stirred into the blues in many a Bland con-concoction. Indeed, there is only one other singer in the field whose sex appeal is stronger than that of Bobby Bland.

He is Riley B. King, better known as B. B. King. You can't listen to B. B. King without being struck by the rich timbre of his voice and the direct, no-nonsense quality of his attack, musically speaking. For B. B., perhaps more than any living blues singer, is dedicated to the blues. He not only sings the blues, he is *concerned* about their survival as a musical form identified with his race. This former disc jockey is, in my judgment, the most articulate and sincere exponent of the blues today. That statement is not intended to diminish the stature of other blue singers; it's just that B. B. King is special. His musical debts to others are acknowledged freely and quickly. T-Bone Walker influenced his guitar styling more than anyone, but the great gypsy guitarist, Django Reinhardt, comes in for his fair share of acknowledgment as an influential force in B. B.'s musical world. Other influences were Lonnie Johnson, Blind Lemon Jefferson, Sam McQuery, the great jazz guitarist Charlie Christian, and B. B.'s cousin, the blues man Booker White. As for B. B. King's musical appeal to the women, if Bobby Bland stirs their blood, B. B. literally makes some of them faint.

"See See Rider," "Do You Call That a Buddy?" "I'd Rather Drink Muddy Water"—the records have rolled out without surcease. Some of them were done by other blues artists of note. B. B. did "Goin' to Chicago," which was almost a theme song of Jimmie Rushing. "Cherry Red," another B. B. specialty, was done in a more rural, down-home style by Eddie "Mr. Cleanhead" Vinson. But the most interesting contrast is to be found in the recording of "I'm Gonna Move to the Outskirts of Town." Originally recorded by also saxophonist and singer Louis Jordan, it was a major hit. In Louis' hands it was a showman's piece, delivered with humorous inflection, with eyes popping, with all the consumate showmanship Louis Jordan could muster. B. B. King sings it as straight blues. Whether you prefer his version or Jordan's depends on how serious you want to be about the song. Jordan was always an entertainer; B. B. King is always an artist, and perhaps that is the difference. It is a difference in kind rather than in degree.

In the United States, the blues have always been held in rather low esteem by the white community and during the last twenty-five years, they have been relegated to the back burner by the blacks. A portion of the white community has accepted them eagerly in the couple of decades and perhaps that explains part of black rejection. The blues deserve, in my opinion, a wider popularity in both communities than they have ever had.

For there are many functions that the blues fill. They are catharsis for both singer and listener, the former unburdening himself, the latter being given an artistic soulmate. In the history of the blues the themes they have followed have been many and varied. The most obvious one has been sex, but the blues contain more. There were prison songs, love songs, songs of protest, songs of frustration. Blues lyrics ran the emotional gamut from anger to tenderness, from restraint to overt hostility. They encompassed, in short, the whole range of human emotions. But with all that, the blues are primarily an art form. Ralph Ellison, one of the greatest black writers, had this to say in *Shadow and Act:*

> For the blues are not primarily concerned with civil rights or obvious political protest; they are an art form and thus a transcendence of these conditions created within the Negro community by the denial of social justice. As such they are one of the techniques through which Negroes have survived and kept their courage during the long period when many whites assumed, as some still assume, that they were afraid.[13]

LeRoi Jones, in his provocative book *Blues People,* commented: "Classic blues . . . represented a clearly definable step by the Negro back into the mainstream of American society. Primitive blues had been almost a conscious expression of the Negro's individuality and equally important, his separateness."[14]

Jones is making some subtle distinctions. Note, for instance, that he refers to *classic blues* as the black's step into the mainstream, *primitive* blues as an expression of his *isolation.* The former, then, was an attempt by the Negro to become part of American society; the latter expressed his earlier inability to do so. In the whole range of human emotions there are none, I think, that are as acutely painful as that mournful and melancholy feeling of utter aloneness, rejection, and sense of abandonment by society. Jones further notes: "To understand that you are black in a society where black is an extreme liability is one thing, but to understand that it is the society which is lacking and impossibly deformed because of this lack *and not yourself,* isolated you even more from that society."[15]

The essentials of the blues, perhaps, are best encapsulated in the lyrics of the song "Black and Blue" by Fats Waller and Andy Razaf. The title explains it all.

The blues in their classical form may have been rejected by blacks, but nothing could be more basic in current musical use. They may be disguised as soul, they may have evolved into rhythm-and-blues, and on into rock and roll, but they are still the blues. And if only Joe Turner, Eddie Vinson, and B. B.

King are still singing the old-style blues, a thousand others from Diana Ross to James Brown to Lou Rawls are still wailing them in slightly different form.

NOTES:

1. Tony Heilbut, *The Gospel Sound* (New York: Anchor Books, 1971), p. 90.

2. Duke Ellington, *Music Is My Mistress* (Da Capo Press, 1973), p. 417.

3. LeRoi Jones, *Blues People* (New York: William Morrow, 1963).

4. In the world of jazz there are certain notes that have been labeled "blue notes." They are notes not normally found on the diatonic scale because they fall in between certain others. The blue notes impart a mood of melancholy and are in common use among virtually all jazz musicians.

5. Samuel Charters, *The Poetry of the Blues* (New York: Oak Publications, 1963.)

6. Bruce Cook, *Listen to the Blues* (New York: Scribner, 1973).

7. Dickie Wells, *Night People* (Crescendo Publishing Co., 1971), p. 79.

8. Ellington, *Music Is My Mistress*, p. 418.

9. Giles Oakley, *The Devil's Music: A History of the Blues* (New York: Taplinger Publishing Co., 1977), pp. 216-17.

10. Ray Charles, interview in *Playboy*, 1969.

11. Oakley, *The Devil's Music*, p. 178.

12. Charles Keil, *Urban Blues* (Chicago: Univ. of Chicago Press, 1963).

13. Ralph Ellison, *Shadow and Act*, (New York: Random House, 1953), p. 250.

14. Jones, *Blues People*, p. 86.

15. Ibid., p. 185.

Here Come the Clowns

10

"Open the Door, Richard"

Between the first black comedian's appearance in a post-Civil War minstrel show to Bert Williams' stardom in the *Ziegfield Follies* more than a half century elapsed. And from the heady days of Williams' early appearances on Broadway to Flip Wilson's stardom on a nationwide television series, still another fifty years passed. Yes, it took a long time for white America to wake up to the uniqueness of black humor. Today, black contributions are numerous. For instance: Redd Foxx's *Sanford and Son* has set new styles in situation comedy, Richard Pryor on the screen and TV is an international superstar, Nipsey Russell now appears on everything from TV "Roasts" to quiz shows, and Bill Cosby is nothing short of an American institution, doing standup comedy and starring in commercials. Funny, funny, funny Eddie Murphy joined Pryor in becoming an internationally known superstar.

Tracing black comedy's roots way is both fascinating and depressing, exciting and bewildering. Its origins lie in the early minstrel shows of the nineteenth century, those white spectacles that were dedicated to parodying blacks and rationalizing the institutions of slavery. When black artists finally gained admission to minstrelsy around the time of the Civil War, they too adopted the prevailing attitudes laid out for them by their white predecessors. It was either conform to the prevailing order of things, starve, or be left out entirely.

The white originators of minstrel shows "blackened up" by smearing burnt cork on their faces, then adding the huge white lips which became part of the whole grotesque stereotype. The final picture of the "black man" that emerged was one the audience and performers wanted. In their eyes, he was humorous, gay, contented, and of course subservient! As recently as thirty years ago most black comics were still wearing cork, the same cork their brethren smeared on

---

Clad in a crushed opera hat and a tramp's get-up, taking pratfall after pratfall, Dusty Fletcher intoned "Open the Door, Richard." The song became his theme song. It also became a national craze during the forties, setting the stage for this story of the clowns.

already dark complexions almost a century earlier! They weren't "Uncle Toms," those early black comics; they were survivors in the daily grind for jobs, money, and status. The great Bert Williams was paid several thousand dollars a week even in the twenties, for doing his pantomime, songs, and dances under a layer of cork and confining himself to a segregated dressing room backstage. No wonder a contemporary said that he was "the funniest and the saddest man I ever saw!"

Among others who "blackened up" were Pigmeat Markham, Miller and Lyles, Dusty Fletcher, "Spider Bruce," even Rookie and Joyce, a pair of female comics. Of the major black comedians of that early period, only Jackie "Moms" Mabley probably went corkless, but that was because she started as a dancer. (Though Honi Coles "seems to recall" that even Jackie once wore cork.) Even Willie Bryant and Leonard Reed, whose skins were white but who worked in that part of show biz called "colored," loaded on the cork. Leonard now recalls: "In one show I came in late and rushed onto the stage to do my act without making up. An indignant white lady rushed up, pulled me down from the stage, hissing, 'Don't let me ever catch you up there with those niggers!'" Laughed Leonard, "It was the first time in my life I knew there was a difference, but I found out more about prejudice later. The black performers hated me because they thought I was white; the white performers shunned me because I was black. Hell! I couldn't please nobody!"

Some of the early white critics expressed genuine astonishment when they first noticed that blacks were not all the same color! They learned that when they saw their first all-black minstrel shows, for unlike the white minstrels where *everyone* blackened up, only the comical "end men" wore cork in the black shows. Blackface had become the traditional makeup of the black clown.

Sometimes the use of cork accidentally developed unexpected humorous overtones. Doll Thomas, who traveled with minstrel shows shortly after the turn of the century, recalls being with a show in the South when the great comic, Billy Higgins, got himself in trouble with the law. "Billy," said Doll, "was in jail sleeping it off that night, but doing a show without the comedian was unthinkable. Even though I wasn't a comedian [he was a stagehand] I put on the cork, went out, and did Billy's routine, which I knew by heart, and no one ever knew the difference! I almost died laughing myself when it was over!" Without benefit of makeup, Doll is barely cafe au lait in skin tone, while Higgins was dark. But under the makeup, "We are all alike."

Some of the most illustrious names in show business came out of the black minstrel shows. James Bland, for instance, wrote hundreds of songs, none more famous than "Carry Me Back to Ole Virginny." William C. Handy, father of the blues, was another early minstrel man as were the "mother of the blues," Ma Rainey, and her protege, Bessie Smith. And then there were such legendary artists as William Henry Lane, who danced "the Juba," Sam Lucas, and Billy Kersands, who could get two billiard balls in his mouth at once. He said of himself, "If God wanted me to have a bigger mouth, He'd have to move my ears."

In the early days, every minstrel show included a dramatic sketch. Generally, they contained little homilies portraying the "American Way," minstrelsy's euphemism for rationalizing slavery with its "benefits" to family life, and generally glorifying the status quo. Out of those corny little skits sprang the early patterns of black comedy, the black comics gradually being able to modify the more obvious stereotypes.

In today's theater, most comedians do "standup" comedy; that is, they stand straight before the audience and deliver their lines and gags right "at them." But with only a few exceptions and until the last twenty years or so, most blacks did situational comedy, their work usually being done in skits and sketches. Even some comedians who worked as "singles" (for example Dusty Fletcher) or even in pairs (Miller and Lyles, Butterbeans and Susie, Apus and Estrelita) were basically situational comics. Their acts told stories or presented humor in more dramatic contexts than the more one-dimensional standup variety.

Dusty Fletcher, for instance, played the part of a drunk in doing "Open the Door, Richard." He staggered out on stage carrying a ladder with which he was going to climb to Richard's apartment. Disasters overtook him in the form of pratfalls and spills as he tried to climb the ladder, and finally he had a brush with the law when a cop took a dim view of the noise he was generating. In his monologue, part of which took place with Dusty seated on stage all tangled up in his ladder, was his recollection of that "churchified" lady who laced him down for "being D-R-U-N-K." With his mobile face screwed up in appropriate mimicry, Dusty told Richard that "she talked about my being saved—hah!—about my being made white as the driven snow. Harrh!" he intoned, "can you pitcher *me* being white as eh-nee-thing?" In sweaty blackface, makeup running down his white collar, no audience, most especially a black one, could visualize Dusty as being "white as the driven snow." Their response, therefore, came in gales of laughter, especially if they were comfortably ensconced in the friendly confines of the Apollo.

Comedy of a different sort came with the "indefinite" routines pioneered by Miller and Lyles, authors of "Shuffle Along." In this style of comedy, the lines are never finished by the comics; as you can see, it isn't necessary.

> "I'm gonna see my girl tonight. She's——"
> "You goin' with her?"
> "Yeah, I been going with her since——"
> "You been goin' with her *that* long? Heard she was sick."
> "Yeah. Had to git a doctor for her."
> "Who'd you git?"
> "Old Doc——"
> "You got him? He ain't no good. You outta try——"
> "Naw! Heard he ain't no good neither——"

Miller and Lyles also pioneered in those comedy sketches where the underdog was mocked by the city slicker, but finally won out in the end. Those situations, used in many subsequent scenes by Pigmeat Markham, were replete with country-cousin lines, like the following:

> "Cousin, I noticed some new land down the lane a mile or two. I'm gonna get me a plow, I'm gonna plow it up an' plant me some collards an' some taters."
> "New land. Fool, there ain't no new land here. All we got up here is old land. Where'd you see that new land?"
> "Saw it down to Uncle Ernie's place."
> "Now listen to this fool! That ain't no new land. That's Central Park!"

When Aubrey Lyles, disgusted with the treatment of blacks in the United States, left the country for a while, Flournoy Miller continued his work in comedy aided by such partners as Mantan Moreland and later by Johnny Lee. When Mantan left for Hollywood and stardom in the old Charlie Chan movies with Warner Olin, he left this farewell letter with my father.

A purer, more overt kind of situation comedy evolved in the burlesque-type sketches best remembered as performed by Pigmeat Markham, John "Spider Bruce" Mason, and a whole coterie of others, including Eddie "Rochester" Anderson, Tim Moore, Johnny Lee, Sandy Burns, Jimmy Baskette, Marshal "Garbage" Rogers, "Slidin' Billy" Watson and Crackshot Hackly. When Rochester later performed with Jack Benny, he was actually performing the role of "end man" out of minstrelsy; funny, provocative, teasing, but basically respectful to "the boss."

Others who worked in blackface doing situations were Eddie Green, who starred in radio's "Duffy's Tavern," Montella Steward, Buzzen Burton, Rastus Murray, King Brown, Happy Donover, and Henry Drake. Then too, there were Glenn and Jenkins, Jones and Jones, Gulfport and Brown, and Travis Tucker.

Teamed together were George Williams and Bessie Brown and Joyner and Foster. Pop Foster (not to be confused with the legendary bassplayer Pops Foster) was long a leading comic who put together and produced entire shows and took them on tour with the TOBA. Joyner, his sometime partner, was also a leading comic and, as Doll Thomas recounted, "People came from miles around just to see Joyner *lean,* for somehow or other he could lean at a 45 degree angle without falling." In the midst of a dialogue with Pop, Joyner, without blinking an eye, would go into his lean, the audience straining with him, wondering if he would fall over. He never did!

Then there were the "blackout skits," in which the stage was blacked out at the end of the sketch to add emphasis, signify the end of the bit, and permit the stagehands to strike the scenery and reset the stage for the next act. These evolved in the performing. Although there are synopses of the comic sketches, there are few if any actual scripts around. Indeed, the late George Wiltshire, an actor who played straight man for many of the great comics, once described a typical Apollo rehearsal. "We would walk around the block and talk over the situation. We would trade lines and correct each other, go over the material once or twice and by the time we had circled the theater a couple of times, the rehearsal was finished."

Like the famous "head" musical arrangements of many jazz bands, the scripts of most of these comedy scenes merely "developed." Their themes evolved almost directly out of minstrelsy, and mostly concerned the battle of the underdog against superior odds, somehow managing to win. The character of these themes is well-nigh universal. Here is such a scene performed at the Apollo in 1954 by Pigmeat Markham, George Wiltshire, and Barbara Velasco:

> Pigmeat and Barbara return to her apartment house after "a night on the town." They are both a bit tipsy and Pigmeat is trying to accompany her into her apartment. Barbara may be a bit drunk, but she is not that drunk, and she resists his efforts. As they are arguing and jockeying back and forth, George appears as a cop. He demands to know why they are raising such a ruckus, and then he becomes somewhat threatening. In an effort to smooth things over, Barbara tells him that Pigmeat is her husband and they are just "having a little family argument." The cop's attitude suddenly becomes benign and finally he "orders" them both into the house. Pigmeat, of course, is delighted. So is the audience.
>
> The scene ends in a blackout! The comic underdog has somehow won out.

Nobody had a more expressive face than Dewey Markham, probably the most endurable comic in the history of black show business. Black minstrelsy, carnivals, and the vaudeville stage have successively received the inimitable stamp of his comic genius.

Typical, I suppose, of the comedians masked in blackface was Crackshot Hackly. You can see the "Sad Sam" nature of his comedy in Illustration 64c—the exaggerated mouth, which was outlined in white. Since Crackshot's face was enlivened by a small diamond, set in the middle of a front tooth, one might say

64a. Pigmeat Markham

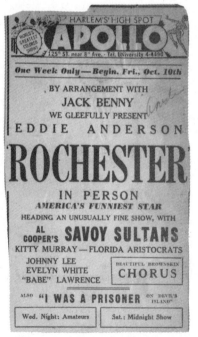

64b.

64c. "Crackshot" Hackley

he had a dazzling smile.

Sometimes the underdog won out but then authority would once again assert itself, leaving him holding the bag. Here is a scene frequently performed by Dusty Fletcher, with George Wiltshire and Vivian Harris doing the "straight" parts.

> A policeman, George, is chasing a man when he drops his handcuffs. Dusty picks them up. The policeman turns around and accuses Dusty of stealing them. Dusty protests that he doesn't even know how they work and when the policeman innocently shows him how, *he* suddenly finds *himself* handcuffed by Dusty. Dusty is not about to let such a golden opportunity go by, and he uses the situation to make things tough for the cop. "Remember that time you hit me with your club?" he asks as he jabs the cop in the ribs. "And remember when you gave me a parking ticket and I didn't even own a car?" he asks as he pushes the cop *over* his own extended leg. "I believe I'm gonna git me a cane and refresh yo' memory," he says as he heads for the wings.
>
> Enter Vivian. The policeman convinces her to open the handcuffs just before Dusty returns. When he does return with his cane, he raises it to strike, only to find the policeman pulling out his pistol! "You were gonna do what?" demands the cop as Dusty stares in disbelief. The audience howls.

Sometimes sex and the color angle enter into a situation, which is tailor-made for laughter. This scene was often performed by John "Spider Bruce" Mason, one of the funniest comics, assisted by Edna Mae Harris and Monte Hawley. As always, Spider was in blackface and as always, even his walk was funny. Germane to the plot is the fact that Monte was light-skinned enough to "pass," had he so chosen.

> The scene is in a hospital corridor and Spider is pacing up and down as the expectant father. A cry announces the birth of a child and a few minutes later, Edna Mae and Monte as the Doctor enter carrying not one, but two bundles. "Twins," she shouts. "Your wife has just given birth to twins!" But when Spider looks, he sees that one baby is very light, the other is black and asks, "How come one of them is so black and the other so light?"
>
> MONTE: That's just the way they were born. Must come from the father.
> SPIDER: Yeah. Well I don't think I'm gonna pay that bill for $200 I just got.
> MONTE: Here's my half.

Sometimes the scenes were unvarnished humor; sometimes they even had a touch of the ghoulish. One of Pigmeat's most famous sketches was the old "graveyard bit," where he and his stooge are looking in the graveyard, which is filled with moving ghosts, revolving tombstones, and the like. As the scene progresses, Pigmeat actually sees the ghost, which so terrifies him that he starts to run, pursued of course, by the apparition. As he runs he is lit up by a flashing spotlight (a gadget called a lobsterscope is attached to the spotlight, making it flash on and off), which creates the illusion of both speed and fear as the two run faster and faster with Pigmeat looking back at the ghost in wild-eyed terror. At the end, Pigmeat becomes so frightened that he "flies" through the air (assisted by a piano wire secured around his waist), the blackout coming as he is in midair.

One blackout ended in near tragedy in 1948. Now Pigmeat was a large man. Six feet tall, he easily tipped the scales at two hundred and twenty pounds. In the midst of his "flight" that weight proved too much for the piano wire that supported him. It snapped just as he reached the apogee of his flight, about eight feet off the stage. In the midst of the blackout, then, Pigmeat shook the rafters and almost put a hole in the stage as he crashed down. He broke both ankles in the jarring fall. One of my early chores, while working at the Apollo, was to visit him in Sydenham Hospital. It was a depressing experience, not because Pigmeat was in great pain but because it was the first time I had ever visited a hospital ward in Harlem. One final note must be added: After months of watching Pigmeat try to reach a settlement with the insurance company, my father advised him to "sue us." The resulting $10,000 settlement, no small sum in those days, helped Pig out substantially. He used the money, I recall, to buy a Cadillac.

Still another scene had an element of the bizarre about it.

The scene is a darkened stage. In the center is a table with what appears to be a sheet-covered body lying on it. As the lights come up very slightly, a deep-toned bell starts tolling offstage.

BONG! BONG! BONG!

Suddenly, a phone starts ringing. It rings once, twice, three times—nobody answers. The figure on the table suddenly sits bolt upright. "Will somebody answer that damn phone?" he yells.

Aside from Moms Mabley, one of the most beloved comedy acts was the team known as Butterbeans and Susie, in real life Mr. and Mrs. Jodie Edwards. They made comedy records as far back as the early twenties. Butter also specialized in doing the eccentric dance known as the Heebie Jeebies. They sang songs telling about the eternal conflicts between men and women. Sue would play the demanding and sometimes demeaning matriarch, while Butter was the blustering male, threatening all sorts of revenge and harsh treatment of her, which was a bit hard to swallow since his face was as round and innocent as a new-born lamb's—with or without cork.

In their version of "When the Real Thing Comes Along" Butter sings a long recitation of how he'd take on any dangers, including lions, tigers, and virtually all the rest of the zoo, just for her, but when Sue demands to know "'Till when, 'till when?" Butter replies, "Until a bigger fool comes along!" They also recorded a tune earlier made famous by Bessie Smith titled "I Need a Little Hot Dog for My Roll." It contained some mind-boggling chatter.

SUE: I need a hot dog for my roll.
          I want it hot, don't want it cold.
BUTTER: My dog's *never* cold.
          Here's a dog that's long and lean.
          Now here's a dog that's short and fat.
SUE: I don't really want one like that.
BUTTER: I'm known as the champion hot dog man.
SUE: Don't want no excuse.
          It must have lots of juice.

The history of black comedy can't be told without reference to Lincoln Perry, whose stage name was Stepin Fetchit. On the screen and in such diverse places as the Lafayette and Apollo Theatres and the old Cotton Club, he portrayed the lazy, shiftless "darky." Many blacks insist that Stepin Fetchit made a career of portraying the worst lies about black character. There are, on the other hand, those who point out that he opened the way for later black performers to become part of show business and the movies. They also add that although Fetchit played the shiftless type of clown, true to post-Civil War Afro-American traditions, he usually "won."

The "racial" aspect has become more prominent in black comedy in the past two decades, but it was always there in one form or another. Doll Thomas tells of one old comic scene in which two men are talking about a "gal" who is standing with her back to the audience. They are talking the relative merits of the "high-yaller" and the "tan-skinned gal."

"Ain't nothin' like a high yaller," says comic number one. "Man! When you is walkin' down the street with one of them chicks on your arm, you in the high cotton."

"No, man! They alright, but as for me, I likes one with a little more color than that. Now looka there," he intones, as the chick on stage switches her stance from one hip to another, "I'll betcha ten to four that she's a tan."

"No, man! I kin tell by the looks of her from here, she's a high yaller. Betcha five."

The betting continues for a while, always going higher. Suddenly the lady in question turns around and to the consternation of the two men and the delight of the audience, she's as black as the ace of spades!

"There was a kind of a poem," Doll adds, "which was popular at one time."

              She rides in a lovely surrey,
              brownskin gal does the same,
              ole black gal rides a billygoat,
              but she gits there just the same.
              Yellow gal smells like sweet perfume,
              Brownskin she does the same,

ole black gal smells like a skunk,
but she smells just the same.

There were a few standup comics in the old days. One of them, Leonard Reed, claims that Allen Drew (later known as "the black Milton Berle") was among the best. "He didn't work theaters," says Leonard, "because his material was too blue." Others who worked standup were Willie Bryant and Nipsey Russell.

But sometime you had comedy by accident. It happened to a comic named Dina Scott, who, as Leonard Reed described him, "was just a so-so comic who worked like hell to get just a few laughs." Like most comics of the 1930s, Dina finished with a dance routine in a costume that included a pair of closely fitting tights. One night, Dina swung into his dance routine, when unbeknownst to him the tights split right up the middle, and since he wasn't wearing a solitary stitch underneath, "everything hung out." Suddenly, and for perhaps the first time in his life, Dina Scott had an audience that was not merely laughing at his antics but was rolling on the floor hysterically. With a grin on his face that creased it from ear to ear, Dina continued his dance routine, which he thought had suddenly and mysteriously caught fire.

His associates on stage were half whispering, half shouting at him, "Dina, your costume's split. Dina, look down below!" but Dina wasn't looking or hearing. "Outta my way," he stage-whispered. "I got em now, got em pissing in their pants! Gonna lock up this house tonight!" The audience by this time, was almost begging for mercy and the more they hollered the more Dina swung it; the more he swung it the louder were the audience's screams. Suddenly Dina looked down! If a blush could have shown through cork and his own dark skin, it would have shown through his. With a sob, he dashed off stage.

Said Leonard, "We had to throw cold water on him to revive him. He wouldn't go back on stage for the rest of the week." Poor Dina Scott! His one great moment of glory was smothered in humiliation. The worst of it for him was that he could never look back on those hysterical roars of laughter or visualize those helplessly laughing patrons convulsed in his one great moment of triumph, without starting to blush all over again!

Moms Mabley was a clown from beginning to end. She could stand out there in stage center and just look out at the audience and break up the house. Sometimes the audiences would laugh for several minutes before she had said a single word. And when she talked, she created images that were ludicrous, absurd. Clad in gingham, an apron hanging down in front, those large shoes on the wrong feet, she talked of romance, of love affairs, of sex. Clad in that unlikely outfit, she talked about the president and going to the White House, talked about it as though she were really going as honored guest and confidant.

But mostly it was young romance which centered her humor. On old men: "I ain't got but one nerve—and they get on that!" Or: "Old man can't do nothin' for me. Ole man can't do nothin' for hisself! When I married him he answered the preacher, sayin' 'I will.' I found out he *couldn't!*"

It was always young men she talked about. To Basie, "Please, Count, you know I love you, but can't you jest let me have that young drummer boy?"

The older she got, the fewer teeth she had, the more outlandish her costume, the more Moms talked about young men, young romance, young love. And as she talked about it, the deeper her voice became, the less feminine she appeared to be. And that was the point of it all. It was all a big fat joke and somehow she worked her magic and almost made you believe it. At any rate, you believed it enough to laugh out loud, to laugh till your sides ached, and you loved every raucous, uproarious minute of the charade you *knew* was a fake but wished were true.

An older pair of comics who didn't use blackface was Patterson and Jackson, two ponderous guys whose byline read "640 lbs. of humor." They could tap dance with amazing agility considering their girth, but it was their rapid-fire dialogue that endeared them to Apollo audiences. One of their stories was the beginning of a vertible chain of social-protest comedy. Patterson led off:

> Got on the train in Tampa, Florida, on the way to New York. Conductor came around, said, "Give me your ticket, boy." Gave him my ticket, he punched it and gave it back. Came around again in Richmond, Virginia, said, "Give me your ticket, boy." Gave him my ticket; punched it and gave it back. In the Lincoln Tunnel on the way into New York City, conductor came around and said, "Give me your ticket, boy." Turned around to him and said, "Who the hell you callin' boy?"

That early gag aimed at the South didn't merely bring "yocks"; it brought roars of laughter and sometimes a standing ovation.

Comedy has been used as a method of delivering a message since the Greek comedy-writer Aristophanes. Indeed, the highest forms of humor are those which contain some kind of message. Way back in the early days of black minstrelsy mild and careful elements of protest respectfully reposed deep within the by-play between the interlocutor (the emcee) and the end men, the black comics. The end men gently chided the interlocutor:

> "Mr. 'Locutor, Sir, who gits into heaven?"
> "You know, Mr. Bones. The white people do."
> "Iff'n that's so, then who opens them pearly gates for 'em?"

In the thirties and even more strongly in the forties, the expressions of social protest became stronger and stronger. One of their targets was the cork itself, for it reduced all comics to a single common denominator, it deprived them of individuality, and it marked them with a demeaning stamp. Just who is responsible for the demise of cork is doubtful, but Honi Coles insists: "It was your father. He went to the comedians and said 'You don't need this anymore.'" Some of them no doubt abandoned it with reluctance, but all of them complied.

65a. Patterson & Jackson

65b. Dick Gregory

History will record that one comic was ruined by the demise of cork. He was a pantominist named Johnny Hudgins, who really needed the cork and the wide white lips to render his clown act intelligible. "I feel nekid out there without it," wailed poor Johnny. But abandon the cork he did. There was too much pressure from the black community for him to keep it.

The disappearance of blackface was a symptom of the changing times, but what was still needed was a true spokesman. He came in the form of an articulate and dedicated fighter named Dick Gregory. Dick not only revolutionized black comedy by the material he used, he also showed that black comics as standups were every bit as capable as whites. But it was his lines that added the shock to protest, a shock like ice water down an unsuspecting back on a hot summer day.

> "I'm sorry but we don't serve niggers here," the waitress said to me.
> "I don't eat niggers. How about bringing me a ham sandwich?"

Or he threw this one at unsuspecting audiences:

> Where else could I ride in the back of the bus, live in the worst neighborhoods, go to the worst schools, eat in the worst restaurants, and average $5000 per week just talking about it?

There are few people in show business for whom I have more respect that I have for Dick Gregory. This man has almost sacrificed his career and his health to campaign and fast for his beliefs in human rights and peace. Nor have those beliefs been applied exclusively to black people. Indeed, Dick has often included a clause in his nightclub contracts permitting him to leave the job if his services were required for marches and protest speeches. With his flair for comedy, his incisive intelligence, and his all-around decency, Gregory could be a superstar today. He has not achieved that exalted position, because outspoken activity on behalf of causes he believed in were more important to him than material success.

There are comedians who "trade" on the issues surrounding the racial problems in their world. In no sense do I offer criticism of them, for their efforts are worthy. Other black comics use "ethnic" material as it seems important, useful, or worth their attention. Such a comic was Godfrey Cambridge, whose unfortunate premature death deprived the entertainment world of a great person. Says my brother Bobby, "I believe that Godfrey Cambridge was the finest black comedian in the business." He was as much an actor as he was comedian. Indeed, he died of a heart attack while hard at work in the role of Idi Amin in the movie *Entebbe*. Idi Amin is not exactly a pretty character; a man careful about his "image" might not have wanted such a part. Nor could one find a more effective statement of the depth of feeling that rejection-on-account-of-color can bring than in Godfrey's portrayal (in *Watermelon Man*) of a man who suddenly, mysteriously, is transformed overnight from a white to a black man. Rejected by his business associates, abandoned by his wife and family, the last scene of the film shows him attending a karate class that provides an outlet for his pent-up violence along with ammunition for some future action against the system that has destroyed his life.

You would never know that Nipsey Russell was born in Alabama, because he has abandoned all his Southern accent. Nipsey's humor is well-structured, intelligent, and articulate; it isn't especially ethnic, rather it is broadly democratic. A typical Nipsey Russell statement is:

> Our great land is the only place in the world where you can work in an Arab home in a Scandinavian neighborhood, find a Porto Rican baby eating matzo balls with chopsticks.

For years, Nipsey's "home" was a small nightclub called the Baby Grand, just one block west of the Apollo. Although we had a long-standing policy of not playing acts that had recently played the neighborhood, we made an exception with Nipsey Russell. He was too good to be victimized by a mere rule. And if our respect for Nipsey was deep, his for the Apollo was profound. In a recent conversation, he said, "To Frank Schiffman, the quality of the show was the all-important thing. It didn't matter if you were the biggest drawing card in the world; if the show wasn't any good, your ass was out after the first show no matter who you were."

There is a universality to Nipsey's brand of humor. Along with Bill Cosby, Nipsey is perhaps the least ethnic of all the black comics. In the last few years, he has blossomed out to join a legion of white comics on Hollywood talk shows, Dean Martin's "Roasts," and the like. It is probable that his career was given a major boost when the black musical *The Wiz* was released, for along with Richard Pryor who also starred in it, the name Nipsey Russell was high on every reviewer's list.

Back in the late forties we played a team called Foxx and White at the Apollo. Each of that pair went on to become a major black comic. Redd Foxx played the Apollo as a single in 1957 for a weekly salary of 375 dollars. His last Apollo engagement was in 1974, when his show *earned* $76,212.33 during one sensational week. Our private file of comments on Redd Foxx in the period between those two engagements in replete with such comments as "Very funny material . . . excellent . . . cool, casual and entertaining . . . did a yeoman's job . . . held an hour spot beautifully." The most frequent comment was "Dirty, but good."

If there is a single criticism to be made of Redd's work, it is that he has relied too heavily on material known in the theater as "blue." I am no prude about such things, but I compliment Redd when I say that a guy who sustained the likes of *Sanford and Son* for season after season needn't rely that heavily on such material. In terms of the humor labeled "ethnic," Redd's falls between that of Dick Gregory or Richard Pryor (with their heavy accent on matters black) and Bill Cosby or Nipsey Russell, whom most show-biz aficionados label "white comics," white, that is, in the sense that the humor has little ethnic slant. The tremendous popularity of *Sanford and Son* is testimony to the almost universal appeal of the Foxx brand of humor. Although unmistakably black, it is obviously very American.

As for his former "sidekick," Slappy White, Slappy is an entirely different specimen of the comic fraternity, and his career has run an unusual span. For Slappy was a visual comic and an oral one at different stages of his career. He started out as one half of the comedy team known as the Two Zephyrs. That act was what was called a "knockabout" comedy act (the label clearly placed the act in the slapstick category), featuring patter, songs and dances, and ending in a mock crap-game fight done in slow motion, with special lighting effects dramatizing the "fight."

When Slappy left the Two Zephyrs, he teamed with one of the most naturally funny comics I have ever seen. He was named Willie Lewis, and he was the kind of comic who could stand there, open his mouth, let out a few slow words and fracture any audience. Head hung low, shoulders hunched forward, floppy hat pulled down over his ears, Willie would drawl, "Ah was so tahred, ah wuz so lazy that ah couldn't even hoe in mah garden. Then ah took some of that there Had-ee-call—and now, ah'm the best hoer in town." The double-entendre gag never missed. Somewhere along the way Willie Lewis would do his cane trick, a trick I still don't understand, for Willie would take a plain, straight cane, do a little twirling with it, then balance it on one thumb, moving his hand back and forth so that the cane would move from side to side so slowly, that you wouls swear it was glued to his finger. The act ended with Slappy and Willie dancing.

Slappy White remains one of the most intelligent, careful comics in show business. He is the type of man who can write comedy material for other comics, as well as doing most of the writing for his own act. The world is Slappy White's oyster; he uses any situation that appeals to his fancy, be it ethnic or not. Versatility is his keynote.

You can scarcely talk about versatility in black comedy without bringing in George Kirby. Now George is not, strictly speaking, a comic, but a mimic. But what other show-business specialty will encompass the mimic's work unless it is comedy? You have to hunt far and wide to find a mimic with George Kirby's flair. We played him at the Apollo from the forties to the seventies and watched him develop from an excellent supporting act to a first-rate headliner. During all that time, George's act never stayed static; he changed it, added names and personalities, subtracted them when their usefulness no longer suited his purpose. His ear, his comic flair were impeccable, and whether it was an imitation of Joe Louis or Ella Fitzgerald, you could swear you were watching the real thing. His most famous was an imitation of "Pearlie Mae," Pearl Bailey. Indeed, it was so good that Pearl herself used it in her own show on more than

66a. Nipsey Russell

66b. George Kirby

66c. Lewis & White

one occasion.

At this writing, probably two of the leading black comics are Bill Cosby and Richard Pryor. We first played Richard in 1965, paying him a huge 600 dollars, for he had already "killed" a few national television audiences. Our file card commented: "Fresh young comedy star with a unique style and a marvelously poised delivery for so young a performer. This boy is going places." A year later, with a salary jump to 1000 dollars per week, we wrote: "Hit of the show! Excellent material and delivery."

In 1967 Richard jumped to 2500 dollars and was still drawing rave notices, and by 1974 his earnings had moved into the high-percentage category and our comments read, "Dirty! Dirty! But Funny! Funny! Absolute control of the audience." Bobby said, "I have never seen an audience react with such laughter as they did to Richard Pryor during that week. They were almost hysterical!"

It is hard to classify the guy. At this writing he is more than a comic, more than a comic actor; he is a developing and charismatic personality with a tremendously varied talent, a difficult and outspoken man with a penchant for getting people to adore or abhor him. He is, without doubt, a movie star of the highest rank; as a comic, his material runs the gamut from that of a kind of black Sam Levinson to an offbeat Puck. His stories of growing up black are warm and humorous, but from time to time bitterness creeps into his material, making you laugh with what is known in Yiddish as *schöner gelächter* (beautiful laughter).

And no one can throw more pure and undulterated vulgarity into a routine than Richard Pryor. (I suppose I betray my own prejudice when I use the world *vulgar*. Sorry! It's just that there are times when *motherfucker* and similar terms seem tiresome and offensive.) Still, there is something roughish about Richard's delivery. He squints, he leers, he raises his eyebrows and throws his eyes around as though daring you to be angry. It's hard to feel provoked, because he is so talented, so undeniably wickedly talented! Taking the good with the bad, the tasteless with the rest, Richard Pryor is today probably the most outrageously funny man in show business! It is no wonder that he was signed to a five-year, forty-million-dollar contract in 1983.

Bill Cosby doesn't choose to use—and doesn't seem to need—a spate of four-letter words to make his audiences laugh. Still, no one can deny that Cosby is one of the most successful and respected comedians today. We booked Cosby into the Apollo in 1968, but when the theater opened to the first show on a Friday, my brother Bobby almost had a heart attack. "I couldn't understand it," he said. "I mean, this guy was a superstar and there was hardly anybody in the audience! And by that night," Bobby continued, "I confess that I thought I had made a dreadful booking mistake, for we were dying with the show." Bobby paused, smiled, and continued with, "We stood outside and listened to people passing by, watched them as they stopped to look at the displays out front. They said, 'Hey! I know who that guy is now. He was on *I Spy*. Yeah!'

"By Saturday matinee the word was getting around and the theater was

STARTS
FRIDAY
JUNE 14th.

★ WORLD-FAMOUS ★
APOLLO
AMERICA'S GREATEST STAGE SHOWS
~125th St. near 8th Ave. • Tel. RI 9-1800

AMERICA'S NO. 1 COMEDIAN

BILL COSBY AND HIS SHOW
O. C. SMITH • KING CURTIS
VIVIAN REED • AND THE KINGPINS

TICKETS ON SALE: MANHATTAN - THE APOLLO THEATRE; 253 West 125th Street —
68 ST. PLAYHOUSE 68 ST. & 3RD AVE. / JAMAICA RONNIE'S CASUALS 163-08 JAMAICA AVE.
BROOKLYN: LOOKING GLASS STORE BROADWAY & HALSEY ST.

67.

starting to fill up. So was my hope for the show. And by Saturday night, we had them standing in the aisles." It was the oft-repeated story of a show where the advertising known as "word-of-mouth" made the difference. It's the cheapest and most effective kind. The only trouble is that it's hard to plan it in advance!

Our comment in the file on the Cosby show was: "One of the finest, most natural humorists ever. Clean, funny material that borders on incidents that touch everyone's life. Audience howled. Funny, funny man!" Bill Cosby had come into the Apollo a "Who's that?" headliner. At the end of a single week, he left about as close to a "beloved figure" as it was possible to be. Bill is a natural comedian, whose intelligent approach is through the retelling of those humorous situations that occur in the lives of all of us; but he tells them in ways that point up the essentials that make those situations funny.

Scoey Mitchell's *Barefoot in the Park* sitcom won him high praise and an enthusiastic audience. Scoey played the Apollo as a single, but since those days his activities have been enlarged to include serious acting in addition to writing and comedy.

Still hard at work are galaxies of other black comics. Clarence Muse, for instance, played at the Apollo back around 1950, long before he became a television star. Timmie Rogers, who wrote songs for Nat "King" Cole and comedy material for Redd Foxx and others, is one of the more enduring black comedians on the scene today. The late Sam Theard, known in the trade as Spo-Dee-O-Dee, not only appeared in situational comedy at the Apollo and elsewhere for years, but he also immortalized himself by writing "I'll Be Glad When You're Dead, You Rascal You." Nor can I leave off this listing without mentioning a team called Stump and Stumpy. Jimmie Cross, known among the cognoscenti as "Big Stump," would glare at his partner, little Harold Cromer, and say, "You're too small to talk so long" and the act was off and running.

Jimmie "J. J." Walker has surfaced to add to the comic din, but the newest and the best of today's newcomers, already a superstar, is Eddie Murphy. I wonder how much of his humor is "scripted" and how much represents his own natural talent.

I have saved Flip Wilson for last for several reasons. One is that Flip is not only one of my favorite comics, but one of my favorite people. Another is that along with Dick Gregory, Flip is a critical, transitional figure in the history of black comedy. Flip Wilson sometimes uses racial material, but he is not a strictly ethnic comic. He is a comedian who merely happens to be black. Or, as Flip himself put it in a recent conversation, "Black was just the thing which got their attention while I walked out on the stage." There is a universality in his humor that strides the subtle demarcation between strongly ethnic humorists like Redd Foxx and Richard Pryor and the more neutral comics like Nipsey Russell and Bill Cosby.

One incident tells more about Flip's attitude toward the color issue than anything I can think of. It took place during the making of a two-hour television called *Uptown*, based on my book of the same name produced by Bob Hope

Enterprises in 1979. Flip was included in the cast as both a comedian and a co-host. In the former role he was called on to perform an old comedy bit in which he played the dumb stooge with Nipsey Russell playing the wise guy. It was suggested that since this was an old burlesque sketch, his role might be better played in blackface. The decision was left strictly to him, but we all felt a twinge of trepidation while awaiting his decision.

"Understand, you don't *have* to do it," said the director, Gary Smith. "It's just that it makes some sense to do it that way." Then he added, "I remember when we were doing the Irving Berlin show there was a Bert Williams number, and Sammy Davis said, 'You know, I always wanted to do a part in black-face!'"

"Look," said Flip. "I dig what you're saying. In my opinion blackface *is* a social commentary in itself. Bert Williams put on blackface so that he could get a job working as a black guy! I'll do it in blackface."

I looked at Flip with new and heightened respect and recalled a conversation I had had with him while I was writing *Uptown*. "There are times," I had said, "when I'll write some material and leave it on my desk for a week or even a month, then pick it up and discover I hate it—or love it."

Flip got excited. "Yeah! I dig that, 'cause I do it all the time when I'm writing my own material. When I wrote the Christopher Columbus routine, I wrote and rewrote it over a period of seven years before I was satisfied with it."

Seven years! Look at his record titled "Cowboys and Colored People" containing a dozen or so routines, and in tiny print in the lower-right corner of the album a phrase declares "all material written by Flip Wilson." (However, that is not an exclusive with Flip Wilson; other comedians write a good deal of their material as well.)

The guy seems so young and fresh that I cannot quite believe my own file, which gives the chronology of his career as exemplified in his Apollo appearances.

> 1962: $300. Good M.C. and good comedy. Should be watched.
> 1966: $600. Good comic and improving as M.C.
> 1966: $900. Very funny man. On the upgrade.
> 1968: $2500. Excellent comedian. Improving each time.

Besides being the first black performer to host a continuing TV show, Flip is the creator of a beloved character, Geraldine, who falls alongside Charlie McCarthy and Mortimer Snurd in popular affection; he also created the Reverend Leroy, who has contributed as many rollicking and hilarious moments as anyone on television since Milton Berle.

If I were to try to pinpoint the essential charm of Flip Wilson's humor and delivery, I would call him "infectious!" He even infects himself with the spontaneous stuff rolling out as he performs. With more than two people present, Flip is always "on stage." During rehearsals of the *Uptown* TV show, he kept cast, executives, and crew in a state of constant hilarity, and his deft comic touches added pace and humor to much of what was ultimately done. In Gary Smith and Dwight Hemion's office, for instance, he told us this story, which tells as much about Apollo audiences as about Flip himself. It is impossible to convey his inflections and the contortions of his mobile face in words, so I ask my readers to try to project that comic guy's face, twisting from side to side as he followed the action of this scene:

> Walked out on the stage and before I was barely started, a cat on the left side of the balcony hollers, "Do the junkie bit." I say, "Okay, Broth—just give me a couple of minutes to warm up and I'll do it."
>
> So, a few minutes later I start to tell this junkie story, when a gal on the right side of the balcony hollers, "God damn! Another junkie bit. Why the hell do I always have to hear that?" I turned my head toward her, when from the left I heard—"Bitch! Shut up and let the man tell the story, sheeeit!"
>
> "How come every time I come in the damned place I gotta listen to that shit?" comes the lady's voice from balcony right.
>
> "Bitch, now shut up and let the man talk," comes from the left again. Well, I'm just standing there looking from left to right as all this is goin' on. Ain't had time to tell half the story myself.
>
> "Damn it all to hell," starts the gal on the right when the voice from balcony left booms out once more, "Bitch! If you don't shut up and let the man talk, I'm gonna come over there and throw you the hell over the balcony!"

By this time Smith and Hemion, the writers and staff assembled, Jack Schiffman and Wilson himself are almost on the floor. His infectious humor and the way in which he reenacted that scene got all of us. We were all, once more, back in that faded old showplace listening to the audience dictate to one of its favorite sons how the show should and shouldn't be done.

The history of black show business and the story of the slow acceptance of black artistry by the American public follows an episodic course. There are leaps, pauses, regressions, and changes of pace, which show up as history is viewed in retrospect. It took some doing, for example, before jazz was gradually accepted by even a small coterie of white Americans. Despite the fact that jazz is primarily a black phenomenon, the impact of black artistry was played down; despite the obvious debts white musicians owed black ones, that debt was rarely publicly acknowledged until recently.

Comedy was the last form of entertainment to gain acceptance. That fact, in my opinion, has a special significance. It is the last on a tragically long list of "put-downs" of black efforts by white America. That is, the efforts of black comics were rejected as "unworthy" of attention, for years and years. The principal reason, I believe, is that comedy is a more intellectual art than say dance, which is directed toward our visual senses, or music, which *may* be enjoyed intellectually, but *must* be enjoyed aurally, emotionally, sensually. Comedy has to be thought about to be understood at all. It may seem strange to think of it as intellectual, but its appeal is to ideas rather than to feelings or even images. In my judgment, according comedy its due place would have required an acknowledgment by white America that blacks did, in fact, possess intelligence and the ability to think. It would have required a tacit admission that all the slander about a lack of black intelligence was false. White America, until now, was not prepared to make such an admission.

The result was that we deprived ourselves of the richness of black humor even as we deprived black comics of a broader forum, a more generous livelihood, and a more respectful acceptance. The worm has turned, for today black comedians are kings of the mountain, superstars among superstars. Even black musicians and singers have been forced to take a back seat as Bill Cosby, Nipsey Russell, Redd Foxx, Richard Pryor, Flip Wilson, Scatman Cruthers and Eddie Murphy are doing their acts before wildly appreciative American audiences.

If there is a hierarchy of values in comedy, the top position belongs to the comedy with a message, the comedy that makes us more human even as we clutch our sides in laughter. It is the ennobling art of Aristophanes and Shakespeare rather than the simpler stuff of knockabout comedy. And sometimes the true story is the one which has the comedic-tragedy strong enough to touch us with its pathos. Accordingly, I am going to finish this chapter by recounting a true story. It was told to me by my friend Leonard Reed, a close friend of Joe Louis. They were buddies, traveling companions, and friends over a long period, stretching from the days before Joe won the heavyweight championship until Joe's death.

Now Leonard is an excellent golfer, despite the fact that at about five feet nine or so he doesn't weigh much more than 130 pounds. Joe's addiction to golf was legendary.

Joe called me one day to tell me that he had an exhibition coming up in New Orleans. He suggested that we take an early plane to that city and give ourselves time enough for a golf game. He asked me to call some golf courses there and make the arrangements. Although it was long before New Orleans dropped the restrictions regarding blacks in public places, I called one of the clubs there, told them I was calling on Joe's behalf, and was told, "We would be honored to have the Champ play here."

We arrived in New Orleans before noon and discovered a limousine waiting for us. I got our bags and clubs, put them into the limousine's trunk, and Joe and I waited to leave. We waited—and waited—and waited. Finally Joe said to me, "Listen, Leonard, we're going to miss our golf game if we don't leave soon. Find out why we haven't left yet."

I got out of the limo and saw three drivers in uniform over to one side, talking. I walked over and said, "Would one of you gentlemen mind telling me when the limousine will be leaving? We have a golf date coming up."

"Are you with the Champ?" asked one of them.

When I told him I was he said, "Listen. We've been talking here, trying to figure out what to do. The truth of the matter is that it's against the law for us to carry colored passengers in our limousines. It's not that we wouldn't be happy to take the Champ, but we can't."

"To hell with it," said Joe when I told him. "Let's take our stuff and go over in a cab." So I moved our bags and clubs into a cab, we got in, and waited—and waited—and waited.

Again I got out. Again I found the driver. Again he said to me, "I'm sorry, Mister. But I'm not aloud to carry colored people in my cab." So once again I move our bags, put them in another cab, a colored one this time, and Joe and I get in. Cab driver turns around and says to me, "Sorry, Mister, I ain't allowed to carry white people in my cab."

"Leonard," Joe says, "You know white folks ain't allowed in this cab. Better get in another one!" Now we're in two cabs, and mine follows Joe's to the golf course, where we finally get our game in.

It takes us two cabs to get to a hotel, but when I got to check in, the clerk at the desk says, "You want to stay here, sir?"

"Yes," I answered.

"Sorry, sir. We ain't allowed to have white folks here."

Now I'm really stuck. The cab I took has gone and since we're in the middle of the colored section, I have no way to even get out of there. We compromise by getting in a colored cab with me on the floor! Not a lot of people realize what a sense of humor Joe Louis had. But he looks at me and says, "Leonard, it's a pain in the ass to have white folks around all the time." I'm too cramped down there on the floor to answer.

Well, I checked into a hotel, take a shower and change my clothes, when there's a knock at the door. It's the manager. "Mr. Reed," he says, "are you colored?"

"Hell, no," I answered, wondering what in the hell this is all about.

"Well, there's a dark-skinned colored lady down in the lobby. She's got three kids with her and she claims her husband is staying here and his name is Leonard Reed."

I tell you, I could have killed that Joe Louis. Turned out he hired the woman to play that part. Hell, turned out that he tried to get Dinah Washington to do it, but because Dinah and I have been close friends she wouldn't.

11   Explosion

"Heat Wave"

Like a portending clap of thunder, the rumbling, pulsating rhythms of Bo Diddley rocked the entire street as well as the Apollo in the summer of '55. Things have never been quite the same since. Depending on your bias, it was the beginning of the most productive or useless, the most influential or detrimental, the most profitable or ultimately destructive era in show-business history.

Said my brother Bobby, "If there is any musical form with the possible exception of jazz, that was created in this country, it was rock and roll, and including jazz, it was the most remunerative and productive, the most outrageously important musical form of all."

Said Honi Coles, who for sixteen years staged and rehearsed these same rock and roll shows, "I hated it."

If it did nothing else, rock and roll emphasized once again the distinctions between the successful and the excellent, for there are those (Bobby and our father) who equated the two, while there are others (Honi and myself) who insist that aesthetic values were lost in the pell-mell flight to the bank. But Dad's position was, at best, ambivalent. Honi said, "Your father and I kept arguing with Bobby, pleading for some relief, some variety in the shows, but he insisted that only acts with proven box-office value be included in each show."

That the rock and roll shows brought a new, heady excitement to the theater is undeniable. That they also brought immense throngs in their wake is easily attested to by the Apollo box-office records hung up by James Brown, Gladys Knight and the Pips, and The Temptations. A listing of the major stars who headlined in this era is impressive in its length and depth: Aretha Franklin,

---

Nowhere else in this book is the title of a song and the contents of the following pages more appropriate than here, for the age of rock and roll was, indeed a "Heat Wave," and Martha (Reeves) and the Vandellas' recording of it was as characteristic of the era as any song I can think of. If Bo Diddley's rocking guitar started the rhythm pulsating, the Motown artists picked up the beat and rode it out, as did a galaxy of other stars.

Diana Ross and the Supremes, Marvin Gaye, Al Green, Stevie Wonder, Martha and the Vandellas, Smokey Robinson, Dionne Warwick, Gladys Knight and the Pips, Otis Redding, Sam Cooke, Jackie Wilson, Ray Charles, Chuck Berry, The Jackson Five, The Spinners, The Temptations, Chuck Jackson, The Fifth Dimension, and James Brown. Week after week their names graced theater, nightclub, and arena marquees from coast to coast, and the beat refused to let up. The period stretched from the mid-fifties to the late-seventies; its impact is with us still.

In the interest of simplification, this chapter calls the period under consideration "rock and roll" or simply "rock." But many divergent artistries are encompassed, like James Brown's and Roberta Flack's; like Sly and the Family Stone's and Smokey Robinson and the Miracles'. It is the music which will concern us and if we have limited it too much with the label "rock," be advised: it transcends all labels.

You can divide the artists into two principal groups: the performers and the creators, although most who wrote music also performed. The creators include Stevie Wonder, Marvin Gaye, Quincy Jones, Smokey Robinson, Ray Charles, Curtis Mayfield, and nonperformer Berry Gordy, just some of this elite group. But artists like Al Green, Diana Ross, Isaac Hayes, and Aretha Franklin probably also belong if only for the impact they had on other artists. Several of these presented a whole new sound; Isaac Hayes, chains, seminudity and all, brought a new look and a raw sexuality to the stage.

Of the creative souls just mentioned—and they form only the hard core in an ever-expanding fraternity—nonperforming Berry Gordy is the most unique. For Motown, the organization he headed, supervised music, costumes, choreography, publicity—the works. No longer was the sound static, much less was it predictable. It ebbed and flowed with strange new rhythms, pausing, even halting in unexpected places, rushing when you least expected it, stirring you to your fingertips. If its musical father was Smokey Robinson, its godfather was Berry himself, for he was producing new and startling costumes (gone the tuxedoes and white dinner jackets) and intricate dances dovetailed into the music. Some were concocted by Cholly Atkins and Leonard Reed.

Rock music is compounded of blues and folk music, and as the form developed, its lyrics took on significance and a form bordering on the poetic. The lyrics of Paul Simon are crystalline gems, often moving in their profound complexity.

As for the other creators, Marvin Gaye was always more comfortable behind a piano, blank music paper in hand, than behind a mike. By his own admission, he was scared of audiences, although they never knew it. Once, he flew to New York for an Apollo engagement, then turned right around and flew back to Detroit rather than face "that audience." It took strong persuasion by Bobby and a flying trip to Detroit by Pete Long, the Apollo's jack-of-all-trades and prime publicity man to lure him back. Still, alone or in tandem, first with Mary Wells, then with Kim Weston, and for three years with the late Tami

Terrell, he poured out the discs. He teamed with Diana Ross in some dazzling productions. Singles, duets, movie scores—there seemed to be no limit to the creative genius and impact of this introverted, shy, and somewhat insecure man, who was always afraid of "making a fool of" himself.

It is easy to throw around a term like *creative genius*. Yet to no one does it apply more aptly than to Quincy Jones, whose musical versatility and accomplishment is truly incredible. Quincy's career now spans more than thirty years. Arranger, composer, musician, producer, he is entitled to all labels. He wrote for Sinatra, Tony Bennett, Johnny Mathis, Ray Charles, Aretha Franklin, Al Jarreau, and Michael Jackson. He's done scores for movies (*The Pawnbroker, In Cold Blood, In the Heat of the Night)*, and won Grammy Awards in 1962, '72, '73, and he took a handful in 1984. Quincy's first professional gig was as a trumpeter with Lionel Hampton before he graduated from music school.

Say the word *creative* and you can interchange it with the name of Curtis Mayfield, whom Bobby called "the nicest of men." With or without The Impressions, with and without his long-time friend Jerry Butler, Curtis Mayfield has done it all. With his unique, high-flying tenor voice and his prodigious composing abilities, he's done singles, scored movies, worked with Gladys Knight and the Pips and The Staple Singers, and given us a legacy of songs, albums, and singles that include "I'm So Proud," "Keep on Pushin'," "Back to the World," the immortal "Amen," and the equally enduring sound track for that classic movie *Superfly.*

Save for Berry Gordy himself, Motown's prime mover has been Smokey Robinson. Through composition and arrangements for others as well as himself and The Miracles, he established what is known to the public and the music industry as the "Motown Sound." Some of his compositions are the kinds of classics that will endure through the years: "My Girl," which he composed for The Temptations, and "My Guy" for Mary Wells. (He even composed for Marvin Gaye.) A great singer, with a tender, lyrical voice and a high, soft falsetto, Smokey's association with Berry Gordy dates back to their high school days, when the original Miracles were formed. (Their "Shop Around" was the galvanizing force in the group's early days.) Had Smokey written nothing except "Tracks of My Tears" and "Tears of a Clown," he would have assured himself a place in musical history. As it is, his career as soloist, composer, and arranger shows not the slightest sign of slowing down.

On a small record card kept in the Apollo's office, the words "genius! genius! genius!" appear. This man transcends all pat categories; he has done rock and roll, country and western, blues and ballads. I was approached, one day in the early fifties, by a musical conductor named Reuben Phillips. "I've got a kid I'd like you to hear," Reuben said. So down into the Apollo's rehearsal hall we went where I heard a blind piano-playing singer do his stuff. I was so impressed that I put him in the show then and there. Thus was born the Apollo career of one Ray Charles Robinson. (He later shortened his name to Ray Charles to prevent confusion with another Robinson named Sugar Ray.)

You can't hear Ray Charles sing two bars without recognizing the influence of gospel and blues in his music. Yet he was originally a disciple of Nat "King" Cole and Charles Brown (the "Driftin' Blues" man). That early influence faded as Ray's own genius began to emerge. His unique career shot skyward in 1959 with his recording "What'd I Say," combining as it did, gospel and blues with African call-and-response shouts done with his female group, the Raelets. Later, he did "Them That Got," "Outskirts of Town" (the old Louis Jordan hit), "Georgia on My Mind," "Hit the Road, Jack," and "I Can't Stop Loving You," a country and western tune and a record much criticized by some "experts," but a daring move into a supposedly alien field. Experts or not, there is not the slightest suggestion of doubt that Ray Charles is a living legend, a creative genius for the ages.

His full name is Steveland Morris; he was called "Little Stevie" early in his career, but the world now knows him as Stevie Wonder. Bobby once commented: "Because he is blind, because he couldn't go out and play baseball, he became totally mesmerized by music. He didn't just bring his clothes into his dressing room. He brought his recorder, a piano, a synthesizer, and between shows he'd be working, trying to create something new. He had an unquenchable thirst, a desire to create. It's where he got his kicks."

As a result, Stevie Wonder's musical outpourings have been prodigious. He had mastered half a dozen musical instruments by the age of eight; he signed his first record contract with Berry Gordy at nine. When he first appeared at the Apollo, the audience was as intrigued with his harmonica playing as with his piano and voice.

Who doesn't know "My Cherie Amour"? Only someone tone deaf and without a radio. When his "Songs in the Key of Life" was released in 1976, it may have been the most keenly awaited album in history. It was an album, by the way, that took months to record. The listening public has little awareness of the sheer concentrated labor involved in recording sessions—enormous, when done by musical perfectionists like Stevie Wonder.

The variety theater that evolved into rock and roll is the world of emotions. And indeed, judged by the self-same emotional standard, the rock era may have been the most exciting of all. The gospel shows engendered an almost hysterical response; it was short-lived and intense. Rock and roll, on the other hand, endured for two decades. It resulted in more paying customers, more performing artists, and more creative souls hard at work than in any period in modern entertainment history. Like it or not, its influence was all pervading—indeed, it still goes on—and in Harlem, often the trend-setter, record after box-office record fell as excited fans queued on down to Seventh Avenue, turned the corner northward, and sometimes even snaked on around 126th Street. To those unfamiliar with New York topography, let me say that that is a long, long line.

For years, the Apollo's box-office record was held by Lionel Hampton and his house-rocking crew. Then Duke Ellington and Pearl Bailey (following her marriage to Louis Belson) teamed for one glorious week. Their record held firm for years. But in the rock days, Gladys Knight and the Pips broke it, held it briefly, and relinquished it to the slickest vocal group of all, The Temptations. And finally, in another convulsive, unforgettable engagement, the "godfather of soul," James Brown moved in with his blockbuster show to explode the record for once and for all. The lines waiting patiently for their chance to invade the 1700-seat auditorium were so long that James himself went out on the street and served coffee to his patient fans!

An extraordinary man, James Brown. In the entire rock and roll era, he is a towering figure. Said Bobby, "The funny thing is that there were better singers than James Brown around. Not that he was bad, but Jackie Wilson, for example, was better. And yet, he was the showman personified. He had more tricks to keep the audience stirred up than anyone else. Even now, when his career seems somewhat faded, it wouldn't surprise me a bit to see him do something extraordinary and rise to the top again."

James is a short ex-pug with a high-flying gospel style. He once supported no less than twelve black medical students at one time. His charities, often quietly given, were monumental. During the famous Boston race riots, he went on the air and on the streets to pour oil on troubled waters. Still, it was on the stage where he truly lived, an artist to his fingertips who knew how to stir an audience to the very heights of excitement. It all started with his gospel-slanted "Please Please Please" in 1955. It was followed a few years later by "Try Me." Then, this dynamic entertainer with the keenest of business senses, aided and abetted by his manager, the late Ben Bart, really took off. With the dazzling footwork and body movements an acrobat could envy, he poured it on. His monumental album "Live at the Apollo" is his most enduring hit, with "Prisoner of Love" and "Say It Loud, I'm Black and I'm Proud" not far behind.

If James created bedlam at the Apollo and elsewhere, so too did the legendary Jackie Wilson. Although Berry Gordy wrote hit songs for him as far back as 1957, it was with Brunswick Records (under the leadership of its president, Nat Tarnopol, who was also Jackie's manager) that he made his biggest splash. He was dubbed "Mr. Excitement," and no one deserved this press agent's dream label more than he, for only James Brown or the gospel shows were ever able to stir more excitement than he. What a tragic loss to musicdom and the world of entertainment was Jackie Wilson's stroke, which left him with irreversible brain damage and finally death at the age of 49.

Conventional wisdom has it that performers are an irresponsible lot to whom money is meaningless and who always end up broke. As usual, conventional wisdom is wrong. Stage-door scuttlebutt has it that the first millionaire among black performers was Johnny Mathis. It is true. Whether his status is due to his efforts or his manager's is irrelevant. What is relevant is that he has managed a trick only a few performers can boast of: maintaining his popularity with the youngsters and their parents at the same time.

In 1956, Bobby heard his record "Wonderful Wonderful" at Bobby Robinson's hole-in-the-wall record shop a block west of the Apollo, and was so impressed that he urged Dad to book him (at 350 dollars for the week) three months from then. By that time, his record was number one in the United States. Unfortunately, the demands of new success put a strain on Johnny's vocal chords, and he closed himself out after the first show with a bad case of laryngitis. He returned a few months later (at 1500 dollars) and hasn't looked back since. Today, at the age of forty-eight, Johnny is truly a living legend; his liquid voice is recognized all over the world. "It's Not for Me to Say," "When a Child Is Born," "Gone Gone Gone," his duets with Deniece Williams, and dozens of other records have made him one of the world's most durable stars.

Superstar Jerry Butler is almost as well-known for his business acumen as for "Your Precious Love," the record he cut with The Impressions that made him a star. He is, for starters, the largest importer of foreign beer in the Chicago area. Add to that his Chicago Butler Music Workshop, which caters to writers, arrangers, and artists. But that's only the beginning for Jerry. He was the soloist with The Impressions (with his old friend Curtis Mayfield), having arrived at that position from his early gospel days with the Northern Jubilee Gospel Singers and afterwards from a group called The Quails. Many hit albums rolled out when he starred with The Impressions, but more were to come when he soloed. In his spare time, Jerry wrote songs for Jackie Wilson and Count Basie. He waxed "The Ice Man Cometh" and "Ice Man."

And speaking of business, how about Bo Diddley and Lloyd Price ("Lawdy Miss Clawdy")? Both are legendary for their business acumen. Lloyd was involved in Mohammed Ali's famous fight in Zaire and is now actively working with a new African nation. And Chuck Berry, it is said, drives up to his one-nighters in a limousine and asks to see the promoter. Before he alights from the car, he has his price—$10,000 per concert—or he doesn't alight!

Business considerations aside, the rock and rollers (who were the historical successors to the rhythm and bluesers), produced a plethora of female groups and individuals, many of whom became superstars. Of these, none is more charming or deserving than Gladys Knight, who sang along with the Pips to become a living show-business legend. Many a producer remarked of her, "She's a sweetheart."

It's debatable whether Gladys Knight or Aretha Franklin should be called the "Queen of Soul." It is also irrelevant, for Gladys, a gospel-trained woman (she sang with the Wings Over Jordan group early in her career) is surely one of the most charismatic, dynamic singers in show business. Gladys Knight and the Pips (named after a cousin James "Pip" Woods) is a family group (a brother and two cousins), which has sung under various labels (among them Motown, Buddah, Brunswick, and Columbia), has worked under several managers including Bobby Robinson and Sidney Seidenberg, and has recorded some of the best music extant. "Neither One of Us," "Help Me Make It Through the Night" (by Kris Kristofferson), "Midnight Train to Georgia," and "The Way We Were" are merely samples of the dozens of discs they have cut.

Bobby, said "We played Martha and the Vandellas and The Supremes on

the same bill and I thought Martha was one of the great singers in the business."
It isn't that he didn't think Diana Ross and the Supremes were great, but
Martha hit his special chord. Intense, dramatic, Martha's career has ebbed and
flowed, soared and plunged. "They were one of the most popular groups when
'Heat Wave' hit the charts," Bobby said, "and we did great business with them.
Besides, in an early appearance, The Supremes were the opening act and I didn't
pay more attention to them than one normally pays to an opener." It is probably
true that Martha never quite got over the tremendous success of The Supremes.
She no doubt thought her group would walk off with first prize. Nor is Martha
Reeves finished, musically speaking. It's just that Diana Ross and the Supremes
became legends beyond their time. In a recent concert in New York, 350,000
people came out to hear Diana sing!

In recent times, no vocal group has had a stronger impact on musicmakers
and fans alike than Diana Ross and the Supremes. Whether their style was due
to Berry Gordy, Smokey Robinson, or the girls themselves is open to question.
Suffice it to say that The Supremes, originally called The Primettes, became
America's singing sweethearts, and Diana Ross, an early friend of Smokey
Robinson, became their leading light. "Baby Love," "In the Name of Love," and
"You Can't Hurry Love" are just a few of the discs that won them international
fame. They may have originally patterned themselves after Frankie Lyman and
the Teenagers, but they had the imagination to develop their own style. When
Jean Terrell replaced Diana Ross, the quality of the group was not diminished,
but the new Supremes never achieved that same degree of success again. Like
fashions, musical styles change and only the inventive survive. In the eyes of the
public, The Supremes and Diana Ross are inseparable.

At the time *Lady Sings the Blues* was being filmed with Diana Ross
playing the part of Billie Holiday, my father wrote Diana a humorous letter.
"Why didn't you choose me as your leading man?" he queried, to which Diana
responded in kind, "If I had only thought of it I would have done it."

Some women became superstars in the age of rock and roll, and of them
Aretha Franklin may be the most talented and enduring. At this writing, two
decades have felt the impact of her style. Her singing can best be summarized by
the word *explosive*, for that is what Aretha's soaring, scorching voice is.
Throughout her long and turbulent career, the gospel touch, spawned in her
father's church and influenced by her aunt, Clara Ward, has held. Aretha has
transcended "race" records, sliding easily into the pop field while her gospel
roots remained clear and clean. She was first signed to Columbia Records by my
friend John Hammond, but Atlantic's Jerry Wexler later became one of her
prime mentors. She has won Grammy awards, singer-of-the-year awards, even
an honorary Doctor of Music. "Chain of Fools," "Baby, I Love You," "Son of a
Preacher Man" and "Let It Be" are only a few of the enduring Franklin
numbers. "Ain't No Way" was composed by her sister Carolyn, and she has
sung songs penned by Stevie Wonder, Elton John, Ashford and Simpson;
albums have been produced by Quincy Jones and many others. To hear Aretha

at her best is to experience one of the most original of all modern talents. It is also to understand why lines of fans crowded into theaters and clubs by the thousands to hear her.

Then there is Dionne Warwick, a show-stopper and a heart-throbber. In the Apollo's history, few artists have engendered a more excited response show after show. Like nesting doves, her fans descended down to the stage's apron reaching up to express their appreciation. Like the gracious lady she is, Dionne responded.

An early member of the gospel group called the Drinkard Singers, Dionne studied music from childhood on, won a scholarship at the Hartt College of Music, and worked, worked, worked. But it was her discs "Walk on By" and "Anyone Who Had a Heart" that propelled her into the international big time. Her biggest hit is "I'll Never Love Again." "She's a pro," said Bobby. "When we were hanging the scenery the night before her show began, Dionne would show up in blue jeans to add her bit to the operation. She'd tell us exactly where she wanted the piano or how she'd like the stage set. She'd cue us in advance on her lights. I never saw a performer as thorough as she." (I did: Fats Waller.)

Dionne interrupted her career to have a family, then did the unusual. She resumed it and zoomed right back into the stratosphere. By the way, in her Apollo shows she always included her younger sister Dee Dee, a genuine talent in her own right.

Not one, but two stars sprang from The Temptations: David Ruffin and Eddie Kendricks. The act, however, is owned by Otis Williams and Melvin Franklin, the only originals left in it. The Temptations remain one of the true class acts of the rock and roll era. They are always costumed in a dashing array of original outfits; their choreography is always timed to perfection; but it is their vocalizing, running the full gamut from rhythm to slow ballads and, sometimes, even containing a dash of comedy, that has kept them on top. "My Girl," "Since I Lost My Baby," "My Baby," "Superstar," "All Directions"—the list of their hits is long and rich. David Ruffin left in 1968, and although he was missed, The Temptations then became more group- and less solo-oriented after his departure. Franklin's incredibly rich bass was used more frequently in striking contrast to the high tenor of Dennis Edwards, for example, and the result was a less strident, more mellow sound. They have endured for almost two decades.

It's a long step from Aretha Franklin to Roberta Flack, for smooth-singing, low-keyed Roberta is far distant, vocally, from the explosive, sometimes violent sound of Aretha. And yet, Roberta Flack is in the time framework of the rock era, a cool oasis of sound calculated to relieve any offended ears. Trained in the classics, educated at Howard University, Roberta won a record-of-the-year Grammy right in the center of the rock decade, in 1973 for "The First Time Ever I Saw Your Face." She lit up the musical firmament with "Killing Me Softly." Her mellow style can calm jangled nerves or soothe a tormented spirit. A bittersweet chapter for her was the brief period when she recorded with the late Donny Hathaway, who committed suicide. A gifted woman with roots deep in classical and church music, the world of entertainment will see her star on the horizon again and again.

It would be hard to find a greater contrast than that between the mellowness of Roberta Flack and the sock-em-in-the-jaw stridency of Tina Turner. Oddly, this beautiful, energetic, bombastic singer was more popular with white audiences than with black. It isn't that she was a dud in the Harlems of the United States; it's just that Park Avenue seemed to like her better than Beale Street did.

Sometimes an artist, wittingly or otherwise, can alienate an audience. If they do so at the Apollo, there's hell to pay. Such was the case with Nina Simone, ultra-talented but sometimes abrasive. She recorded George Gershwin's "I Love You, Porgy" in 1959, and an impatient audience called out for it. Nina's reponse was to lecture that audience. "The amateurs are not back here," she said. "You are." Then she added, "I'll sing it when I'm good and ready." Oh, brother! The audience calmly filed out and waited in the lobby until she finished her routine, then filed back in again. An entertainer scolds an Apollo audience at his or her own risk.

But you can sometimes flim-flam the managers. At least Big Maybelle did. Now Big Maybelle was King-Kong size. She could belt the blues like nobody's business and the audiences loved her. Her only trouble was money. Handling it—that was her problem. Somehow it flowed through her hands like water through a sieve. She got to be a pain, coming into the office for a "loan until payday," because by week's end her envelop was stuffed with I.O.U.'s instead of greenbacks. So we stopped making loans, which was, in Big Maybelle's book, an act of war. She came into the office one day and announced, "I've got a cab outside and I don't have a dime to pay for it. Lend me twenty bucks." Sure enough, a cab sat out there waiting. It wasn't until later that we discovered she'd picked it up on the corner of 125th Street and Seventh Avenue, a fare of perhaps fifty cents! Or there was the time she came into the office, toothless. "Need a hunert eight bucks," she seemed to be saying, "to get my teeth. They're at the dennis'." She won; we lost. How can you ask a lady to open her bag so you can check to see if her teeth are there?

But there were wonderful people to work with, whom we didn't have any trouble with. There was, for example, Patti LaBelle, born Patricia Holt. She teemed with her friend Cindy Birdsong and a couple of other women and called the act Patti LaBelle and the Bluebells. They made a high-flying record called "I Sold My Heart to the Junkman," which quickly propelled them into the front rank. Cindy later left to become part of The Supremes, and Patti and the Bluebelles had a long, successful career until they also parted company. Today, Patti LaBelle is carving out her own career as a single.

Single also are Dakota Staton and Lavern Baker, two hard-singing chanteuses. I don't know the present whereabouts of Gloria Lynne, whom I started as part of a girl quartet called the Dorsey Sisters. She was a supertalented thrush. Briefly, all too briefly, Gloria was a major headliner. Not so brief was the career of lovely Joyce Bryant, exotic in appearance and voice. She pitched her voice soft and low until Bobby said to her, "You're too soft. It's hard to hear the lyrics." Responded Joyce, "The quieter I am, the quieter they'll be." She was absolutely right.

"The first artist to come into the Apollo with enough electronic equipment to frighten an engineer was Sly Stone," said Bobby. Christened Sylvester Steward in Dallas, Texas, calling his band The Stoners, the man is little short of a musical genius. In his first Apollo appearance, the speakers and other gear was piled so high that they almost obscured the stage. It produced sounds that ranged between frightening and deafening. It was so loud that people in the first ten rows had to scramble for cover, and even then the noise was enough to shatter eardrums.

"I knew if I went backstage and told him to lower the sound, he'd tell me to jump in a lake," said Bobby, "I played it cool. Told him I loved it. Told him how great he was. And on the way out of his dressing room I turned around and innocently asked, 'Is the lyric important?' 'Course it's important. Why?' 'Because we can't hear it—can't understand a word.' The result was that for the next show, the sound was cut back by half!"

Sly composes, and he is sometimes called the father of psychedelic music. He has had immense difficulty with drugs and has acquired a reputation for being undependable. In one year, the amount of money his record company laid out in payment to musicians for recording sessions called and never completed because of his absence ran well into six digits! And yet, this incredible man recorded "Dance to the Music," "Everyday People," and the song that became the theme song for Woodstock, "I Want to Take You Higher." The thrust of that title seems obvious to anyone who knows anything about this troubled and troublesome genius.

Unlike Otis Redding, who died in an airplane crash one week before his scheduled third Apollo appearance, Sam Cooke was already an established superstar in 1964 when he died only three weeks before his next Apollo gig. A graduate of the Highway QC's (where he sang with Lou Rawls) and the Soul Stirrers, Sam's life was a long tussle with conflicting desires to sing gospel and pop. His record "You Send Me," with its lilting phrasing and unusual musical concept, propelled Sam to national prominence and a number-one rating in a matter of weeks. Most likely, the shooting that took his life at age thirty-two was an accident. Accident or not, it was a tragedy that deprived us of his extraordinary talents.

As for Otis Redding, his every Harlem appearance brought him closer to top stardom. At the time of the plane crash, he was on the verge of it. He composed, he danced and gyrated, and he has been recognized as a great balladeer since his untimely death. His last legacy was "Dock of the Bay," but the great number of Atlantic records he cut will make him remembered.

At this writing, there is no more successful artist than Michael Jackson, formerly of the Jackson Five. He is, to use an overworked term, simply fabulous. This family group were in New York some years ago, and they had run up a hotel bill too large to handle. Their father spoke to my father and a date was quickly arranged. They were a smash! But a short time later, Diana Ross had them on her show and they zoomed so hard, fast, and high, that we were never able to arrange for a repeat performance. Once again, lightning!

No recitation concerning stars of the rock era can be complete without including Al Green. He has shuttled back and forth between gospel and soul and funky pop. At his peak, Al Green was a major black headliner; his appeal to the women was phenomenal. In the heyday of his soul career, the promoter was required to furnish him with a dozen roses per show, which he distributed to the ladies! All the stops—gospel tones, clear tenor, high falsetto—are pulled out on "Tired of Being Alone" and later "Let's Stay Together," "I'm Still in Love with You," and "You Ought to Be with Me." But his play to the females brought disaster when a jealous female broke into his apartment and burned him badly with a pot of hot grits. The result was a long, painful layoff, a soul-searching experience that took him back to religion and his gospel roots. Full circle for Al Green.

From our Amateur Show winners, another transitional group arose, The Spinners. The group is transitional in the sense that their style is modern but lacks the hard overtones of other rock groups. For us, The Spinners hold a special place both because their every Apollo engagement was a "return home" and because in one magnificent week back in the early seventies, they teemed with The Temptations to rack up a box-office record which endured until James Brown came along. And if their incredible performance that week made The Temps work doubly hard to hold their audience, that is precisely the stuff of which exciting shows are made.

In this day of change, one rarely finds an act that hangs together through thick and thin, yet that is the case with the Four Aims, renamed the Four Tops by Berry Gordy. They were designed to be the male equivalent of The Supremes and in many respects they were. The act took a cue, perhaps, from the old Orioles in making their lead tenor, Levi Stubbs, the central figure. Levi's voice radiates power. Their "Reach Out and I'll Be There" has all the earmarks of an enduring classic; it was a landmark both for the Tops and for Motown. Although they left Motown in 1972, they continue to record and make successful appearances the world over.

There is an added significance to be found in ruminating over such artists as I have been discussing. It is to be found in their relaxed mellowness. Somehow, the public has gotten the impression that rock and roll (formerly rhythm and blues) and the word *noisy* are synonymous. But stars like the Four Tops, Roberta Flack, Nancy Wilson, and Dionne Warwick also belong to the rock era. They are part of it and who is to say that they are less typical of it than, say, Otis Redding, Jackie Wilson, or James Brown?

Chuck Jackson is "King of Soul," who went "soul" down the line, even

125th STREET
APOLLO
BEG. FRI., JAN. 16th

"Love Me"
JERRY BUTLER
"16 Candles"
CRESTS
"Lovers Never Say Goodbye"
FLAMINGOS
"So Much"
Little Anthony
IMPERIALS
"Musical Touch"
DOC BAGBY
BAND
"Here I Stand"
WADE FLEMONS
"Down the Aisle"
QUINTONES
CLAY TYSON
WED. NITE: AMATEURS
SAT.: MIDNITE SHOW

68a.

HARLEM'S HIGH SPOT
APOLLO
125TH ST., near 8th Ave. • Tel.: UNiversity 4-4490

ONE WEEK ONLY—BEGINNING FRIDAY, NOV. 18

JACKIE WILSON

"Alone at Last"
"Am I the Man?"

"DEAREST DARLING" **ETTA JAMES**

SUGAR PIE DESANTA | DELORES COLEMAN
SPANIELS • JOHNNY & JOE

WED. NIGHT: AMATEURS — SAT.: MIDNIGHT SHOW

68b.

DR.
JIVE
RHYTHM 'N' BLUES REVUE

CLOVERS
SANTO & JOHNNY
BEN E. KING
OLYMPICS
ETTA JAMES
ROBERT & JOHNNY
WADE FLEMONS
BILLY BLAND
VINES
JEAN DUSHON
BOBBY MARSHAN TICK-TOCK
Wed. Nite: AMATEURS
Sat.: MIDNITE SHOW

68c.

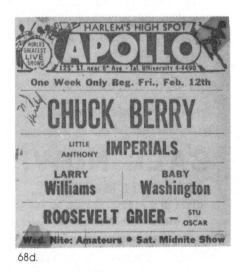

HARLEM'S HIGH SPOT
APOLLO
WORLD'S GREATEST LIVE SHOWS
125" ST. near 8" Ave. Tel. UNiversity 4-4490

One Week Only Beg. Fri., Feb. 12th

CHUCK BERRY

LITTLE ANTHONY IMPERIALS

LARRY Williams | **BABY Washington**

ROOSEVELT GRIER — STU OSCAR

Wed. Nite: Amateurs • Sat. Midnite Show

68d.

HARLEM'S HIGH SPOT
APOLLO
WORLD'S GREATEST COLORED SHOWS
125" ST. near 8" Ave. Tel. UNiversity 4-4490

One Week Only — Beg. Fri., Feb. 17
"Mr. Tutti - Frutti"
LITTLE RICHARD
MASTER OF GUITAR & BLUES GUITAR SLIM
POPULAR VOCAL GROUP THE FLAMINGOS
JACKIE "Moms" MABLEY Lloyd Lambert Band
Wed. Nite: AMATEURS @ Sat. MIDNITE SHOW

68e.

featuring a nine-piece band all his own. "I Wake Up Crying," "Any Day Now," and the album he dedicated to Elvis Presley are among his big hits.

Fats Domino sold twenty-two million single records! "Ain't That a Shame," "Blueberry Hill," and "Red Sails in the Sunset" are Fats' trademarks. If you don't know them, you've never been into rock.

Remember Hank Ballard? No? Remember "The Twist," which Chubby Checkers recorded and started a dance craze? Hank wrote it. In the fifties, Hank and The Midnighters waxed several million best-selling discs. An irony in Hank Ballard's career is that he didn't show for a record date to do "The Twist," thereby relinquishing it to Checkers.

Says Bobby, "The Drifters made records more than twenty years ago and some of them still sell thousands each year." "Save the Last Dance for Me," "Saturday Night at the Movies," "Honey Love"—all are living standards. Originally Clyde McPhatter, then Johnny Moore sang lead with the group.

Wilson Pickett is a macho, soul-brother superstar. During the sixties, a plethora of highly charged hits made him a sure-fire box-office and record star. His is a vibrant, full-throated, electric sound, overlaid with gospel tones. With Steve Cropper he wrote "The Midnight Hour" and it was a smash. His every performance is a vigorous, athletic experience.

And how about Little Richard? Born Richard Wayne Penniman, he was steeped in the Seventh-Day Adventist tradition from which he strayed and then returned. His "Tutti Frutti" is a classic. His performances were laced with muscle and shouts. In midstream, Little Richard suddenly switched and began to cut gospel songs, then returned to soul rock, and back once again to evangelical gospel.

Esther Phillips starred, in the early fifties, with Johnny Otis' revue, but then she was Little Esther (born Esther May Jones). She is the possessor of an unusual style and voice. Early in her career she recorded "Double Crossing Blues," and we brought her to the Apollo as a precocious fourteen-year-old. She recorded "Misery," and we brought her back again. Shortly thereafter, she virtually disappeared. When she did return it was as Esther Philiips. She had gone through a drug scene, and it showed in her performance and in her emotion-packed, highly charged records. Listening to those records, it is hard to sit in your chair. It is my judgment that Esther is one of the relatively unrecognized artists in the United States. To listen to her is to go through an emotional experience.

There has been a shift in the power structure of the entertainment business, which has had a serious impact on the business itself. Perhaps the reader will be pleased to learn, for example, that the role of the booking agent (much abused in the public's conception of how the system works) has been seriously eroded in favor of record-company executives. During the last two decades or so, the money flowing into that industry has been so stupendous that the executives are indeed a vital, a controlling force in the destinies of the artists. "There were times," said one aficionado of the business, "when you could only get a booking through the record company and if they thought your engagement important enough, they'd pay part of the act's salary!"

If that seems to be good, the answer is "not necessarily." For if power has the potential to corrupt, it can corrupt one side of the equation as easily as on the other. I shall go into the question of power and its consequences later.

The questions surrounding money are eternally fascinating. What was once a terrific weekly salary for an act is now a poor stipend for a single night! And the back-breaking schedules of Honi Coles' era would be looked upon with disbelieving horror by artists today. (In days gone by, thirty-one shows per week was standard, but today that same number of shows would occupy two weeks.) The fortunes made by artists and record companies in the sixties and seventies eroded the control promoters and exhibitors have over the acts they hire.

"If I were to go backstage as we used to and tell an artist what numbers to eliminate or change, most of them would tell me to go——myself," said Bobby. If you are an artist, that might seem good, but some impartial observer must question the quality of the shows.

There is no question about it: the rock and roll era has generated more income, seen to the birthing of more stars, probably created more job opportunities than any movement in theatrical history. Furthermore, it has stirred more excitement, involvement and controversy than anyone would have dreamed possible. If it has brought adverse reactions, even wrath, that is not to say that it has been bad.

When Honi Coles said, "I hated it—every minute of it," it was because rock was a revolution and overturned all his earliest training and experience.

The impact of this prodigiously productive era goes on today. For just as every revolution brings changes and influences the next generation of artists, the offspring of rock are still being spawned. It is hard even to conceive of today's musical beats, of reggae, of psychedelic music, and the like, without thinking of the rock sounds that preceded them. And once again, an important point must be made: the revolution was led by black artists. It isn't that whites didn't make contributions, but chiefly they built on the work of Sonny Til, Berry Gordy, Stevie Wonder, Hank Ballard, Smokey Robinson, Quincy Jones, and all the other black rock artists.

The fact that Elvis Presley became a multimillionaire and virtually a national hero following in the footsteps of the black artists, with scarcely a backward glance at them, has left mountains of resentment and bitterness in black ranks. What's the bottom line? What conclusions can be reached about the impact and significance of this rock era? I try to separate the bits and pieces of my own experience as a theatre operator and I say this:

The era of rock and roll was exciting, productive and profitable. It permitted—no, it encouraged artists to experiment with their own creativity. In a way, it was the logical extension of the bebop and progressive jazz era, for they too really started out as experimental modes, as attempts to find new ways to use old disciplines.

69a.

69b.

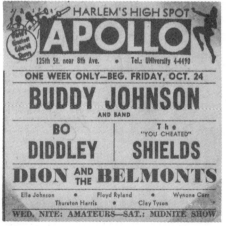

69c.

My show business training tells me that the rock shows traded on monotony in the succession of like-sounding acts which performed, substituting as they did, excitement for musical quality. I question those musical values which place the sound mixer in recording sessions above the musicians themselves in the scale of values. Still, I cast a nervous glance backwards and I am restrained by history's admonishing finger. History has been kinder to the experimenters than were his contemporaries. Perhaps, God willing, I may look back at the rock era twenty years hence and wonder at the contention and controversy surrounding so casual a form of musical development. Perhaps, after all, it is merely the next logical step in the eternal march of self-expression. Perhaps! After all, the familiar is comfortable; the new and different always stir our opposition because they are there. Today's strange and exotic becomes tomorrow's commonplace.

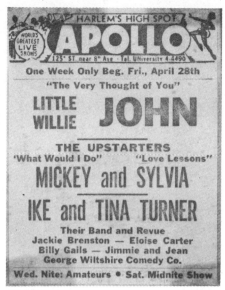

70a.

70b.

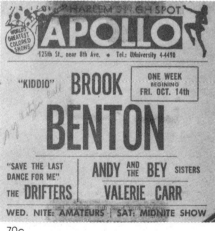

70c.

Blackout

"Unforgettable"

When we closed the Apollo's doors in 1977, almost exactly three years after my beloved father's death, more than personal losses were consigned to history. The Apollo's shuttering signalled the end of the Heyday Years. Of course, show business, with its vigorous, ambitious, hungry practitioners will continue in new and innovative ways. Indeed, so too will the Apollo, which was, in 1978 and again in 1982 transferred to other hands. But the particular era I have called the Heyday is over. It is over partly because the black variety theater itself is gone. It is over, too, because that special elan that characterized it has been displaced, first by the spirit of rock, then by numerous other changes culminating in the disco scene.

I would be the last to argue for the continuation of a segregated theater, but the black variety theater's demise is at least as lamentable as it is a sign of progress. If the black variety theater wasn't the Heyday in its totality, the Heyday without it is unthinkable. During its glory years, there was that special magic, that electrical current which passed back and forth between audience and artist. By the mid-seventies that magic was virtually gone, not because it had been somehow exorcized but because its home had perished. The audiences were still "out there," out on the streets of the Harlems of America but luring them back in to reconsummate the emotional marriages with performing artists had become less feasible, more costly, and finally, utterly impossible.

Frank Schiffman and the Apollo Theatre were an integral part of the black variety theater. Flip Wilson, speaking of my father, said, "Frank Schiffman wasn't just the Apollo Theatre; he was the whole damned block!" One could reasonably add that Dad was a significant part of the spirit of that social, economic, and political entity known as Harlem.

The title of one of Nat "King" Cole's most enduring hit records, "Unforgettable," is suitable for this final chapter. For the Heyday Years themselves and "our theater" were just that. The reader, I trust, will forgive me this last touch of sentimentality. Everyone who admires these years will agree that the description really fits.

Variety, known affectionately as the "Bible of show business," had this to say about him on January 23, 1974:

> Frank Schiffman, 80, founder and president emeritus of Harlem's Apollo Theatre, New York, died January 15th at Surfside, Florida, where he maintained a winter home for many years . . .
> Schiffman, a white man, was instrumental in changing the direction of black entertainment in New York. Before his acquisition of the Apollo, patronage was shunned, even though black actors were on stage. Schiffman introduced an open house policy and knocked down the color lines in that theatre long before it became fashionable. The Apollo for many years had racially mixed bills, although the predominant color motif was black. Until the advent of rock, he had a policy where no one race would be in total command. Thus, there were bills in which big bands such as Charlie Barnet came in for a week. Comics would play that house before hitting a major theatre downtown just to test new material. He was the first to introduce all-rock bills in that house.
> Originally, showmen deemed it disastrous to have complete programs of band and a succession of singing groups. However, Schiffman proved the efficacy of completely rock bills. It became the mecca of new talent and was a showcase which agents had to attend. Lena Horne got one of her first casings there. Headliners such as Bill Robinson and Jackie "Moms" Mabley among others, felt a need to play for the homefolks a minimum of once annually at the Apollo . . .

The Heyday Years were an era of growth, change, vitality and excitement in the theater. A singular *joie de vivre* never seen before or since permeated the whole period, infected its audiences, and gave the entire country a long-remembered emotional lift. As long as energetic and creative men and women are active in the theatre, it will live and, no doubt, prosper. Still, those years had their own special vibrations, and they are gone forever.

As black artists developed their styles and honed their crafts, gradual public acceptance of their work and presence was parallelled by development and acceptance in other fields in American life—sports, economics, politics, and other arts, for example. I do not mean to be overly simplistic; for black Americans the promises of democracy are far from realized. But there has been movement, and it has occurred in a variety of locations at the same time. In particular, black performing artists spread their wings and flew, especially as confidence in themselves and in the ultimate acceptance of their efforts become more apparent. The first area of acceptance, of course, was in the mainly black music halls like the Apollo, Washington's Howard, and Baltimore's Royal. In the faded confines of those dimly lit theaters, black artists developed and presented their acts, working them into the gems which, step by step, were almost reluctantly absorbed into the mainstream of white America. It wasn't easy, that acceptance, but what new events of history are?

When the early rock and roll shows were first presented, they were a revolution, for as *Variety* points out in Dad's obituary, they altered the accepted format of vaudeville shows by presenting a procession of singing acts without benefit of the "relief" normally offered by the comedians, dancers, and novelty performers. To me, the rock shows were aesthetic monstrosities, but to our audiences they were the quintessence of excitement. Viewed from the box office point of view, they were a "hype," which changed the profit-and-loss statement's bottom line from bright red to black.

However, I think history will blame the rock shows at least in part, for the demise of the variety theater itself. But as my brother Bobby said to me, "Every act on those shows had to earn its keep at the box office. Every act had to be a drawing card. The cost of those shows was so high that there was simply no room in the budget for anything less than a star record act." The obvious expendables under such a formula were the variety acts that might have added spice to the show, but could never be accused of being "box office."

In formulating the rock shows, the age-old battle between aesthetic quality and practical reality was once agian joined. It was really no contest. The financial requirements of the theater's continuing operation virtually demanded that the rock shows be presented. Nor was the decision merely the Apollo's. Every promoter in the country quickly recognized the box-office appeal of the rock and roll show, and they hastened to consign the variety show to the garbage heap of history in the headlong dash for profit. Although I recognize that the requirement of cash in the till often supersedes all the rest, I cannot agree, however, with the argument that good business and artistic excellence are synonomous. That argument was one I had with my father over and over again. We never agreed.

The attitude toward "box-office value" is even more pronounced in the field of television, where stringent budgets are set up and there is precious little room for less-experienced acts. "If I have 10,000 dollars budgeted for an act," said one top TV producer, "then I must have a 10,000 dollar act. Two 5000 dollar acts simply will not do, regardless of how good they might be." As a result of that attitude, dozens of able, even talented artists are permanently barred from television on grounds that have little to do with artistic merit. An example is Helen Humes, a great jazz singer, who sang for many years with Count Basie. Helen registered an outstanding performance on the public television salute to John Hammond several years ago, but as she remarked to me, "I've never had the luck to appear on a top, nationwide television program." Why? Too short and stout for the tastes of the TV producers, that's why. In that spirit, girth control rather than voice control becomes a show-business standard.

And then there are the technical innovations that changed the stage. The camp followers of jazz and rock concerts these past dozen years could not fail to notice the mountainous array of electronic equipment used by some acts. "It takes a qualified electrical engineer merely to hook up all those instruments to their amplifiers," said one director with tongue only slightly in cheek. At the Apollo, we had to abandon the two tiers of box seats located on either side of the stage because the speakers totally obscured the stage from those perches. Thus, the growing trend toward electronic music required drastic changes in the shows' format and contributed still one more blow to the already reeling variety theater.

And then for clinchers, there was the disappearance of the "grind," those four-, five- and six-shows-per-day schedules that were so characteristic of the early Heyday. The "grind" became increasingly unpopular with artists as demand for their talents grew. With their new-found power, they simply raised an eyebrow or shook their heads when the subject of "extra shows" arose. To the owners of large arenas or the money machines known as Las Vegas nightclubs that was no problem. They could gross enough during two or three shows per night to pay the stupendous salaries of the superstars, but for small theaters such as ours, it was another in a growing string of impossibilities.

I do not fault the performers for refusing to continue in the "grind." They are in the marketplace; if they can draw enough patrons to pay their enormous salaries and permit the owners to make a profit while on reduced schedules, then so be it. The exhibitors complain, of course, about the "arrogance" of the artists, but they have merely chosen to forget their own arrogance of yesteryear, when the shoe was on the other foot.

In today's highly charged world of entertainment, the entertainers are clearly in the driver's seat. I am sure that some of them take malicious glee in pressing their power to the utmost, but that isn't always the case. During the taping of *Uptown*, a large cast of artists cooperated far beyond the call of duty. Not one of them ever disputed the instructions and decisions of Gary Smith and Dwight Hemion, the show's directors. Said Gary, "We've never had a show where the cast had such spirit as this one. Some of it is undoubtedly due to the fact that it's an Apollo special, but still it's been unusual."

Anyone with a modicum of show-busines acumen and a well-equipped stage can present a good variety show, providing, of course, that there is good talent available. A more vital function of management is in developing such talent. And that was our function as we saw it. After all, we had nothing to do with whatever talent the artists possessed. They either had it coursing through their veins or they didn't. But we did have something to do with their artistry. For artistry is a learned function; it comes from exposure to audiences, from coaching, and from the suggestions of professionals. It springs from the accumulated experience gleaned during long years of observing, watching, synthesizing the reactions of both artists and audiences.

Take, for example, the case of little Edna McGriff, about whom I have heard nothing in the last decade. Edna was a beauty. But she had more than beauty; she was a composer, a singer, and a graduate of the Apollo's Amateur Hour. She composed a song called "Heavenly Father," which zoomed unexpectedly to dizzying heights on *Billboard* magazine's charts in the early fifties. Happily, we arranged for Edna's initial professional Apollo appearance. She was a dud—a beautiful, talented dud. For Edna had all the stage presence and excitement of a cigar-store Indian. We coaxed, coached and wheedled, trying to help her inject more showmanship into her stage appearances. It helped a little, but not much. And then, about a year later, we bought her services again, this time on the basis of a new record. Dynamite! That lovely young girl had absorbed in a single year enough showmanship to put her in almost any league. Her artistry had been acquired through the combined experiences of many personal appearances and when added to a natural talent, had converted her potential into exciting reality.

Edna's triumph was not due merely to the Apollo. It was due to an accumulation of experiences culled from dozens of one-nighters, scores of theater appearances, and many a nightclub "gig." She started out as an amateur and through training, she became a professional. All of that makes me feel that the greatest loss from the demise of small theaters is the loss of a training ground for young talent.

Juanita Uggams asked, "Where are they going to learn their trade if all these places close?" Pleaded the Negro Actors' Guild's Ernestine Allen, "You've just got to keep it [the Apollo] open or there'll be no place for the youngsters to learn and grow." Wailed Leonard Reed, "There are hardly any places where young talent can try out their acts today."

By 1978 the Apollo was in deep trouble. We were closed, we had financial difficulties, and we saw an agglomeration of problems that made us feel somewhat hopeless. The theater was too small to generate the income needed to buy the big acts; there were simply not enough seats for that. We felt we had lost the touch of creating exciting enough shows using less-expensive talent. The public seemed to have been schooled either to buy big names at the box office or stay home and watch it free on television. The terrible decay that had engulfed Harlem didn't help either. It brought a trembling fear to the populace, a fear which kept them locked securely in their apartments at night rather than parading up 125th Street to the Apollo. The peopleless appearance of the street on bitter wintry nights was now being repeated in mild springtime, warm summer, and balmy fall.

Surprisingly and ironically, the biggest factor in the Apollo's problems was the collapse of the ghetto as a containing influence on performer and audience alike. I do not mean that Harlem isn't a ghetto any longer. It is just that its inhabitants are no longer forced to stay there in their quest for jobs or entertainment. And if freedom of movement is true of those living in Harlem, it is doubly, triply true of the performers themselves. For now black artists and audiences are welcome in places far removed from the ghetto. The owners of those places could care less where artist and audience come from or go after the show is over. They are welcome.

Here is the irony: the very success of our efforts to help broaden the acceptance of black artistry everywhere helped bring on the death of our theater, our business, our lifework. My family has long felt a keen interest in the expansion of black goals and accomplishments, and when they came, our business was one of its victims. But I'm certain my father wouldn't have wanted it any other way. Indeed, we had all long felt that the Apollo belonged in black hands. It is part of black heritage and history, even if a few soul-brothers who helped on the way happened to be white.

In 1978 we sold out to black interests. The historical process that started many years ago when black talent was first presented at a dozen theaters in Harlem had come full circle. We were no longer a part of the scene.

History is replete with many surprises, and for the Apollo's black ownership there are no exceptions. They have already discovered many of them, for merely being in black hands in no way assured success to the new Apollo owners. Indeed, their experience was that the gigantic financial, commercial, and artistic problems of the theater combined with the seriously deteriorated economy of Harlem to create a disaster. Their tenure was relatively short-lived, and regretfully we were forced to protect our investment by repossessing the theater several years later. We did so without a serious thought of resurrecting the dead by reintroducing stage shows. For it seemed to us that would doom us to failure too. Only an entirely new concept can make a viable institution of the old Apollo.

In 1982 the Harlem Commonwealth Council acquired the Apollo from us, and simultaneously leased it to a group headed by ex-Manhattan borough president Percy Sutton. The facilities have been altered, seating (up to 1500) has been added and the theater will be used as a performance center and a studio to make television products for the black cable market. The shows themselves will be performed before a live audience. The Apollo will live again!

The Apollo reopened in February 1984, and a new Amateur Night was held before an audience of a thousand people. "Harlem residents, leaders, and business people view the reopening as the return of an economic anchor that could help reclaim some of the luster of the deteriorated area," commented Sheila Rule in the *New York Times.*

In July of 1983, the Apollo was accorded landmark status by the landmark commission. As with all history, the theater's growth was accomplished in a series of steps, one following discreetly behind another—expanding, enlarging, altering, growing. In each entertainment field—music, dance, song, and comedy— evolution and revolution joined forces at various times. The black variety theater died when the climate and need for it as a separate entity no longer existed. When black artists gained a more universal acceptance and when black patrons were welcomed in previously restricted showplaces, the singular world of black showdom became a kind of historical relic.

I do not mean to imply that the total integration of blacks into American society has been accomplished, nor has black artistry been completely and unreservedly accepted. But the *need* for an individual and separate black theater has diminished and it has therefore receded into history. Perhaps one can say that the black variety theater *had* to perish in order for blacks to find a larger acceptance. If that fact is not entirely to the good in that there are black elements that have not yet been completely developed and presented to all of us, it nevertheless says a great deal about the ultimate democratizing process.

Looking backward over the past fifty-odd years, it is obvious that the creative efforts of black Americans have met with increasing acceptance. In the history of our democracy that is no small thing. Still, one can mourn the demise of the black variety theater and not solely from sentimental nostalgia. There are singular and unique aspects to be found in any ethnic group's efforts, and the loss of their unique product is a loss indeed. I have the feeling that we are being deprived of some singular black offerings because the black variety theater is no more. Before the mixed audiences of today, the spontaneous thrusts of black offerings may be lost or at best neutered. It is for this reason that I wish the present Apollo ownership good fortune. They may be the only ones left who can provide a way-station for some black artists to express themselves in an exciting milieu of their own. And that milieu may be the one essential ingredient they need to express their unique talent.

For my own family, "our theater" is now a nostalgic, historic relic. We look back at the Apollo with understandable regret. Even driving past its rejuvenated façade brings a pang of pain. And yet there is a sense of pride in our ruminations, for our contributions to the Heyday Years were considerable. Those years, too, have ended. They have ended not with a clap of thunder, not with the rolling of drums, but in the way of the variety theater itself—in a blackout!

INDEX